INDEPENDENT MONTHLY LITERARY MAGAZINE

REVISTA LITERÁRIA INDEPENDENTE MENSAL

ADELAIDE

Independent Monthly Literary Magazine
Revista Literária Independente Mensal
Year III, Number 18, November 2018
Ano III, Número 18, novembro de 2018

ISBN-13: 978-1-949180-44-2
ISBN-10: 1-949180-44-1

Adelaide Literary Magazine is an independent international monthly publication, based in New York and Lisbon. Founded by Stevan V. Nikolic and Adelaide Franco Nikolic in 2015, the magazine's aim is to publish quality poetry, fiction, nonfiction, artwork, and photography, as well as interviews, articles, and book reviews, written in English and Portuguese. We seek to publish outstanding literary fiction, nonfiction, and poetry, and to promote the writers we publish, helping both new, emerging, and established authors reach a wider literary audience.

A Revista Literária Adelaide é uma publicação mensal internacional e independente, localizada em Nova Iorque e Lisboa. Fundada por Stevan V. Nikolic e Adelaide Franco Nikolic em 2015, o objectivo da revista é publicar poesia, ficção, não-ficção, arte e fotografia de qualidade assim como entrevistas, artigos e críticas literárias, escritas em inglês e português. Pretendemos publicar ficção, não-ficção e poesia excepcionais assim como promover os escritores que publicamos, ajudando os autores novos e emergentes a atingir uma audiência literária mais vasta.

(http://adelaidemagazine.org)

Published by: Adelaide Books, New York
244 Fifth Avenue, Suite D27
New York NY, 10001
e-mail: info@adelaidemagazine.org
phone: (917) 727 8907
http://adelaidebooks.org

FOUNDERS / FUNDADORES
Stevan V. Nikolic & Adelaide Franco Nikolic

EDITOR IN CHIEF / EDITOR-CHEFE
Stevan V. Nikolic
editor@adelaidemagazine.org

ASSOCIATE EDITOR
Raymond Fenech

MANAGING DIRECTOR / DIRECTORA EXECUTIVA
Adelaide Franco Nikolic

GRAPHIC & WEB DESIGN
Adelaide Books DBA, New York

CONTRIBUTING AUTHORS IN THIS ISSUE

Charlotte Freccia, Nancy Lines, James Brennan, Thomas Tomlinson, Libby Belle, Zia Marshall, Kyle Labe, Libby Copa, Don Dussault, Cristina Oramas, Cassie Lawson, Malcolm Garcia, Maggie Slepian, Joseph Washburn, Emelyn Grace Jaros, Leslie Johnson, Kedrick Nettleton, Jessica Olivos, Ross Dreiblatt, Henry Simpson, Heide Arbitter, Effy Rose, Lazar Trubman, Juanita Tovar Mutis, Gregg Williard, LaDonna Friesen, Jeffrey Loeb, Cynthia Close, Walker Thomas, Tamas Dobozy, Rebecca Kirschbaum, Raymond Fenech, JR Solonche, Howard Sage, C.H. Coleman, Amelia Abdullah, William Snyder, Jan Little, Daniel Jackson, Jhier Wells, Leanne Talavera, Austen Roye, Tim Wenzell, Jessica Sabo, Rick Adams, Andrew Hubbard, Mark Hurtubise, Thea Tomaini, Bray McDonald, Amanda Leigh, Louise Lever, Ken W. Simpson, Lisa Zaran, Michael Anthony Istvan Jr., Bikal Paudel

CONTENTS / CONTEÚDOS

POETRY

EDITOR'S NOTES

Stevan V. Nikolic

ON HOPE

It was nine thirty Thursday morning when Michael entered the lobby of the National Library of Portugal in Lisbon. He sat on the sofa opposite of the security desk. 'Carlos should come soon. He is never late,' he thought.

Carlos entered into the lobby, approached and sat next to Michael. He was in his office in the Santa Maria hospital all morning and didn't have time to change. He was still in his whites.

"Olá Michael.

"Hi Carlos. Thank you for coming. You are a real friend."

"Listen Michael. I don't know why I am doing this. Everybody is saying bad things about you. Wherever you go, whatever you do, there is a noise after you. If I tell our Masonic friends in New York that I am helping you, they would say I am crazy. In spite of everything, I respect your courage to go after your ideals, no matter what. Men like you make this world spin around. I know that the road you chose to go is covered with thorns. But I also know that it must be a road to the stars. So, I brought you money that you ask for. If you are careful, it will last you for three months. I am sure you can find a room in Lisbon for two hundred a month. So try to manage. It is my gift to you. No need to repay me ever. If you ever get in a position to think about repaying me, give instead a donation to some animal shelter in my name. And please, don't call me any time soon to get you another ticket to New York," Carlos started smiling here, "In last three months I

bought you two tickets already. Or maybe, just give me enough notice in advance so I could find a good deal, ha, ha."

"Not to worry Carlos. This time I have everything figured out."

"I really hope so. You are expensive friend to have Michael. So what did you figure out?"

"I figured out where the key to my purpose is."

"Where it is?" Carlos asked.

"Right here." Michael said.

"Here? In this Library?" Carlos asked.

"Yes. Or better to say, this is where the key will unlock the door of my purpose."

"I am not sure if I understand you? Carlos asked.

"Don't you see? I was going after a woman believing that the key is in being with her. But the key is in writing about her. The key is in words that are in me. Longing for her is just an impulse for words to come out. And the whole purpose is for words to come out. Words are important. Words about love. Words about life. And they are not mine. They are just channeled through me. Remember, in the beginning there was the word, and the word was with God, and the word was God, and the word was made flesh. The whole purpose of all my life was to accumulate enough impulse for all the writings that need to be done. That is my mission. That is the Holy Grail I was after. There is so much despair in the world today. People are losing fate in God. Nobody believes in love anymore Carlos. Nobody. Hope, Love, and Kindness are today only empty phrases from the Sunday Bible school. People need love. They need hope. Hope of the Rose. But before they understand what hope of the Rose represents, they need to hear truth. Truth is important."

"Truth according to Michael?" Carlos said.

"Yes...according to Michael. It could be also according to Carlos, according to Maria, according to anybody. Name doesn't matter. But in each of us is a little bit of Michael, ha, ha," Michael said, "and some don't like me because they recognize themselves in me. My truth belongs to all."

"And I assume this is where you are going to write it? Carlos asked while pointing at the entrance of the reading room.

"Yes. I love this space. I can sit here in the reading room surrounded with books and write all day. It is so quiet and inspiring. They have wi-fi. And it is free." Michael smiled.

"And young girls from the Lisbon University writing their school papers next to you." Carlos said with a bit of irony in his voice while shaking his head.

"Yes, I was thinking about the same thing. Isn't that nice ha, ha. But it won't make difference to me. I'll be with my Maria."

"Whoever that is..." Carlos said and smiled.

About a year later, in New York, Director Keith was passing by the Barnes and Noble book store on Union Square. He saw a familiar face on a poster in the store window. It was an announcement of the book signing, Truth According to Michael by Michael Nicolau." He smiled and continued walking. 'Yes, Michael was right - he was under protection,' Director was thinking, 'I wonder if Michael ever passed through the eighth door...I'll ask him. I'll go to that book signing and ask him.'

(From *Truth According to Michael* - A novel by Stevan V. Nikolic

WILLOUGHBY

by Charlotte Freccia

Clara Richardson had two sisters, and of the three of them, Clara was the least beautiful and had the least interesting name. Clara's older sister, Eliora, had a long neck and symmetrical, almondine eyes. Clara's younger sister, Opal, had generous, well-lit brown hair and the most elegant nose anyone had ever seen. Their mother, Violet, herself quite beautiful, had evidently distributed pretty names and genetic gifts unevenly among her three daughters, though of no real predetermined fault of her own. However, as the light came up on the long entr'acte of the Richardsons' shared girlhood, it became abundantly clear that Violet, perhaps unintentionally, perhaps helplessly, had allocated her affection for her daughters proportionally to their beauty, and to the beauty of the names she'd chosen for them. Clara didn't consciously catch on to this pattern of preference until she was about nine, and now, thirty years later, the moment when it dawned on her was blurry around the edges. She remembered walking down Clinton Street toward Radio Park Elementary School, her sisters side-by-side, in step, their gleaming hair and gleaming tin lunch boxes catching the watery September sunlight as it peeked cautiously through the canopy of ancient, reaching oaks which shaded their street. She remembered walking behind her sisters, uncomfortably close, stepping on heels in order to enforce her own inclusion, because the sidewalk was not wide enough for three girls to walk across it together. Her own lunch box, as she remembered it, was scuffed where her sisters' were shiny, a hand-me-down, cast off by a neighbor's waste-

ful only child. There had also been the times, in childhood, when Clara would wake up in the bedroom she shared with her sisters and one or more of them would be out of bed, and she would stumble from the room and stand on the stairs and listen to Eliora or Opal or sometimes both sitting at the kitchen table with their mother, slurping juice, and Clara would calmly acknowledge her frank segregation from this loose coalition of feminine alliance as if it was another person, another less-loved sister, in the room with her.

Clara had grown up relentlessly utilitarian, and as an adult she figured that her pragmatism was a result of not being spoiled by sponge-soft adoration in her childhood. In a way, she liked to think, she had been spared from a more unhappy adulthood by the lovelessness she had experienced as a young girl. Retroactively, she thought, and with tongue placed firmly in cheek, she ought to thank her mother for loving her so haphazardly, so incompletely, that she would never be let down or disappointed when she looked for love in the real world. Retroactively, she admonished herself for believing that there was a real world of romantic love out there for her to yet discover. Retroactively, she wondered if she'd broken her own heart by believing that her mother had really loved her less than her sisters: in her worst moments, she fretted that she made it all up, that the moments she remembered from her childhood hadn't happened to her at all but were merely things she had seen done to unwanted children in fairy-tale movies.

No one in Willoughby had to know this, though. No one in Willoughby had to know any of it.

Clara worked part-time at Cup & Caboodle, the charming, well-lit coffee shop where Willoughby wives stopped mid-morning for post-yoga, pre-tennis cold-brew cappuccinos, one part almond milk, one part fat-free foam. Clara couldn't think of anything more specific or more professional-sounding than Worker when Facebook asked her what she did at Cup & Caboodle, because she felt she was too old to self-seriously identify as a barista. Despite—in fact because of—its unremarkable implications, Clara appreciated her job at Cup & Caboodle, because every day the stakes of her personal performance were about as low as they could possibly be. Clara had really only ever wanted to work in coffee shops, bookstores, and ice-cream parlors, because she had never had any career ambitions beyond providing people with their simplest and most durable pleasures.

In fact, the only thing she could really remember *wanting* to be when she was a girl had been quickly and convincingly talked down by her mother herself. Enamored of the look of her dull-brown hair in a hairnetted, bobby-pinned, lopsided bun and her spindly limbs contorted into some contrived posture in a wall-to-wall panelled mirror, Clara had for a time nursed dreams of becoming a ballerina. She had been, at the time, conventional enough to believe that a ballerina was the most glamorous thing a girl could be. She must have believed that the glamor of her chosen profession would imbue her with the kind of beauty that her sisters had simply been born with. The ideas of beauty and balletic talent were constantly negotiated and renegotiated in her own mind. She was ironically encouraged by the child at the helm of *The Nutcracker,* every budding dancer's favorite ballet, with whom Clara shared a name as well as an overactive imagination. Her sisters were in many visible respects more special than Clara, but neither of them shared a name with a balletic heroine. Clara could—and did—hold onto that.

Understanding this, and somewhat sympathetically fearing the fate of her unloveliest daughter who so affectionately harbored dance dreams, Clara's mother yanked her out of lessons at age six, signing Clara up for gymnastics at State College Family YMCA in dance's stead. This change to Clara's burgeoning artistic life proved inconsequential. The differences between a ballet leotard and a gymnastics leotard, and how an unbecoming child looked in both, were scant enough to replace Clara's fondness for ballet with a tolerance for gymnastics. Both involved mirrors and padded floors and the making of the body into something more powerful and more beautiful and more frightening than it already was. She had actually been quite good at gymnastics: she had the kind of compact, muscular density that suits a gymnast's body better than a dancer's, and at night she stretched her rectangular back while her mother rolled her little feet over a sealed mason jar filled with boiling water so she could evolve in both flexibility and stamina at once. She competed in gymnastics until the seventh grade, when early puberty widened her hips so that her balance suffered, and she fell off a beam onto an ancient, petrified blue plastic mat at a competition site in Lewiston and damaged her rotator cuff, ending her gymnastics career preternaturally and permanently.

Nearing middle-age, Clara appreciated her job at the Cup & Caboodle because it gave her ample free time to explore interests she'd pushed aside in her pursuit of an adult life. She lived in a one-bedroom studio above a hair salon down the block from the Cup & Caboodle with new carpeting and lots of light and the smell of sodium thioglycolate moving in through the cracks in the floors which did not require too much housekeeping. Between her small, well-kept apartment and her undemanding entry level job, Clara made plenty of time for what she called her extracurriculars, and slowly they became the most reliable thing in her life.

Clara had recently engaged with an extracurricular named Peter Price. He was the seventh-grade science teacher at Eastlake Middle School, and he came to her apartment twice weekly: Monday afternoons, just after the final bell rang at the middle school at 3:30, and Thursday evenings, after he finished coaching the boys' seventh-grade basketball team at 7:20. Peter fucked the way a seventh-grade science teacher might be expected to, with the glaring exception of his active katoptronophilia. Clara did not mind indulging this taste, and furnished her apartment with panelled mirrors of the kind she had loved to dance in as a child. Peter appreciated this touch. Peter had spectacular ear hair and a concave chest, and he unselfconsciously wore long-sleeved polo shirts. Peter's wife, Erica, was a teacher, too— eighth-grade U.S. History—and as such drank her coffee in the teacher's lounge at Eastlake, so Clara had never met her. She could imagine her well enough, though.

Another extracurricular Clara enjoyed was named Caleb Bunting. He was the most success-ful residential real estate agent in Willoughby, or at least the one whose name and face appeared the most frequently on for-sale signs planted in yards throughout town. Caleb came to her apartment three or four times a week. He was fond of afternooners, and she could easily fit him in on Mondays at 2 before Peter, ever reliable, came over at 3:30. Caleb fucked the way a man who would willingly invoke his own smug face in strangers' lawns might be expected to. He loved Clara's breasts, and she let him. He appreciated her amenability, as far as her own breasts were concerned. Caleb had thinning sandy hair and a stubby little dick, and he drove a fire-engine red Mazda Miata. Caleb's wife, Bethany, had a pinched little face and long white-blonde hair which she wore clipped back in barrettes, like a middle-school girl. Bethany owned the dog-grooming service which operated adjacent to the salon below Clara's apartment, so she had seen her coming and going many times. Caleb himself had to have had seen his wife coming and going many times, but Clara got the feeling that such

frequent narrow misses made his involvement with Clara so much more thrilling to Caleb. Bethany was a conventional Starbucks bitch, so Clara had never had to suffer the vaguely pleasant indignity of pouring Bethany's coffee at the Cup & Caboodle. Recently, Caleb had begun floating the idea—he must have thought that he was being subtle—of a threesome, and Clara could only imagine the way that Bethany would react to that.

Clara's most demanding extracurricular was named Eli Nicks. She wasn't entirely sure what he did but she knew he worked in the city because he often came to her apartment, sweaty and harried and swinging his briefcase, at 1 or 5:20 PM, saying out of the corner of his mouth that his escape from the office was only temporary. He fucked the way a man who was always in a hurry might be expected to—he took very little to wind up, but quite a long time to wind down. Clara spent the majority of the time which constituted their frenetic trysts with Eli's face buried in her breastbone, feeling clouds of condensation bloom over her heart as he inhaled and rapidly exhaled. He often asked her if she could use suspiciously specific nicknames as she guided him through sex: sugar bun, licorice, honeydew. Eli had a heavy, expensive watch which he didn't take off when he fucked her and a big house out in the subdivisions and wiry hair on his back. Eli's wife, Lena, was beloved in Willoughby because she had spearheaded the Lake Cleanup Initiative and the Moms Against Animal Testing Coalition, and everyone said she was a serious activist. She was appropriately honey-haired and long-limbed and trim, but her ass still moved like Jell-O on a plate in her yoga pants which she often wore when she stopped by the Cup & Caboodle after Samira's 11:30 Tuesday/Thursday yogilates class.

Clara regularly had sex seven days a week, and sometimes more than once per day. It was a tricky game she played, like a high-stakes, sexually-charged version of Tetris, fitting each man, with his own specific demands and constraints, into her daily schedule. As for herself, she had no particular preferences but that her meetings with her various men occur only in her space. Each had, at some point, suggested some sort of romantic getaway—Peter wanted to bring her to a campsite in Cuyahoga Valley where he'd once led his son's Cub Scout troop on a camping trip; Caleb proposed an afternoon at the Renaissance Cleveland; and Eli offered to take her out to his vacation home on the lake—but the idea of moving her sexual life out of the protective boundaries of her own apartment shook Clara. Then again, she hated to think of her place as a pleasure palace. Her little shampoo-scented apartment, decorated with the extensive collection of hummingbird regalia she'd sustained throughout her marriage, the only operative brothel in Willoughby! But she had to admit she did little to prevent this conception from developing. It was a funny thing how open secrets in small towns were only open to certain people, while remaining closed, or at least closeted, to others. She knew that the men of Willoughby knew that if you wanted to cheat on your wife, you could get away with doing it with Clara Richardson. She knew it by the way wives—in their recognizable getups of yoga pants or frumpy sundresses or ancient corduroy pants with the asses worn saggy—moved away from her in the supermarket, at the car wash. She knew it in the way their husbands looked at her while looking over the lunch meat, while unhooking the vacuum tubes. It was like she couldn't help it: peoples' husbands were drawn to her. She had started seeing Eli—his words—when they met across the vitamins aisle of Sweeney's Pharmacy. Her relationship with Caleb—his words—developed after he came into the shop for a cup of coffee with a client. Peter had simply approached her in the street.

Nothing shocked her anymore. This was Willoughby. She knew it like a dog knew a fire hydrant—innately, intuitively, indifferently. She had come here with her husband and she remained here without him. After her divorce but before she began engaging so enthusiastically with her extracurriculars—there had been

a little window of time—she had had little reason to stay in Willoughby, but she took it as a sign that she had chosen to rent the apartment above the salon before the divorce papers were notarized that she should not go away. She had nowhere to be, really, but here, and she would stay here indefinitely. She would not wait until heartbreak or boredom chased her away. She had, already, in certain senses, had her heart broken. She had, already, succumbed to boredom. And here she remained. Among the men who wanted to fuck her and the women who drove them, panting and desperate, to her apartment door. The women who believed that a ring, a ceremony, a solemn promise meant they could finally give up the dieting and the waxing and the pushing the progressively bluer pills through clear plastic and the long nights of masturbation and the short nights of anorgasmic sex and the men who knew that the women would never actually give up on any of these things because even after the marriage there was no way to call off the competition among women to get picked first, picked fast, picked well, and stay picked. Clara knew that men would always continue the hunt no matter how many women threw their bodies against theirs, gave their bodies up as prey. She knew the Willoughby wives knew this too, but they had more reasons to keep quiet about it than she did. And with her extracurriculars, she never had to worry about staying picked. She knew the terms of her trysts not by heart but by body, and they were the only terms she had ever trusted.

Clara fucked reliably and patiently and sufficiently. When she had sex she was almost without fail on the bottom, where she could fix herself exactly and expertly according to the certain gaze of whichever man hovered waitingly above her. She had a low, sweet voice and a very expressive face, and both of these augmented her sexuality greatly. She took care of herself. And, besides, she had that apartment! So pretty, so fragrant. The men she fucked often swore she was the perfect woman before kissing her sinking cheeks like an unmarried aunt with bad breath and returning home to their wives.

Clara loved divorce. She loved the defensive, savage vocabulary of it: loved the words alimony, condonation, corroborative witness. She loved the easy out of it—to others, marriage may have seemed like the biggest and most important commitment one could possibly make in their whole life, but Clara failed to see how marriage was protected or protectible when divorces existed and in fact colonized marriages with such reliable speed and frequency. "You shouldn't refer to divorce as an 'easy out,'" admonished her sisters when they went to Clara for advice in dealing with their hapless, handsome husbands and she urged them to divorce, as she was, she believed, inevitably going to do one day, as she, eventually, did. "I think most people who have been through divorce would argue that it's anything but easy." Clara only smiled, close-lipped, polite, when her sisters tried to lecture her.

Clara believed in divorce. She believed in it the way some people believe in love or money or God. She believed that she had married just so she could one day divorce. Clara did not care about getting picked, which was, she thought, the whole point of marriage: picking someone and expecting that they picked you in return. She had, after all, never felt picked in childhood, and she had expected this lack of being picked to be rectified in that larger world she saw of men and women and the unspeakable things between them. As it happened, she had been picked out in that world, and it didn't do anything but put her off to the idea of picking entirely. Like the way babies, who had no identity or experience were given names or beauty or dancing lessons, the way that people tripped into marriages on the basis of loose pickings seemed distastefully arbitrary to Clara. Not picking required flexibility and stamina while picking, and being picked in return, required nothing—no nerve or wit or beauty—except a mindless desperation to prove that you meant something—anything—to at least one other person on Earth.

When she married, Clara's older sister's name became Eliora Ransom. Clara thought that the poetry of Eliora's name was moving from the admirable to the unfair. She placated herself by reciting her sister's full name, first-middle-last-married last: Eliora Renee Richardson Ransom. She stumbled purposefully over the three recalcitrant Rs, standing immobile as mountains. She felt satisfied at the gracelessness of this four-part moniker, just one letter away from spelling the word "error" in monogram. When she married, Clara's younger sister's name became Opal Flood. Clara thought that the sheer natural beauty of Opal's nomenclature was becoming, to use her mother's word for all that was contemptible or inappropriate, a bit *much*. She placated herself by thinking this. She thought about her own name, in mutable variations: Clara Richardson. Clara Kulwanoski. Clara Price. Clara Bunting. Clara Nicks. Clara Richardson, again.

When Clara married Alek, she kept her name. Alek's last name, Kulwanoski, was liberally pronounced by his colleagues, Clara's disinterested relatives, and anyone asked to repeat it over the phone. It also sounded vaguely like "colonoscopy," even when pronounced accurately. Alek was a generally gentle and understanding man, and was characteristically accepting of Clara's decision to keep her name. You'd have to love me a whole lot to change your name for me, he said, and he thought it was a joke, but Clara remembered the couple in the house next door to the one she grew up in, the Hookers, and how she had watched from their adjacent kitchen windows as Mr. and Mrs. Hooker grew old and bitter together, silently and mournfully: she watched Mrs. Hooker cleaning up the kitchen after dinner and retreating upstairs while Mr. Hooker let the blue light of the television lull him to sleep; she watched Mrs. Hooker clip Mr. Hooker's undershirts, yellowed under the armpits, to the clothesline at the end of each week; she watched the racoons and neighborhood strays search through the Hookers' trash cans in the alley behind their houses for Mrs. Hooker's bloodied, curled sanitary napkins, once a month for twenty-three years. Yes, Clara said to Alek, I don't love you nearly enough to do that, and he laughed, and it was all she could do to smile with her lips stretched tightly over her teeth.

Alek Kulwanoski was an in-house accountant at a small firm which marketed technologically sophisticated baby strollers. He had a massive facial blemish, sustained in a difficult passage through the uterine canal, which swallowed up his eye and dripped down his cheekbone, angrily blood-red, so it looked like he was always balancing a raw steak on the right side of his otherwise unremarkable face. Dogs loved him. Clara loved him, for a little while—after all, he was generally gentle and understanding, and he fucked in a kind of gentle and understanding way which did not surprise or intimidate or offend her, and he was employed. They met in college, in Principles of Business Economics in their sophomore year. At least that was the story that they had told people. Really they were set up on a half-blind date by Alek's RA, Clara's friend, Julianne. It was half-blind because Alek had noticed Clara sitting by the door in Principles of Business Economics and had connected her to Julianne and begged his RA to set them up, so she did. This story mortified Clara, and she had managed to subdue him into simplifying the memory, when people used to ask. Clara was Alek's first. Alek never asked Clara if he had been her first. He hadn't been. But he was the first man she loved, and she had loved him in spite of his face. For a while, she'd wondered whether she was a bad person, bad woman, bad wife for loving him in spite of his face and not because of it, before letting the thought dissolve noiselessly in the back of her mind.

When Clara married, Clara's sisters stood at the altar with her. In honor of the occasion—the wedding, and her sisters' presence at it—Clara intentionally picked the plainest bridesmaids' gowns she could find. They were high-necked and boxy through the bodice, in an uninspiring blush-pink, even though it was an August wed-

ding and all the flowers were vivid late-summer oranges, golds, and greens, because the color did little for the sisters' clotted-cream complexions. Still, her sisters outshone her, impetuously, on her wedding day, radiant and warm-skinned and smiling in their pink gowns while Clara gleamed dully in her floor-length white, her lacy veil drawing attention to her wide, prominent forehead and all bunched up in the back.

Before she married, Clara's sisters privately remarked that her apparent love for such a distinctly marked man proved the oft-reported depth of Clara's generosity of heart. Once, Clara overheard them, and privately agreed. Before they married, Clara and Alek had had that brief, decisive conversation about her name, and Alek had assumed that she would not take his name because of its coarse, un-American sound. He had only been partly correct in his assumption: it was as if Clara sensed, even before the orange and gold and green August ceremony, that the marriage would eventually expire and that the last thing she'd want to be left with as an immovable talisman of the futility of love was a last name as dubious as Kulwanoski, dead-bolted to her forgettable first name with all the permanence and unloveliness of a license plate dead-bolted to a car.

It was Alek who had led them to Willoughby, and Clara who had followed. They had lived in Philadelphia with everyone else who had attended their college for a few years after graduation, but after a while Alek tired of the sooty history of the city, the groups of high-school students, who moved between monuments in their school-color polo shirts and their long rectangular tour busses. As a grotesquely birth-marked and fundamentally uncompetitive child growing up indoors outside of Allentown, his favorite film had been *Major League,* and Clara remained convinced that this juvenile proclivity was what put the idea of Cleveland into Alek's head to begin with. Alek had never mentioned the connection between the film and his desire to move, Clara thought, because even he knew that it would sound absolutely unjustifiable to argue for a move to a city based upon an affection for a Charlie Sheen movie. Instead, he invented a parade of reasons for the move, each one more absurd than the one that came before.

He told Clara he no longer wanted to live in a city on a river and wanted to relocate to a city on a lake. "There's a river in Cleveland," Clara had told him as he raved. "It's actually kind of famous because it was so polluted with chemical waste that it caught on fire, a couple of times."

"I'm sure that's not true," said Alek. "Where do you come up with this stuff, anyway?" He wasn't being cruel when he said it. He was just being positive. Then he told her that they should move while they were still young, explore the world a little. Clara flinched at the thought that moving to Ohio constituted a global adventure in Alek's mind. He insisted that his employment as an accountant was elastic because people needed accountants everywhere. Before they moved, Clara had worked in the bookshop at the Museum of Art, and Alek had suggested that her employment was mobile too. "Cleveland's got a great art museum," he told her. Eventually she tired of trying to convince him otherwise. Her desire to remain in Philadelphia, an unspecial, violent city which she would never love, was just as groundless as Alek's desire to leave it.

They married shortly after they landed in Willoughby, at Abundant Life Community Church. Clara had not been raised in any religion, and Alek, by birth a Polish Catholic, told her he'd forsaken God as a small child because he could not believe that God would give him a face so damaged without also giving him a superpower. He had told her this on their third date, over ice-cream sundaes brittle with ice in the Student Union. She had not known him long or well enough by this point to know that such a epistemologically consequential decision was radically uncharacteristic of Alek. She also did not know that by that date that Alek

had already fallen in love with her. She took his virginity that night, because she guessed that Alek was the kind of boy to lose his virginity after an ice-cream date. Just as he was the kind of boy to insist on getting married in a church on a rocky peak above a lake he pointlessly worshipped, despite his high claims of atheism. Abundant Life was one of those terrifying non-denominational churches common to the midwest, with parking lots like wastelands and cavernous entrances. The most beautiful thing about the space in which Clara and Alek had married had been Clara's sisters.

Clara had never got around to making friends in Willoughby after she was married, and now that she was divorced, she'd managed to make one. Her name was Claudia and she was a shift manager at Cup & Caboodle and a student at the Institute of Art and sixteen years younger than Clara. She had all manner of exotic facial piercings and no tattoos, though she frequently drew trees and people and fire hydrants up and down her arms with Sharpies. She knew all about Clara's extracurriculars, and she was the only one who did. Despite her flamboyant appearance, Claudia was actually rather conventional when it came to sex—she had, after all, been raised in Cuyahoga Falls by overweight, evangelical parents named Burt and Rhonda—and asked Claudia innumerable questions about the state of her affairs.

"Why do it?" was the most common one which Clara had only answered once. They had been sitting over chipped mugs of house coffee one morning before their shift started.

"I don't like monogamy," Clara responded, because it was the simplest true answer she could give in the fewest words. "Is that so wrong?"

"No," Claudia had said, drawing back. "I know a lot of kids at art school who are non-monogamous. But they're all in their twenties, and it's *art school.*" Clara shrugged. "What I'm saying is it's okay to be non-monogamous in certain social spaces," said Claudia, pushing her pink cat-eye glasses with the non-prescription lenses up her freckled nose. "But this is like suburban Ohio. All the dudes you're 'non-monogamous' with are other people's dads. And you're...." She trailed off, suddenly enthralled with something at the bottom of her coffee cup.

"I'm what?"

"You're not in your twenties, is all I'm saying." Claudia had not lifted her head from its dropped position, staring intensely into the depths of the mug.

"So maybe I should get out of suburban Ohio, is what you're saying. I can't be free to pursue my sexuality because I live in suburban Ohio, and there's a certain code of conduct that mandates monogamy in suburban Ohio," Clara said, affectless.

"Where did you grow up?" Claudia asked, tracing the new Sharpie tattoo she'd drawn in the shape of the state of Ohio on the inside of her wrist. The lines that formed the shape had blurred and bled as Claudia stood over the steamer earlier that morning, so the state now took the amorphous shape of an a-frame house tipped over on its side.

"Pennsylvania," Clara said flatly.

"Pennsylvania," Claudia repeated, seeming to chew the word in her mouth. "I've never been there. But from what I've heard it sounds like a pretty monogamous place to me." Clara squinted into her coffee mug at the distorted, big-eyed reflection of her own face in the oily, blank blackness. "Why did you come here?" Claudia asked. Her voice filled up the room, sounding hollow and far-away by the time it reached Clara's ears.

"Monogamy," Clara said, and swallowed a voluminous mouthful of coffee, feeling the gritty dregs crawl along her tongue.

When Clara and Alek divorced, Clara coordinated meetings in family court, found an apartment to move into, and signed some paperwork. She did not book a venue or buy a dress or worry about the bloody politics of seating

arrangements. She was the only one of her sisters to get a divorce. They had transcended her cosmetic, limited beauty all their lives, at her wedding even. But they would not surpass her in this. As far as she was concerned, the divorce was one of the easiest things she could have ever claimed to accomplish. Far easier than the wedding, or the marriage itself.

About the Author:

Charlotte Freccia is a third-year student of En-glish, Creative Writing, and Women's and Gender Studies at Kenyon College in Gambier, Ohio, where she also enjoys an associateship with the Kenyon Review. She is a 2016 winner of the Philip Wolcott Timberlake Writing Award, and has recently published poetry in Zaum Magazine, short fiction in Potluck Magazine, and creative nonfiction in Newfound. Her short story "Young Enough To Be Afraid" was published in Adelaide Literary Magazine in July 2017.

THE MAYOR OF JOESTOWN
by Nancy Lines

As the car began losing speed, all the lights on the dash lit up, leaving no question there was a serious problem under the hood. It was more than just a dead battery. Ann aimed the car toward the curb and coasted into a long, open spot. There were few cars parked on either side of the street because many of the buildings were boarded-up or razed, scattered among vacant lots full of debris and waist-high weeds.

This was the kind of neighborhood where only the poor and the elderly still lived. They could not afford to move, so they stayed in apartments that grew more rundown by the year. Ann had not seen a grocery store – or a store of any kind, except liquor stores – and no schools or medical facilities for blocks. When she drove down this street as a shortcut, she always drove quickly and made sure her windows were up and her doors locked. Now she regretted taking this route, although to stall on the freeway would have been more dangerous.

The only business nearby that appeared to be open was a tavern. The tavern windows were painted over, but through the peeling paint, she could see lights on inside, and she could hear faint music from a jukebox. She had to call Joel. She had left her cell phone on the kitchen counter—at least, that's where she usually left it –so she headed for the tavern with the red door and black lettering announcing this was "Joe's – An Uptown Bar." She thought "Joe's – A Nowhere Bar" would be more fitting now.

Hopefully, she could call Joel and wait here for him to pick her up. He would be irritated and would find some way to blame her for the dead car. Either she had waited too long to get the oil changed, or she had blown off the routine maintenance. Take your pick. Joel was a master at figuring out how all their problems were her fault.

It was much too hot to wait outside, and with no air conditioning and being afraid to leave a car window open, she would have to trust her luck in the tavern.

The bar was surprisingly dark inside, considering it was mid afternoon. Although it was cooler than outside, the air was anything but refreshing. It was more than stale smoke and stale beer. The air had a chemical top note that burned her nose and made her eyes tear. She thought it was probably decomposition of the building's insulation and walls. She wanted to get out of there as soon as possible, but Joel was not likely to change his schedule just because she wanted to go home.

As soon as her eyes got used to the layers of dust floating just below the tiled ceiling, she could see there were more patrons than she would have imagined from outside. A pool table had pride of place in the center of the room, and three men, all in their late 40's or 50's, with pool cues in hand, glanced up as she entered. She noticed apprehensively that she was the only woman in the bar. A couple booths were occupied with other older men, who had bottles lined up on the table, indicating they had been there for quite a while.

Didn't any of these people work?

The bartender nodded to her as she walked toward the bar. He put down the grimy rag he was wiping the glasses with and flipped a paper coaster in front of an empty barstool.

"What can I get you, young lady?"

She appreciated the insincere compliment, but all she wanted was a phone.

"My car stalled out down the street, and I don't have my cell phone with me. Do you have a phone I can use to call someone?"

He motioned to a wall-mounted phone at the end of the bar past the pool table.

"It's for local calls only."

A man sitting at the bar near the window, blocked by a layer of white paint, watched as she dialed. She supposed he was harmless enough, and the bartender was a burly guy, capable of handling most of the customers that might cause trouble. The pool players went back to their game, and the conversations in the booths resumed as if she were not there.

Joel, of course, did not answer his phone. She left a message, reading the phone number off a label pasted on the handle of the phone and gave him directions. She had not seen a phone like this for years, but this one was probably necessary for calling taxis when someone was too drunk to drive or, even, walk home or to make a flimsy excuse why he would be late for dinner again.

She sat on the barstool near the bartender. She felt she needed to order something to justify using the phone and taking up space while she waited for Joel, so she asked for a bottle of beer, which seemed the most sanitary choice. At the end of the bar, she watched a neon sign that showed fireworks arcing over a city scape. She remembered a Coors beer sign her father had in their family room, which was very similar. Her mother made him take the sign down when the religious relatives came to visit.

The bartender went back to polishing glasses with the dirty cloth, oblivious to the conversa-

tions going on around her and, apparently, totally uninterested in her broken down car.

An older man, who had been sitting in one of the booths with a couple other men his age, sauntered over.

"Welcome to Joe's. I'm the mayor of Joestown, right , Joe?"

The bartender nodded absently. He had probably heard this line many times before.

"Right," he said, without raising his head or even his eyes.

"I'm Sal. What brings you to our fair town?"

Ann wished she could be invisible until Joel got there. She didn't want to get into a conversation with a drunk. She assumed everyone in the bar was drunk because of the number of bottles on each flat surface.

"My car died. I've called my husband to come and get me. He should be here soon." She wanted to make it very clear someone knew where she was and was on his way to rescue her, although she could never think of Joel as a rescuer.

"Well, you are safe until he gets here, isn't she, Joe?"

Joe grunted again. She wondered how long it would take him to graduate to a clean rag for the glasses.

Ann sipped on her beer to have something to do to avoid conversation with Sal, although he seemed to be a nice enough guy, probably just lonely, undoubtedly an alcoholic. Who else would be in a bar in the middle of a deserted neighborhood in the middle of the day. As one of her friends put it, "It's the kind of bar where you go to get drunk."

"Would you like me to take a look at your car? I'm not a mechanic, but I might be able to figure out the problem."

She could think of nothing she would like less than to be outside in the boiling heat with a man she just met.

"Thanks, but Joel will be here soon. He'll probably have the car towed."

Sal sidled up to the stool next to her and ordered himself another beer.

"Can I get you another drink?"

"Thanks, but no. I'm not really a drinker."

"I'm not much of a drinker either, right, Joe?"

Joe smiled and nodded again. He was definitely not the kind of bartender you would tell your troubles to.

"My last car was like that, too," Sal said. "Couldn't depend on her to get me to the end of the block."

Ann could tell Sal was not going to go away. He seemed harmless.

"So what happened to the car?"

"Let my ex-wife take it. Didn't matter. I had lost my license anyway. Bum car to a bum wife. Seemed right."

Ann didn't think asking why Sal had lost his license – or his wife -- was necessary.

"How do you get groceries without a car? I don't see any markets nearby." She was genuinely curious how people like this lived. Where did they shop or go to the doctor? She hadn't even seen a church.

"Oh, Joe serves tacos on Tuesdays and chili on Fridays. I get by."

She had a lot of questions, but she didn't want to get too involved. This life was as far from her comfortable suburban life as she could get. Her first impression of Joe's customers, based on the fact that they were in a bar in the middle of a work day, was they were unemployed, maybe living on welfare. She hated to be judgmental, but the customers in Joe's were not the kind of people she would normally come in contact with.

She sneaked a look at Sal while he was taking a long draw on his beer. He was thin, and he had the look of someone that never got any sun on his skin. He had an alcoholic's broken veins on his nose and cheeks, and his eyes were rheumy beneath gray brows. His sparse hair was combed back from his forehead and poked out around his ears and overlapped the collar of his shirt. He looked like a man that lived alone.

"I don't see a kitchen. Where do they make the tacos and chili?"

"Joe and his wife live upstairs. He's been really good to me."

That explained it, Ann, thought. Joe could keep this place going because he probably owned the old building and had no expenses except taxes and utilities.

"Do you have children?"

"No, not yet." Ann answered. She wanted to say "Not until my husband decides we are ready," but she wasn't going to go into detail about her personal life with a stranger.

"How about you?"

"I've got two boys, but they don't have nothing to do with me after their mother died. I wasn't around much when she got sick, and they've never forgiven me. And then I got married to the piece of trash that divorced me. They hated her. They were better judges of character than I was."

The telephone rang, and Ann hopped off her stool to answer it, sure it was Joel, but Joe beat her to it.

"Ed, it's your wife. She said to send you home for supper."

Ed made no effort to leave, ordering another beer.

"What did your wife die of?"

"She had cancer. I wasn't as strong as she was. I couldn't watch while she died. I was here, and she was all alone. My sons said I was a coward – and a drunk. Can't say I blame them. I got what I deserved with that last one, though. She was a pip."

The telephone rang again, and Joe answered it, raising his eyebrows in the direction of one of the men at the pool table, who vigorously shook his head no.

"He's not here." He hung up the phone with an annoyed click.

Ann wondered if Joe did that all day, relay messages the drinkers ignored and lied about them being in the bar.

"Do any of the wives come in here looking for their husbands?"

"Nah, they don't bother. They know their men will come home eventually. Joe don't let us stay too late."

Ann wondered if some of the times she called Joel and he didn't answer he was at a bar, not wanting to go home. Maybe he was having an affair. At this point, she wasn't sure she cared much. She was also not sure why she stayed with him. Probably it was her fear of being alone, being financially responsible for herself. Although she worked from home doing "overflow" typing for three attorneys with small practices, she wasn't sure she could support herself. She had never had much self-confidence, and Joel's constant belittling had etched away what she had like acid on stone.

Sal finished another beer while she was still slowly sipping hers. She ordered another, not out of any desire to drink it but as kind of an act of rebellion. When Joel found her here, sitting at a bar, drinking out of a bottle, he would be furious and embarrassed. Damn him for leaving her here on her own.

One of the men at the pool table put more money in the jukebox and then went back to where he had been sitting on the corner of the table. A slow bluesy song oozed out and filled the room. It was the perfect song for this sunless place.

Sal got up and slowly began dancing by himself, hands held lightly at his sides, swaying and turning. Ann was amazed at his grace, the sweet sadness of his movements. He extended

a hand to her to join him. She slipped off her stool and danced near him, not touching but turning as he turned. Sal nodded at her and continued his swaying to the rhythms, Ann following his lead. She seldom danced because she felt awkward. Joel said she had no rhythm and was stiff as a mannequin, so she let him dance with their friends when the occasion came up while she watched. Now, she felt free of judgment. Sal smiled at her as she twirled for no reason, and she smiled back.

The telephone on the wall rang again, but Ann made no attempt to answer it.

"Ed, it's your wife again. Get your ass home!"

Ed, head hanging like a dog, finished off his drink, threw a couple dollar bills on the table, and headed for the door.

"See you, Joe, Sal."

A Bill Withers' song "The Love that Made Me Laugh Made Me Cry," one of Ann's favorites, began playing, and Sal continued his dancing. She sat back on her stool and watched Sal, his eyes closed, moving to the music as if it filled his head and drove away all other thoughts. He looked weightless, like he could float away. Whatever he was remembering was making him almost happy.

When the song was over, the pool players resumed their play, and the sounds of balls bouncing off each other and the thunks as they went into pockets echoed throughout the room. Just then, Ann heard a thumping sound, as if someone were banging a broomstick or stomping against the upstairs floor near a set of stairs. Joe looked up and then motioned to Sal, who slid off his stool and went around to the other side of the bar. Their movements were so choreographed, it was apparent these were roles they both knew by heart.

Joe climbed the stairs and in a couple minutes came back down, carrying a plate covered with aluminum foil and set it before Sal, who was now sitting on a stool near the sink. After he went back upstairs, Sal peeled back the foil and sniffed appreciatively.

"Meat loaf night! Queenie is a good cook. I'll be glad to share with you."

So that was the deal: in exchange for a good hot meal, Sal watched the bar while Joe had supper with his wife. The whole silent arrangement spoke of the trust, if not the affection, between the two men. Sal ate his meal and then rinsed his plate in the sink for Joe to take back upstairs after his break. Ann wondered if Queenie ever came downstairs or if this was Joe's private place.

The telephone rang a few more times, but now it was Sal who rushed to answer it. Each call was a wife or girlfriend asking him to send her man home or asking if he was there and then pretending to believe Sal when he said no.

Sal scooted his stool to where he was facing Ann. He looked like a man content with his life, which Ann found impossible to believe. This little, circumscribed life in a dingy bar with deadbeats and alcoholics?

"What did you do for a living, Sal, when you were working?"

"I was a barber." He grinned at her. "I can still do a mean haircut if you want one!" Ann wondered why Sal's own hair was not kept trimmed.

"Why did you stop? Where was your shop?" She thought he would say it was in one of the boarded-up buildings along the street.

"I always wanted my own shop, to be my own boss, but the time was never right. I worked for other barbers or rented out chairs in their shops. I saved, but then I had to put the boys through college, and by that time my wife had cancer, and all our money went to the doctors who couldn't save her. Didn't stop the bastards (excuse my language) from charging me thousands of dollars, though. Then, I just didn't care anymore." He gestured, his hands encompassing the whole of the bar. "This saved me."

"Do you live upstairs, too?"

Sal laughed. "No, but Queenie makes me stay the night if I'm too far gone to make it home. I sleep on their sofa."

Ann was amazed that there was no embarrassment in his tone, no apologies.

The telephone rang again, and she moved to answer it. It must be Joel this time. She had been here for a couple hours. It would be just like Joel to leave her here to teach her a lesson. But again Sal was first to the phone. From where she sat, she could hear a woman's angry voice.

"Jimmy, your wife says if you're not home in ten minutes, she'll feed your dinner to the dogs, and you can sleep with them, too."

Everyone, including Jimmy, who was playing pool, laughed. He walked over to Ann and politely offered her the cue.

"Why don't you take my place. I'm gonna let the pretty lady teach these rookies how to play pool!"

"Come on," Sal said, "I'll help you out."

Ann had played pool at her friends' houses, the friends with swimming pools and "game rooms" with pool tables and pin ball machines. She didn't play well, but she knew how to hold a cue. Joel said if they stuck to their financial plan (his, really, she didn't have any input), they could have a house with a pool and game room, too. The problem was, Ann thought, she was the only one that stuck to the plan. Joel claimed he had to project a certain image to his customers, so he bought expensive cars and clothes and joined the right clubs. As he reminded her many times, you have to look prosperous to become prosperous. And when they were finally as prosperous as Joel wanted to be, he said they could finally start thinking about having a baby.

Ann was beginning to wonder if she was the "right" person to further Joel's success. It seemed sometimes as if he were ashamed of her. If he saw her today, drinking a bottle of domestic beer, playing pool with a bunch of rummies, he might conclude she was the one holding him back. She ordered another beer.

She and Sal finished the game where Jimmy left off. Mickey won, but the players next on deck let Ann and Sal take their turn. Sal was amazingly sure with his shots. They lost, nonetheless, but Ann wanted to keep playing, so she placed a quarter on the side of the table, which meant she and Sal would play the winner of the next game. Sal nodded and patted her on the back.

"Atta, girl. We'll get 'em next time."

Sal brought her a fresh, cold beer. Ann didn't remember if she had drunk this much beer at one time since college. Even then, she didn't drink much because she got sick easily. She really didn't like the taste of alcoholic drinks, but today it tasted good. Maybe it was the company.

A man came in and took an empty booth near the back of the bar. He was dressed in a suit and looked completely out of place here. A few minutes later, a woman, about the same age, came in and joined the man at the back booth. Without their asking, Sal took them each a glass of beer and took their money to put in the cash register.

"They meet here every day, same time, for years. They're both married. They don't cause no trouble. They don't bother nobody, and nobody bothers them." He said it proudly, as if this was part of the reason Joe's was special. He explained the bar had its own rules, and as long as everyone obeyed the rules, they were safe and accepted here.

When it was time for Ann and Sal to play the winners of the last pool game, the telephone rang again. Sal answered and then held the phone out to Ann.

"What's going on there?" Joel asked impatiently. "Doesn't sound to me like this is an emergency. Can't you call a taxi so I don't have to leave work? You have enough for a taxi?"

"And the car? Do I just leave the car here?"

"Have it towed! Our insurance covers that. You can manage that by yourself, can't you?" His voice dripped with disgust.

"Right. I can manage by myself. I'd hate to inconvenience you." She slammed the receiver on the phone. Everyone in the bar looked up to see what was going on.

"Everything okay, little lady?" Sal looked concerned and, surprisingly, protective.

"Everything is fine. I think it's time for me to go home. I'll just call a cab and have the car towed. My husband is too busy to come to get me."

Sal looked doubtful but didn't say anything. He dialed a number he knew well and ordered a cab.

Ann rummaged in her purse until she came up with her insurance card with the number for a towing service. The towing company promised to be there within a couple hours, but knowing Joel was not coming to pick her up, Ann saw no reason to wait.

Joe was back at the bar. Sal announced he was going to stay with Ann until her taxi arrived.

Joe nodded at Ann.

"You can use our phone anytime."

When the taxi stopped in front of Joe's, Sal opened the cab door for Ann and then squeezed her hand.

He smiled, and she smiled back.

"Thank you," she said.

As he closed the taxi door, Sal looked briefly down the street. Ann thought maybe he was ready to go home for the night, but as the taxi pulled away from the curb, Sal hurried back through the red door. He looked relieved. He was, indeed, going home.

About the Author:

Nancy Lines had one long essay published in an area newspaper, and a short story based on a true event is being reviewed by a national military magazine.

A FOUR-LETTER WORD

by James Brennan

Jack Broderick, who worked in human resources at a prestigious university's school of government, had made a career out of playing it safe, so he wasn't crazy about the exposure this year's summer picnic would give him.

At the Harding School of Public Policy, scholars who enjoyed lucrative careers guiding Middle East peace talks couldn't avoid bitter arguments over what kind of rice cakes to stock in the kitchen. Celebrity professors, adept at conversing with presidents and other world leaders, weren't able to say *good   morning* to the guy who watered their plants. The most educated people in the world didn't know how to submit a Spot Award—a nominal staff bonus rewarding extra duty—for an assistant who had given up his weekends over an entire semester to prepare their PowerPoints for a humanitarian summit. As Assistant Di-rector of Human Resources, Broderick had heard it all.

At this school of government, the only thing faculty members enjoyed more than discussing power—its intricate forms and varied uses—in the classroom, was demonstrating who had it and who didn't everywhere else on campus. And it was a place where the trivia contest for the summer picnic was anything but trivial.

The dean liked the trivia contest. And when he'd declared that the picnic was still on, calling it a morale booster, after the University had gone through one of the ugliest layoffs in its history, the contest fell in Broderick's lap like an 800-pound gorilla on steroids.

Hearing the weather report during his morning commute just made Broderick mad. It was sup-

posed to be much nicer on the Cape and Islands today. But not everyone *had* that kind of choice on a Tuesday. He was already resigned to looking like he'd pissed himself. He'd taken the cover off his coffee to let it cool. He liked his coffee hot 365 days a year. But not that hot. He'd barely avoided rear-ending the car in front of him. His mood improved somewhat after he'd squeezed his quivering Corolla, a vehicle purchased new during Reagan's second term, into one of those tight spaces under the concrete eaves in the administration building's underground garage, a place he didn't even consider when he arrived at his usual time.

Broderick and Amelia sat across from each other at the faux-oak table behind closed doors in the HR conference room waiting for one of them to come up with a good idea. Amelia sat with her back to the floor-to-ceiling windows. The sky had opened and it was a real drencher out there. Broderick couldn't see across the campus courtyard.

"Did you burn yourself?" Amelia smiled, not so innocently in Broderick's estimation.

He was sorry that he'd told her about the coffee incident. But what choice did he have? "All this rain may cool things off a bit."

The hang 'n' store file boxes, still not archived from the layoff, were stacked along the front wall. These files were thick. Employment applications, payroll change notifications, a performance appraisal here and there, 403B deduction forms, and, of course, the legal reviews, assessing not only the risk of lawsuits—age discrimination cases were the most preva- lent—but, more importantly, the University's chances to prevail, were all that remained of the recently departed. Many of them had come to see Broderick after their managers, fol- lowing HR's prepared script, told them: *Your position has been eliminated. It is not personal. Please leave immediately.* "They're not going to change their minds," he'd said to each one, a box of Kleenex in hand. He tried to help them leave with some dignity.

Broderick turned from the boxes to Amelia. "Don't ever let them see you grovel."

"Focus, Jack. The picnic's this Friday."

Amelia was twenty-six and had that perfect skin the young take for granted. Her face was framed by dirty-blonde hair cut in a bob. She had wide-set brown eyes, high, angular cheek- bones, a dimpled chin, and her upper lip formed a little heart when she blew on her herbal tea. She had been hired before downsiz- ing began. Hers was a replacement position not an add to headcount, and HR was spared the cleaver because someone had to process all the layoffs.

She'd come east from Missouri, following a boyfriend who was attending the business school. He was no longer in the picture. Greeting her in the reception area of the HR suite the day of her interview, Broderick had liked her right away. "Nice poster," she'd said, looking at his Led Zeppelin U.S. Tour 1977. He was unnerved by the way she scanned every inch of his office, before taking the seat he mo- tioned to in front of his desk, as if he would wait for her to take it all in. He had.

The probing Broderick typically conducted dur- ing his interviews had been nothing more than flaccid inquiry with her. Did she have any expe- rience with payroll in that HR coordinator job listed on her resume? She replied that her only experience with payroll was getting a paycheck every other Friday. He smiled and pretended to jot notes on her resume. He followed up with, "And how did you like that?" She smiled.

"Getting paid? I loved it." Then she pushed back her hair and smiled again.

Her title was HR Specialist. On paper she re- ported to Broderick's boss, but he, Broderick, had trained her during her first few weeks, and she'd go to him whenever she came up against something she couldn't handle, which wasn't often.

Her friend request, when it showed up in his inbox one weekend, had surprised him, in a good way. He clicked on the **accept** button as if she might change her mind at any second. Then he thought of all the reasons why this might be a terrible idea. And as he scrolled through her posts and pictures he thought about what he would say to her on Monday. *Family holidays . . .* The Harding School was like a dysfunctional family where one wrong move could get you disowned. *Barbecues . . .* Cau- tion, like LIPITOR, wasn't pleasant to take, and while it didn't guarantee longevity, it was pru- dent and all you had. Okay, maybe not that. *Having fun at the beach. . . Lots of beach pic- tures. . .* As they say, Facebook's for fun; LinkedIn's where business gets done. *Nag's Head. She's knee-deep in the surf in a turquoise bikini, a hand on her hip, the other hand wav- ing, sunglasses on top of her head, smile sug- gesting, Come on in.* Maybe he had no business offering Amelia social media advice. He deci- ded not to say anything. He also decided to give up beer and to renew his gym member- ship.

Now Amelia was waving her hand in front of Broderick's face. "Are you there?" He could smell the orange she was having with her tea on her fingers. He started writing. He wanted to capture this spittle of inspiration before it evaporated. He pushed his notebook across the table. Then, having second thoughts, he reached for it, but Amelia grabbed it and start- ed reading.

"If you were to take off all your clothes right now and run across the Harding School's South

Lawn, you would be labeled, at best, a political-ly-incorrect nut job. If you had done this in the seventies, however, you would have simply been called a––

"Really?"

This was Amelia's first summer picnic, and their boss had put her in charge of the whole thing. Timothy Dunwright, or Dun, as he wanted everyone to call him, said she was an "up and comer." When Dun had asked him what he thought of Amelia after her interviews, adding that his input wouldn't be a deal-breaker, Broderick had said that he thought her English degree made her interesting.

Broderick had been *Assistant* HR Director for longer than he cared to remember. When they hired Dun from outside, he'd been passed over like a leftover clam chowder no one remembers putting in the office fridge. His involvement with the picnic should have been to make decisions, if necessary, to avert any last-minute disasters, the kind that could derail a career. But he could take solace in the fact that he'd once been good enough to be good at something his heart wasn't in.

His first job at the University had been for a paycheck, and it was supposed to be temporary. He'd wanted to be a writer. But by the time he'd gone from loving everything he wrote to hating everything he wrote, feeling like he'd had a breakthrough, the first layoff in the University's history hit. With a wife and kid, Broderick did what he had to over the years to survive. He was still paying down the loans he'd taken out for his son's college tuition. The undergrad degree was in the court order, but he was paying for the graduate degree too.

Broderick's number one goal in life today was hanging on for the pension. It was simple math: age plus years of service; the higher the number, the higher the payout. Finding love again was a close second, but there was nothing simple about that.

On his good days, Broderick allowed himself to imagine a relationship with Amelia that was more than just colleagues or friends. Sure, he was older than her, but these things happened. And not just in the banal manuscripts he'd read in those writing workshops at the Adult Ed Center, including the interminable one where the Cougar has to decide between her lover and Fluffy her cat, a story that when it stalked his dreams would make Broderick sit up straight, unable to catch his breath as if he had a huge hairball lodged in his trachea.

On his bad days, Broderick saw the future. He was an old man sitting in the hall of some nursing home, staring at the urine puddle on the floor, reaching out for the nurse's aides and flashing toothless smiles at them when they brought him apple juice and his pills. The pleasure of caressing a woman's thigh would be a foggy notion; he would simply be seeking human touch. They would find his liver-spotted, bony hands pushing on their legs annoying, or worse, amusing.

Amelia was pushing her notebook toward him. "What about this?"

What's a four-letter word that sums up the seventies?

The sweat from Broderick's armpits trickled down his sides. He couldn't adjust the AC. The thermostats had been in clear plastic lockboxes since Al Gore's post-White-House speaking tour. *Fuck* was the first word that came to his mind: not the verb of an awkward adolescent when the seventies were waning, wanting to get some before it all crashed and burned, but the noun of a timorous teenager summing up his experience during a decade he couldn't wait to have done. Amelia pushed her hair behind her ears. Then she repeated the motion as if the strands hadn't complied. Broderick thought he'd read somewhere, maybe in one of those sex manuals he started picking up after the divorce, carefully concealing them in the big art books from the bargain table until reaching the cashier, that when a woman played with her hair it meant she was interested. He didn't recall reading how to signal her back that he was interested too. Being direct would've been reckless.

"Give up?"

Broderick handed back her notebook. "A long time ago."

"The seventies are going to be fun."

"If you say so."

"It begins with *I*. Make *love* not war? All you need is *love*?"

Amelia was confusing the sixties with the seventies. But what was a decade or so among friends?

The seventies theme was her idea; giving Broderick the trivia contest was Dun's. He knew his boss hadn't meant it in a good way when he said that the seventies were going to be fun.

The dean *liked* the trivia contest. Dun's predecessor had made the mistake of dropping it at what would be her last summer picnic, opting instead for a mechanical-bull-riding contest. That year's theme was rodeo. With thirty-two years at the School, she should've known better. Maybe she did. Broderick imagined her backing out of the administration building in a blaze of glory, brandishing a severance agreement in one hand, a Harding School-engraved clock in the other. It was a good thing nobody on the outside knew what they were doing. Even the School's most media-tested celebrity professor would have a hard time fielding this question from Anderson Cooper: Your HR people spend *how* much time on a trivia contest?

On Wednesday, Broderick was in Dun's office giving him the update he'd requested. The boss had told the dean that the trivia contest was going to be fabulous.

"So show me fabulous." Dun grabbed the draft out of Broderick's hands. While he read it, Broderick stared at the plants along his wall-length window. His Norfolk Pine needed watering. The sun was trying to come out.

Dun leaned back in his executive leather chair. He wore his platinum hair spiked, perhaps an attempt to create the illusion of height, much like the arrangement of chairs in his office making Broderick look up at him.

"Running naked? Across the South Lawn?" Dun took his glasses off. "What is *that*?"

"Streaking."

"I mean what's it doing in your contest?"

"It's seventies trivia."

"Can you imagine what the dean would have to say about that?"

"He might like it."

"Questions about people running naked in public do not cut it around here. We don't want a call from Legal telling me we have to run another sexual harassment refresher. Do we?"

Dun unfolded the piece of paper he grabbed from his inside suit-coat pocket. The guy was always dressed for business, as he liked to say. "How about this?

"June 1970, this event in New York City commemorated the first anniversary of the Stonewall Rebellion and became the first—

"Oh come on, Jack."

"Sorry."

"In 1975 the United Nations declared this year the—

"Work with me here."

"The seventies were kind of a blur for me."

Dun waved the paper in his hand like he was holding an endowment check from Bill Gates. "I have an entire list of these."

"That sounds like important stuff."

"Right."

"I thought trivia was stuff that nobody cared about."

"Jack, I'm trying to help you. I know you've been at the School a lot longer than I have, but I know what sells. And what would sell better in the Harding School of Public Policy's seventies-summer-picnic trivia contest than important political events from the seventies?"

Broderick knew better than anyone not to trust someone from HR who says he's here to help. He slouched in his chair. He knew his days were numbered: he was a bit old—and expensive—for an assistant director. But he'd studied his younger boss enough to know that he'd want neither an age discrimination suit nor a sizeable severance payout gumming up his career trajectory. That left Dun two options: He could wait for Broderick to do something so egregious that he could fire him for cause. Or he could make him so miserable that he would leave on his own. The legal term for that? Constructive discharge. The trivia contest was going to be an attempt at both—Broderick was sure of it—until Amelia decided to attach her name to the contest too.

Amelia and Broderick were in the conference room finalizing the contest. The picnic was tomorrow. She'd just organized the volleyball competition—another thankless task, but a crowd favorite—setting up an elaborate scoring system that would've been the envy of the NCAA. "I couldn't think of a way to really make it seventies."

"I'm pretty sure volleyball was played in the seventies."

"You know what I mean." The sunlight filling the room brought out the sprinkling of tiny nutmeg-colored freckles under Amelia's eyes. "And I have an update for you on the T-shirts. They're a go. Tie-dyed."

Dun had been reluctant to spend money on shirts for everyone until Broderick told him that he remembered the dean liking T-shirt giveaways. The dean did not like them.

Apparently, seventies retro was in. Broderick wasn't one for knowing what was in and what was out. Freshman year in high school he'd walked into a head shop with hard-earned cash from his bagging job at Star Market and bought a Nehru jacket. Choosing from what they had left on the rack, it was a size too small. It didn't matter. Nehrus went out of style the next day. The rest of the seventies didn't go much better for him.

"What about this one?" Broderick was pointing to his next question.

18. Only three films have won the top five awards (Best Picture, Best Director, Best Actor, Best Actress, and Best Screenplay). What movie from 1975 set in a mental institution was one of them?

"Movie trivia is always good," she said, getting up to adjust the blinds.

No longer squinting from the sun in his eyes, he smiled. "I thought a question about a nut house would play well here." He was thinking how Dun had tucked that list of questions in his, Broderick's, shirt and patted his pocket as if it were on fire.

Amelia came back to the table. She leaned across, put her hand on his arm and said, "How about literary references?"

Jack smiled and nodded. She was great, but she had to be careful. Even up-and-comers only have so much currency to spend. "What is it with you and the seventies anyway?"

Amelia shrugged. "Lots of things, I guess. But mostly that whole question authority thing?"

"That was a hold-over from the sixties, but we did our best with it."

"Well, you don't have to do literary references," she said, breaking the awkward silence. "I was just thinking."

"I love—

"How you think."

The humidity had broken and the weather on Friday, sunny and low eighties, was perfect. The list of things for which Broderick would risk his pension was extremely short, but he was pretty sure it included running naked with Amelia across the lush South Lawn on a beautiful late-June afternoon. He smiled as he tried to keep up with her. She was wearing the tie-dyed shirt, a couple of sizes too big, over black yoga pants. They were coming from reprographics where they had picked up their rush job on the contest.

Fast Eddie, a communications officer in the Media Relations Office, was the DJ, and he stood elevated over Broderick and Amelia on a makeshift platform outside of Mooney Hall. They had set up a table in front of the music, where people could get a copy of the contest and then drop it off in the hemp basket Amelia had found at a yard sale. Passing on the tie-dyed, Fast Eddie wore his own theme outfit as was his practice every year. With white polyester pants flared out from the bottom of his knee to the tops of his black platform shoes and the barely-buttoned purple shirt that looked like it might have been Quiana, he looked more eighties than seventies.

Across the courtyard, it appeared that Marcie and Bibi, staff assistants from Student Services, were on their way to another volleyball victory thanks to the guys they'd recruited this year from the Military Leaders Forum. They'd sent an e-mail with flowers and peace symbols to the entire school inviting everyone to come watch them win another championship. It was signed, *The Rock Star Volleyball Players*. Broderick wondered how you could make yourself relevant simply by declaring it.

"Look." Amelia pointed to the empty basket.

"Is it too late to go streaking?"

"Stop it."

The smell of peppers and onions wafted from the grills. People spilled across the courtyard, some dancing to "Play That Funky Music," others in cliques chatting away and chomping burgers and dogs. The dean, arriving fashionably late, was wearing granny glasses and a Stars & Stripes top hat. He liked to show the hoi polloi that he was a regular guy. Onlookers were cheering the Rock Star Volleyball Players as their team shocked and awed everyone. Their military guys were a hit. This wasn't *really* the seventies. Several folks came by to ask Fast Eddie to pump up the volume, and there were some requests to get imported beer next year. Dun, ever mindful of the budget, had Amelia order kegs of the domestic stuff. Broderick suggested to Amelia that they go grab something to eat.

When they returned, the basket was still empty. Amelia, leaning into Broderick, said, "I think we have a great trivia contest." He detected a vaguely familiar scent, musk or something.

Broderick sipped his Diet Pepsi, trying to come up with something to say to her, when April appeared, waving her contest in front of their faces. Amelia picked up the basket and offered it to April. "Do you want to drop your contest off?"

"What did you say?"

"I said do you want to drop your contest off."

"Oh, this music." April held a hand over one ear. "Too loud."

Over the course of her long career at the Harding School, as documented in her HR file, she had distinguished herself by serving four professors, a department chair, two deans, and by making countless faculty assistants cry. She'd landed into Amelia once or twice over some payroll adjustments.

"I wish to wait while you correct it," April said.

Feeling protective of Amelia, Broderick took April's contest. When he finished correcting it, he longed for the good old days when the prize was a Dunkie's gift card. Nobody beyond their ivy-covered walls would've believed that they were giving away an iPod. A big prize was money well-spent, Dun had said. It showed the dean how big the contest was.

April leaned over the table. "And?"

Broderick couldn't bring himself to tell April that she had them all right.

April picked up the basket. "Where are all the other contests anyway?"

Amelia was about to say something, but Broderick interjected. "They're all locked away in the HR secret vault waiting for our auditors to come in on Monday and validate the results. Only then can we let you know if you have won the iPod."

April paused for a moment and then said, "I see. Thank you so much. It's been a pleasure." She started to walk away, then turned and grinned. "And I'll be sure to tell the dean just what a pleasure it's been."

Amelia looked at their one contest entry. "Why did she have to win?"

"We should've put in your four-letter-word question. She never would have got that one."

"Don't you think this place could use a little more love?"

Amelia had no idea. April was walking over with the dean and his entourage.

The picnic was HR's thing, and that gave Dun the right to tag along today. It might have been the extra layer making him sweat—he was wearing the motif T-shirt over his white long-sleeved oxford, the knot of his paisley tie barely visible—but Broderick had another theory. For all his fawning, Dun knew better than anyone that the dean didn't like him.

The dean had met Amelia at one of his new-hire coffees, but he insisted on an introduction. He held Amelia's hand a little too long in Broderick's estimation. And he wouldn't take his eyes off her. Broderick held a copy of the contest up to the dean, trying to shield Amelia from his gaze. "I think you're going to like this year's."

"I've already heard a lot about it." The dean nodded at April, taking the sheet. "I'm going to take this with me. I have to go over and congratulate Marcie and Bibi for winning the volleyball tournament. Again." He handed the sheet to Dun. "Here. Hold this."

When the entourage was out of earshot Broderick said, "I almost feel bad for Dun."

"That dean would've had his office taken over in the seventies."

Broderick liked Amelia's version of the seventies much better than his. "What do you say then? Monday morning we'll stage a sit-in."

She smiled. "I like—"

"How I think?" Broderick put his hands up as if he were trying to quell the applause.

"That too. I was going to say that I like you."

Broderick was ready to request "Colour My World" and slow-dance Amelia across the South Lawn. He imagined her draped over him, his fingers gently pressing the small of her back, rocking her side to side, her hands cupping his shoulders, head resting on his chest, the smell of patchouli letting him know everything was alright in the world.

But their DJ cut the music. The dean was back and, apparently, Fast Eddie thought he might have a few words for everyone. The dean shook his head and waved away the mic. He handed his trivia contest to Amelia, the fabric of his suit moving with him like another layer of skin. "How did I do?" He smiled behind his granny glasses.

Broderick gave Fast Eddie a nod to put the music back on but he just stood there with the microphone hanging limply in his hand.

With the entourage looking on, Amelia corrected the contest. While he waited, the dean made small talk. He liked the streaking question.

"I *loved* that one," Dun said. He hadn't seen Broderick's final version. "After all, trivia contests are supposed to be light and fun."

The dean, looking at his contest upside down, pointed to the last question and said, "How could that one be wrong?"

20. Some might say this southern writer was for the birds, but her work won a National Book Award in the early seventies.

"You wrote down the wrong name," Amelia said.

Broderick felt a flutter in his stomach as the dean insisted that his answer, Harper Lee, had to be correct because of the reference to the title of her book. Amelia kept shaking her head. He had never seen anything like this. Sure, the dean liked the contest, but he'd never cared about *winning* it. It wasn't like he was eligible for the damn prize.

He had them all right except that one question. Broderick had been thinking peafowl when he came up with it for Amelia. "Didn't she die in the sixties?" she'd said. Amelia didn't know that Flannery's story collection took this posthumous award in 1972. April did.

This was an easy one. They accept Harper Lee and say the dean won. As the second-place winner, April would get the iPod. Everyone happy.

The dean looked at Broderick. "I don't understand."

"You didn't *get* it," Amelia said.

Her defiant look stirred something in Broderick from a long time ago, before fear started waiting for him every day like a schoolyard bully.

Dun lunged across the table and grabbed Broderick's arm. "For heaven's sake. Amelia is simply mistaken. Jack. Is the dean right or isn't he?"

April smiled, arms folded, as if she knew the correct answer to this one too.

That Monday, smoky-gray clouds hung low over the campus. Seventies trivia had had its run. By the time HR would be working on the holiday party, people would chalk up Amelia's faux pas, if it was remembered at all, to youth. *She* would be forgiven. Broderick could see her sitting one day, not quite comfortably, in an executive leather chair perusing the budget report on her desk. By then, she would know that sometimes decisions had to be made to avert disasters.

Amelia didn't have a window office *yet*, so she wouldn't be able to see Broderick on the South Campus lawn. But she'd hear about it. He took one pained step after another. Something was constricting him. It felt like an ill-fitting Nehru jacket that he couldn't seem to lose.

But that's crazy, he thought, lumbering across the lush grass. He was naked.

About the Author:

James Brennan lives and works in the Boston area. His stories and essays have appeared in Charles River Review, Colere, Slab, Edge, and First Line, among others.

HE HAD A LOT OF STUFF

by Thomas Tomlinson

Greg was not a neighbor you would want to have. He would always play loud music. The neighbors were always asking him to shut it off. He would crank it up the very next day. Sometimes the old lady next door would offer him food to shut the music off. She was 88 years old and her house was for sale. She had had enough. Greg was drunk one night and rolled her house. She knew he did it. Another time he put a firecracker in her mailbox and it destroyed it. He was always up to no good.

One time his German shepherd attacked a kid. They sued him and he paid a large settlement. He had a lot of character defects. Rumors had spread that he was seeing a psychiatrist for post traumatic stress disorder and obsessive compulsive disorder.

Greg lived with his son. His son was 17 and a good student. He liked to hang out at coffee shops and do his homework. He was nothing like his dad. Sometimes his dad would tell him he was going to beat him but he never did.

Greg was a hoarder. He loved having things. Any kind of tool or gardening equipment he had He loved fishing. A boat was in the driveway and all kinds of tackle boxes and fis-

hing poles were in the Garage. He liked to paint to. Everywhere were pictures and paintings on the walls. He was a voracious reader and had a bedroom with nothing but books. His obsession was owning whatever he could. He was greedy and competitive. Instead of the saying been there done that it was more like you don't have it but I do. He had a loft in one of his bedrooms with nothing but sports memorabilia. He had a Hank Aaron, Babe Ruth, and Joe DiMaggio baseball card collection. He had shoe boxes filled with baseball cards. He had more sports equipment than one can imagine. He also had saved all his receipts and paycheck stubs. The house was arranged in a neat order because of his OCD. He had bedrooms filled with junk.

One day his son came home from school while Greg was working on a weed eater he garbage picked. He let his dad talk about how he was going to change. Greg felt bad the neighbor was moving because of him. He said she made good food. His son finally said nicely that he needed to change.

His son insisted on no more loud music, drinking, firecrackers, and especially garbage picking. Greg said he shouldn't be doing these things at his age. His son got through to him and told him he knew a good psychiatrist. Greg didn't like the idea of medication for his OCD or PTSD. He

said he didn't know if he could quit garbage picking. Greg liked to fix things that's where the hoarding mostly came from. His son told him no more garbage picking, thrift stores, garage sales, or pawn shops. Greg said he didn't know if he could quit drinking. Greg said he tried Alcoholics Anonymous before and he didn't like the idea of having a sponsor. His son told him to just take one day at a time, and that they weren't going to get rid of everything. Greg was thinking of selling his things on the computer and was excited about all the money he was going to make which would go to the bills.

Greg was thinking of apologizing to the neighbor. He decided no more drinking no matter what happens. No more loud music. No more firecrackers or rolling houses. He would keep the German shepherd in the backyard. Greg even thought about going back to the church he went to as a kid.

His son wasn't sure if his dad really wanted to change. He wondered if the medication would help him get rid of some of his junk. The real motif for change was he didn't want the lady next door to move. She made really good apple pie and cheesecake. He sat on the crowded porch smoking cigarettes and thinking what he was going to fix and sell. He drank some water and contemplated about changing mostly for his son.

THE GIFT

by Libby Belle

The nausea was bad enough to send her jumping out the window, only her house was a one-story and crashing to her death just wasn't possible with a mere three-foot fall. Although, a few broken bones might take her mind off the real reason she is imprisoned in her own home. But in the end, all it would do is add to the medical bills that would never be paid in *her* lifetime – a lifetime shortened by this creepy disease they call cancer. That ugly word doesn't deserve a capital letter until they find a cure for it, and that will be long after Gina is gone. It was a good thing she had decided early on not to bring any children into this world. They'd never have to know the shitty way their mother died.

The bald head was not a big deal, really, because Gina had a very pretty face, tiny features, only a few wrinkles for a woman in her fifties, thin crow's feet that a good make-up could easily disguise, a full set of lips and exceptionally large eyes that when eyeliner was applied, they appeared impishly cat-like. Her hair had always been thin anyway, and when it fell out, she was quite surprised to find that her perfectly shaped head had no lumps or dents. Not one. Altogether a miracle since she had fallen off the bed more times than she could count on two hands.

Bound mostly to her bedroom, the vomit tray within reach, she had plenty of time to ponder simple things like the first time she had hit her noggin during a bout of playful sex. Was it with her first, second, third, or fourth husband? Everything that ever happened in her life was categorized by which husband she was with at the time.

Although, the last two husbands didn't really count because she had given each of them only a six-month trial period during which they both failed miserably. And in both cases, she had filed for annulment, which technically meant she had only been married twice. *Single and married four times* always got a resounding stupefied reaction from the men she dated, as if she'd said "Here, hold this stick of dynamite while I fish through my purse for a match." *Married only twice* worked much better and would usually return a, "Well, you know what they say, third time's a charm," generally followed by a wink and another glass of wine.

One thought always led to another and if she had enjoyed writing, Gina would have put all these tidbits down on paper. Oh well, she'd just have to take them all to her grave!

It was a cloudless, sunny day and hard to stay depressed after she wrapped a designer scarf around her, smooth, hairless head and made up her face to absolute perfection. The nightgown she wore was stunning and if a lover had of been in her presence, he would have told her so just before he ripped it from her body. Yes, ripped! Gina liked her lovers wild and beasty, just teetering on the edge of cruel, and she especially liked them eager and greedy – never satisfied with only one orgasm.

So, if she is such a pretty cancer patient, where are all those exciting lovers now? Not one came to see her, not one called or sent flowers, or even a lousy three-dollar card. Her girlfriends were few and most of them owed her money and stayed away in shame. She figured they must be feeling bad about that, knowing how much Gina could use some extra cash. And hoping to keep her disease private, her boss had told her co-workers that she had a contagious infection, which eliminated any expectations of a visit from a colleague.

Her last hope was her favorite aunt who promised to visit soon after recovering from a bunion removal. "Sure, when will that be? At my funeral?" Gina had blurted, just as she hung up the phone, imagining her epitaph in a sad, drippy font, "Here Lies Beautiful Gina who died of Loneliness."

As for her best friend, Ellen, she was too exhausted from her own miserable life at home with her schizophrenic father, her divorced daughter, and those ungrateful brats. Last, but not least was Frank, poor Frank, the neglected husband who Ellen was gradually losing all desire for. Gina couldn't blame her friend for not coming around anymore. Seeing her like this just added to Ellen's misery.

Thank goodness for daily talk shows and old soap opera reruns and particularly for those magazines pertaining to home design, as Gina loved to decorate – filling her place full of beautiful accessories, sexy lamps and rugs, thick window coverings to darken a room like a cave, and always a touch of leather. Men like leather. She still took comfort in being surrounded by beauty – taking selfies in front of her fancy vases, Scarlet O'Hara drapes, naked statues of Greek gods, and plush bedspreads laced in metallic golds and reds covered with a never-ending line-up of throw pillows trimmed in fur or tassels. She could see her epitaph in a sensual gold font, "The World

Less One Classy Broad!"

It wouldn't be the worst thing to die in all this

lushness, she told her dog, Archie. She had rescued the little canine from her mean step-father who had planned to take him to the pound right after her mother's funeral. People can be so cruel she warned the little Terrier.

Archie was who kept her going. Archie was what kept her believing, because Archie cried when she cried, was happy when she was happy, and never left her bed, like the men in her life eventually did. So, it wasn't surprising that Archie would grow to be over-protective and lunge after anyone who knocked on the door – the pizza delivery boy, always at the wrong address, or that UPS man with those chiseled calves and cute brown shorts. Archie tore through his thin brown socks faster than a Terrier could tear through a rat, clinging tightly to his ankle until the man kicked him loose, upon which Gina quickly scooped him up and admonished the driver for his act of cruelty, not only to the dog but to herself – a very ill young woman on the brink of death. The guy felt such deep sympathy for Gina, none for the dog, he dismissed the threat of a lawsuit and accepted a cup of coffee with her on the porch, while Archie watched him closely with beady-eyed anticipation.

That was six weeks ago – a long time for a woman with her sexual appetite to be without a man to flirt with, toy with, even kiss – just to give him a taste of what she had to offer once that awful uninvited intruder was extracted from her body.

Gina sat at the window, watching for any kind of life to remind her that she was still alive. The birds chirping, and the smell of freshly cut grass heightened her senses. Even the cool air sifting through the screened window felt light and hopeful. As long as Gina kept her thoughts pure she was safe from the impending desolation. It wasn't easy.

She went to the kitchen to get a cup of tea; one of the few things that stayed down longer than the rest. When she returned to her seat, she saw through the window, Frank's car. She had known him since high school long before he married Ellen. She had always liked him, and if Ellen hadn't of swooped down and taken Frank for her own, Gina might have dated him. There was always an undercurrent of sexual tension between them that Gina thought Ellen detected, and even though nothing was ever said about it, Ellen made sure that the two were never left alone. Twenty-five years later, Gina still sensed Ellen bristle up when Frank talked to her, even if it was about something as simple as football. How exciting that he was here now, and without his wife.

Outside it was oddly quiet. She leaned in and stretched her neck looking for Frank, Archie by her side on alert. She heard the water turn on from the outside spigot. "What's going on out there?" she asked her furry friend.

A few minutes passed, and Gina saw a stream of water squirting from the hose to the roof of her car. "Someone's washing my car for me, Archie. It must be Frank." She saw her reflection in the mirror on the wall, the look of delight on her tired face excited her. "Oh, how very sweet."

Knowing Frank would not want her to protest, she stayed hidden at the window and waited to see him as he approached the front of the car. She saw his hand first, grasping a big sponge, vigorously scrubbing the doors. Then as he moved closer in view, she saw his bare back gleaming in the sun, already sweating from removing weeks of filth from her vehicle. He has a beautiful back, she thought, focusing on the muscles moving with each sweep of his arm.

What she saw next, she was not prepared for. When Frank came into full view, she could see that he was completely naked. Stark naked! No shorts, no shoes, no baseball cap on his head.

Gina dropped down to the floor on her knees and giggled. "Don't look now Archie, but Frank's outside washing my car in his birthday suit!"

When she eased back up, she saw that Frank

was taking an exceptionally long time cleaning the side view mirror, feverishly removing the hardened dead bugs, his rear end muscles flexing with each small vigorous movement of his hand, the water hose held conveniently within reach between his thighs.

"Oh, my," Gina exhaled, her eyes half-closed with pleasure when he proceeded to the windows and in slow, broad sweeping motions, wiped across the glass, his body pivoting in rhythm from one foot to the other. It was then that she realized the possibility that Frank was performing for her. She lured Archie to the guest bedroom with a peanut butter cookie and tiptoed out to the porch for a better view.

Frank just had to know that she was standing there, still as a deer listening for potential danger, her heart beating loudly in her chest. But he gave her no sign that he knew and continued washing her car, the spring sun warming his flesh as he performed one of man's favorite weekend rituals just for Gina.

It was a beautiful thing, and something she had never experienced, nor ever heard of anyone doing. She was so entranced by his movements, she had forgotten that she was sick and closer to death than she'd ever been. She swooned when Frank laid his chest across the broad hood of the car drenched in a sea of soap suds. Bent over, she could now see his testicles hard and swollen, his penis strong and erect. She had seen many naked men in her life, but nothing as sensual and exciting as this. When he moved to the other side of the car where he would be facing her, Gina decided to go back inside just in case they might catch each other's eye and break the spell.

Back in her bedroom, she pictured a new epitaph in playful font, "Men Washed Cars in the Nude for Gorgeous Gina." In the excitement of the moment, she felt weightless; the constant dread lifted from her tired body. She fluffed the pillows, eased under the covers and waited to see what Frank would do next. It felt like Christmas Day.

When she heard the water being shut off, she tensed, listening carefully for any other sounds. Then she heard footsteps on the porch and the screen door opening slowly. She grew excited with each creak of the hinge.

"Gina?" Frank called softly from the center of the living room.

"Yes, Frank. I'm in my bedroom," Gina answered in a meek voice.

"Can I come in and say hi?"

She considered asking him if he had his clothes on, but decided against it, since secretly, she hoped he had left them off. "Come on in," she said, biting her lip to keep from giggling.

She heard his wet bare feet slap the tile floor as he approached her room. She sucked in a breath, picked up the magazine on the bed and pretended to be reading.

Frank entered one step over the threshold and stopped. Gina slowly tore her eyes from the magazine and looked up. There he was, like a man who had just gotten out of the shower after a pleasing round of sex, standing there before her, uninhibited, a towel flung over his shoulder, the tightness in his groin now relaxed along with his facial expression.

"How are you, Gina?"

"Well, Frank, frankly, I haven't felt this good in a while. You do know you're naked, don't you?" She blushed and put her hand to her mouth.

"Yes. I do know that. I've been washing your car," he casually spoke.

"Well that was very nice of you. The old gal really needed a cleaning. I appreciate it a lot. But that doesn't explain why you're naked," she said, not scolding him but sincerely wanting to know what was on his mind.

"You watched me. I'm glad. I did it for you, Gina. It's my gift to you."

"I don't understand, Frank."

"Gina, I know how sad and lonely you are here. I know you miss your social life. I know how much you miss being sexy and sexual. So, I thought I'd remind you that you still are." His eyes left hers as he looked down at the floor, concentrating on what he was about to say next. Slowly looking up, he met her eyes again, "If you don't mind me asking, do you think I am still sexy?"

"Hmm," Gina sat up straighter, raised her finger up in the air and motioned for Frank to come closer.

He slowly stepped forward until Gina signaled for him to stop right where a shadow was cast across the floor, the perfect soft light surrounding his body. She studied his torso, trying not to stay too long on the mid-section. When her eyes landed on his feet, baby white from years of wearing boots, she said, "OK, now turn around," still using her finger, like a trainer directing a seal. Frank slowly turned around and faced the door, dropping the towel on the floor. Gina studied his rugged back, bits of wild hairs scattered from his neck to the middle of his shoulder blades, the love-handles not as firm as they used to be, but darn cute, the tan line along his waist framing a very nice bottom, her second favorite part of a man. "OK, turn back around."

She looked directly into his eyes and gave him a full report. "The way I see it Frank, you're still a darn sexy man, and I think you look gorgeous, from head to toe. And by the way you moved out there on my car, it's very possible she's pregnant now."

They both laughed, a hearty laugh between old friends that would've, and maybe could've been more, but both had a mutual love for Ellen.

"I'd love to stay and visit with you longer, Gina, but the way things are sizing up," he glanced down at his groin, "I think it's best I leave now."

"Yes, I suppose you should," she looked away and feeling tears welling up, she dabbed at her eyes with a tissue. "Frank, I have to tell you. That was the nicest gift anyone has ever given me. Thank you. I'll never forget it."

"And thank *you*, Gina."

"For what, Frank?" Gina looked confused. "For being you."

When Frank walked away, Gina slipped out of bed. "Wait, Frank, wait," she cried out breathlessly, rushing toward him, clutching at her gown, the intoxicating scent of freshly sprayed Shalimar bursting from her pores.

Startled by how quickly she had moved across the room and was now just inches from his naked body, he looked at her curiously, "What is it?"

"Will you maybe, please, give me just *one* more gift, Frank?" she asked imploringly, eyelashes fluttering, her hands clasped together on her bosom, her top front teeth biting down on her lower quivering lip as if it were her final plea.

"Will you...will you wax my car?"

About the Author:

Native Texan, Mother of Six, Baby Boomer, Creative Writer, Muse

I live in Austin, a city that thrives on weirdness - a perfect place to nurture my wildly active imagination. Author of four volumes of short stories. Visit me at LibbyBelle.com.

TWENTY-SEVEN VELVET BOXES
by Zia Marshall

Shoma scooped up her hair into a ponytail as she ran down the stairs to get breakfast ready for Farhaan. Soft sunlight filtered in through the large picture window that framed the side of the staircase. Shoma lingered for a few moments by the window taking in the early morning sounds as the world gently came awake. She stared appreciatively at the sky. It was a beautiful medley of soft colors – pale blue tinged with fiery orange and delicate pink hues. She smiled when she saw a snow-white pigeon flying by the window. The pale sunbeams slanted through its pristine white feathers and they glowed in the gentle morning light. If only, Shoma thought longingly, she could be as free as that pigeon flying in the sky.

The striking of the clock announcing the hour startled her out of her reverie. It was already seven and Farhaan would soon be down. He grew impatient if his breakfast was not waiting for him at the table.

Entering the kitchen, Shoma swiftly rolled out the dough for the *paratha*, deftly stuffing it with creamy-yellow potatoes before folding the edges into a triangle. She rolled the dough once more, gently this time, so that the potato didn't spill out. She set the *paratha* on the pan and watched as it puffed up slightly and turned a golden brown. Sliding it onto a plate, she set a bowl of *curds* next to it and dashed into the dining room.

Shoma heaved a sigh of relief when she saw that Farhaan had not yet come down. She neatly folded the newspaper and placed it beside his plate. Then she fished out the letter from the pocket of her jeans and stared at it for a long moment. Should she show it to Farhaan? With trembling fingers, she opened the envelope and drew out the letter reading it once more although she already knew its contents almost word for word. It was an offer letter from a university in Paris. They were impressed by her work and had invited her to attend a six-month art course. Shoma fingered the stiff official-looking stationery. If only Farhaan would relent and let her go. It would catapult her into a different league of artists altogether. She would learn things, which she could never dream of learning here. Then she thought of Farhaan's reaction and unbidden, there rose in her mind, an image of the velvet boxes stacked in the drawer of her cupboard. She shuddered inwardly and was on the verge of stuffing the letter back into her pocket. Then, at the last minute, she changed her mind. She would show the letter to Farhaan, she decided, with a sudden air of defiance. If she hid it away, she would always wonder why she hadn't at least tried. Perhaps, she could convince him to let her go to Paris. After all, six months was not such a long time.

Shoma mentally rehearsed the words she would use to coax Farhaan. Just as she was placing the letter beside Farhaan's plate, he strode into the room, struggling to knot his tie. Settling down on the chair, he opened the newspaper that Shoma had placed beside his plate. The crisp pages rustled as he turned to the Business section and scanned the news, while hurriedly eating his breakfast at the same time. Shoma sat next to him, gazing at the familiar furrow that always appeared at the point between his eyebrows, when he was concentrating on something. He hadn't noticed the letter. Shoma wondered if she should avoid mentioning it. Maybe this wasn't such a good time to broach the subject, she thought. She'd ask him in the evening, when he was more relaxed.

Suddenly a wave of resentment swept over Shoma. Would it always be like this, she wondered. Would she always have to match her words to suit Farhaan's moods? Defiantly, she decided to broach the subject right away.

"Farhaan," she said.

"Hmm, what's it?" he asked from behind the pages of the paper.

"There's a letter beside your newspaper. Didn't you notice it?" Shoma asked hesitantly.

Farhaan glanced down and picked up the letter. He turned it around in his fingers, raising his eyebrows when he noticed the address from the Paris University stamped on the back of the envelope.

"It's an offer letter, Farhaan. The university has accepted me for a six-month art course. I would really like to go. It will give me a chance to learn so much, spread my wings, take my art to a new level," Shoma said, speaking quickly as she stared at Farhaan. She held her breath wondering how he would react. And yet, deep down, in the secret place within her, where truth always rings out loud and clear, she knew what his reaction would be.

Farhaan tossed the letter aside contemptuously and rose from his chair. Shoma knew what would follow. She watched him walk around the table to the chair where she was seated.

"So you want to leave me for six whole months, Shoma," Farhaan said, in a voice that had almost dropped to a whisper. Shoma cowered in the chair, head bent, holding up her hands in a vain attempt to protect herself.

"Look around you," he snarled, holding her hair and yanking back her head. "I have given you so much. And yet you talk of leaving, Shoma! Do you really expect me to let you go to Paris for six months? What kind of fool do you take me for?"

Shoma watched him with detachment, noting the steely look in his eyes as he stared down at her. She knew the danger signs by now. She knew that the sensible thing to do would be to back off and say she didn't really want to go to Paris and wasn't interested in the course. But something within her prompted her to continue.

"It's such a wonderful opportunity, Farhaan. I know I'm attending art classes here, but they are a pale shadow compared to what I could learn out there. Please Farhaan, I really want to do this. Perhaps you could come with me," Shoma said, grasping the sleeve of his shirt, as he relaxed his hold on her hair. She wondered if he would relent and then realized that she had been hoping for far too much.

Gently, Farhaan started stroking her hair. Shoma shuddered for she knew what would follow. She would not scream she told herself, clenching her hands into fists. She would not give him that satisfaction, she thought as the blows rained down on her, as he slapped and shouted and then slapped some more.

"How dare you even think of leaving me," he shouted angrily, taking her by the shoulders and shaking her hard till her head snapped back and forth and she was sure she would black out.

Then it stopped, almost as suddenly as it had started. And Farhaan was in her arms, begging forgiveness, promising it would not happen again. Instinctively, she found herself running her fingers through his thick hair and soothing him, telling him it didn't matter. Tenderly, he cupped her face in his hands and looked into her large tear-filled eyes. He turned away when he saw the hurt and betrayal in them.

"Don't look like that, Shoma," he pleaded,

gently rubbing the blue-black bruise on her cheek. "Shoma," he whispered softly, gently raising her chin till she was forced to look at him. "I'm sorry I lost control. It's just that the thought of you leaving me drives me into a rage. I promise it won't happen again."

She nodded listlessly.

"I have to go," he said, almost apologetically. "You'll be fine, won't you?"

She nodded, marveling at the concern she saw in his eyes.

"I'll make it up to you this evening, I promise," he said.

She stood at the door, watching as he got into his car and pulled out of the driveway. She knew he would bring her a gift that evening. What would it be, she wondered. A diamond necklace? Or a ruby bracelet, perhaps? Her drawer was full of these gifts. Diamonds, rubies, sapphires and emeralds all lay in their deep blue velvet boxes, their blazing brilliance matching the fury that simmered in Farhaan's eyes. She smiled and accepted each gift with quiet equanimity. She stacked them neatly in the drawer but she never wore them. She couldn't bear to put on these mute yet fiery symbols of Farhaan's anger and her submission.

Suddenly she was filled with curiosity. Making her way to the bedroom, she opened the wardrobe. Removing the velvet boxes, she stacked them neatly on the bed. Slowly she counted the stack of boxes. Twenty-seven velvet boxes lay on the bed; twenty-seven times Farhaan had struck her in the year since they had been married. And today she would add the twenty-eighth box to the pile. And so it would go on, she realized. When would it stop, she wondered. Would it stop when the drawer was full and couldn't hold any more boxes? She imagined herself telling Farhaan, *"Stop Farhaan, you mustn't strike me. You see the drawer is quite full and we really don't have any more room to add another velvet box."* She wondered if he would kill her then. Or would it be earlier?

While there was still room in the drawer for a few more velvet boxes.

Chiding herself for being morbid, she picked up the boxes and returned them to the drawer. Glancing at the clock, she noticed that it was almost eleven o'clock. If she hurried, she could still make it to her art class. Practice had taught Shoma how to distance herself from the reality of her situation. She had learned the fine art of stepping away from her body and observing herself like a detached observer. She was totally calm and composed as she dressed, choosing a long-sleeve shirt and jeans to cover the latest evidence of Farhaan's anger. Then she made her way to the dressing table, randomly opening drawers and piling make-up on to the table. She started on her face, adding an extra layer of concealer to the bruises, and then coating her face with foundation. She applied make-up with methodical precision. Then she surveyed the result in the mirror, gazing at her face for a long moment to make sure that the bruises weren't visible.

"God gave you one face and you make yourself another," she recalled Farhaan telling her long ago as he had watched her applying make-up. It was before they had married, while they had still been in college. Farhaan had been fond of quoting literature and Shakespeare had been a particular favorite. She smiled ironically at her reflection in the mirror for it was indeed another face she wore nowadays, one that she often didn't recognize in more ways than one.

She was five minutes late to class. Apologizing to her instructor, Karan, she slid behind her easel. It looked like today would be what Karan called a "free reign" class.

"Draw what you want, or better still draw what you feel," he was saying to the class. "Let your art emerge from the depths of your soul and those of you who can manage it, be your art."

Shoma drew in bold rough strokes, struggling to capture the image that was floating at the gray edges of her consciousness. Soon she was engrossed in her painting, and for a while she managed to block out the reality that was threatening her sanity with each passing day. Her fingers worked feverishly as she gave form to the image – the hot relentless sun, the parched earth, the old and gnarled tree shorn of leaves and the solitary figure crouched beneath it drawing scant comfort from its meager shade. She was so absorbed in the painting that she didn't notice the other students leaving the class. Looking up, she realized that Karan was standing behind her studying her picture.

"It's good," he said frowning at the painting. "You've captured the essence of the emotion or mood you are trying to convey. But you need to work on your technique a bit. Here let me show you." Taking her hand in his, he showed her how to modify the painting, add more depth to the image. "Have you thought of a name for the painting?" he asked.

"A Study in Solitude," she replied in a dull voice.

"The figure under the tree is you, isn't it, Shoma?" he asked candidly.

She started shaking her head, and then found herself nodding instead.

"Are things that bad, Shoma? What's going on with you?"

"It's nothing," she mumbled, shaking her head. "Forget it." She turned away to hide her tears.

"Talking helps, you know. Would you like to tell me about it?"

Shoma shook her head, her eyes filling with tears. "I can't," she whispered.

But Karan refused to give up. She looked so lost and forlorn, that somehow he knew that he had to save her – from herself if need be.

"Come with me," Karan said gently. "Let's have a cup of coffee."

"I can't," Shoma protested, shaking her head vigorously. "I hardly know you and besides it wouldn't be proper."

"Why? Is it because you're married?"

She nodded. "Yes, Farhaan wouldn't like me going out with another man, even if it is for an innocent cup of coffee."

"And do you always do what Farhaan wants?" he asked, raising his eyebrows.

She nodded.

"Well, I won't take no for an answer, Shoma," Karan said stubbornly. "Besides what Farhaan doesn't know can't hurt him."

Taking her hand, he led her out of the studio. They made their way to a tiny coffee shop. After they had ordered, Karan placed his hand over Shoma's. She found the gesture strangely comforting and swiftly bowed her head as tears formed in her eyes. Raising her face, he gently wiped the tears that were rolling down her cheeks.

"You're young, beautiful, and very talented, Shoma. You have everything to look forward to in life."

"You don't know...you can't possibly understand what my life is like," she said.

Karan gazed at her. She seemed meek and suppressed. Yet his artist's eye caught the almost severe lines of her jaw, the firm set of her lips that told him she was made of sterner stuff.

"I'd like to paint you, Shoma," he said.

"Why?" she asked, astonished.

"Because I'd like to strip away the face you are trying to show the world. I'd like to show you what you are actually made of, who you really are," Karan said and she frowned at the intensity in his voice. "But I have to warn you. If I am to paint you properly, I will first have to make love to you," he added, candidly.

He waited, wondering how she would react. Shoma stared at Karan incredulously. What he had just said was outrageous, beyond the bounds of propriety. And yet, something within her craved warmth, comfort and shelter perhaps, even it was fleeting, from the blazing corrosive love that Farhaan offered.

"It won't take more than an afternoon," he said. "You'll be home by this evening."

One afternoon, she thought, as she recalled the twenty-seven velvet boxes stacked neatly in her drawer. Yes, she thought, she had certainly earned an afternoon in which she could live life freely; an afternoon in which she needn't feel like a stuffed animal living in a glass case.

"Why not!" she said, laughing as she threw caution to the winds. She held out her hand to him. "Come, let's go before I change my mind."

Grinning, he took her hand in his and led her out of the coffee shop and back to the studio. The place had a deserted air.

"I don't have any more classes scheduled for today," Karan explained.

He led her to the couch in the far corner of the room. Gently lowering her onto the couch, he undressed her. Then he explored her body with his mouth and his hands, cupping, molding, tasting, till she arched her back with pleasure and called out his name. When he entered her, she wrapped her legs around him, placing her hands on his hips, urging him on.

The whole act seemed surreal; it had an almost dream-like quality to it. Shoma gave herself up to the moment. Karan's arms were strong and comforting. His body felt different; the way they fit together was also different. She drew him closer to her, encircling him in her arms. Closing her eyes, she realized that there was none of the tumultuous passion she was accustomed to. With Farhaan, she felt she was like a wave in the wild sea as it crashed against the rocks. But with Karan it was strangely different, infinitely more tender, like the soft rocking of a boat in a serene sea. Karan was a gentle lover, careful of her needs, and she felt strangely secure in his arms as he led them both to the brink of passion till at last they collapsed in each other's arms.

Rising, he walked to the easel and placed it beside her. Idly, Shoma wondered if she should protest – he was planning on painting her in the nude. But the afternoon had driven away the last of her inhibitions. Besides, she felt too good about herself to move. Settling down on the couch, she watched as Karan's hands flew over the easel in easy rhythmic movements. She felt free and light and happier than she had felt in a long time, as she drifted off to sleep, a smile tugging at her lips. When she opened her eyes, she saw Karan dabbing at the easel with a soft cloth. "Don't move," he said, urgently. "It's almost done."

She lay still, till at last, he laid down the brush with a satisfied sigh.

"Yes," he said. "I think I've managed to capture it."

She was curious. "Can I see it?" she asked.

"Not yet," he replied.

Taking the painting, he carried it to the opposite corner of the studio and propped it against a large mirror that occupied the length of a wall.

"Close your eyes," he instructed.

With a smile, she obeyed, holding out her hands to him. He led her to the painting.

"I want you to see the woman in the painting and compare her with the woman you see in the mirror," Karan said, urgently, almost harshly.

She wondered what he was talking about. But when she opened her eyes, she understood. She gasped when she saw the woman in the painting. It looked like her. The shape of the face was the same and her features were also the same. But it wasn't her! This woman in the painting had boundless energy in her eyes; her own eyes that stared back at her from the mirror were flat and dead. Shoma stared at the woman in the painting, taking in the arched eyebrows, the proud, almost defiant tilt of the head.

"The woman in the painting is so strong and determined," she whispered. "She looks like she can reach out and do almost anything. But the woman in the mirror looks like life has beaten her. She is dead, defeated, a shadow of her true self."

Shoma stumbled away from the painting. "It's not true," she cried. "It's an illusion, an artist's trick. Oh, you are cruel. You make me want things that cannot be, that can never be. You should have left me alone."

Furiously, she looked around for her clothes and dressed herself. She was angry with Karan for showing her who she could be. She was also angry with herself for she didn't believe she had it within her to ever be that woman.

"I am sorry if I have offended you, Shoma," Karan said. "I wanted to offer you a glimpse of what is hidden within you waiting to be released. But how you eventually choose to live your life is up to you, isn't it?"

She walked out of the studio without a word. A growing sense of numbness overtook her as she walked home. She felt she was growing smaller and smaller, while the walls closed in around her. She craved the feel of the paintbrush in her hands and the roughness of the canvas beneath her fingers. She needed to paint what she was feeling. Painting would help her decide what to do next. Reaching home, she walked into the small studio at the back of the house. It was hot and airless, but she didn't throw open the windows as she normally did when she entered the room. She didn't switch on the lights either but painted in darkness. She didn't need to see what she was painting, because it was embedded in the core of her being. She needed to rip out her soul and place it on canvas.

Closing her eyes, Shoma painted. She knew from memory where each color was located on her palette and instinctively she knew the right amount of color to take when she was blending the paints. The hours ticked away and still she painted, eyes closed. She painted the whirlpool that her life had become, and she painted the harsh gray lightning-filled sky. She painted the shore, calm, beautiful, distant, and unreacha-ble. And she painted the small paper boat that was being sucked into the whirlpool, deeper and deeper.

A fragment from a half-forgotten poem flashed across her mind. "Things fall apart, the center cannot hold." Who had written it, she wondered. And then it came to her as she recalled a long ago literature class in college. Farhaan had been sitting beside her as the professor read out Yeats's poem. Her mind flashed back to her college days when she had met and fallen in love with Farhaan. Had she known back then, what was concealed within his charming demeanor? Had some part of her guessed how things would turn out? And would she still have chosen to marry him if she had known?

A dim memory nudged at the gray edges of her consciousness. Farhaan was leaning across the table, telling her he had found a job and begging her to marry him. She remembered how pleased he had been when she agreed. She remembered him promising her he would make her very happy. And she remembered him saying that she mustn't ever allow him to raise his hand on her. If he ever did, she must stop him immediately. Had he known back then, she wondered, about the monster that was lurking within him? Opening her eyes, she stared at the painting before her. "A terrible beauty is born" – another fragment from a poem. Who had written this one? She struggled to remember and then gave up. It didn't matter; she had her answer. She knew what she had to do.

"Shoma, I have been looking all over the house for you," Farhaan's voice cut across her thoughts bringing her back to reality. Walking across the room, he looked at the painting. And Shoma stared at his handsome face, the liquid brown eyes, and the cupid bow of his lips. It was a face she knew so well. Was he the man of her dreams? Or a monster? Or maybe both?

Looking up from the painting, Farhaan stared at his wife in awe. "Shoma, you are so talented. This is the most beautiful painting I have ever seen. Shoma, don't you see! You don't need to go to Paris! You are already so very talented, I bet if you went there, you would teach them a thing or two about art. Shoma, why won't you show your paintings to the world? Why do you want to hide your talent? Shoma, Shoma, Shoma," taking her hand, he whirled her across the room. And she gazed into his eyes, marveling at the love she saw in them. "I won't listen to you this time, Shoma. Paris be damned! You *will* have a show. I will organize it. I want the world to see your paintings. You will be famous. That's what I want for you."

She smiled at his enthusiasm.

"Shoma, Shoma, darling Shoma, I want to make you happy forever. See what I've got you."

She stared at the velvet box in his hand, the twenty-eighth box. She watched him open the box and take out the emerald and diamond choker that lay inside. She felt a strange sense of *déjà vu* as he fastened the choker around her neck. Feeling the cool smoothness of the stones with her fingers, she turned to look at him.

"Come, I want to show you how beautiful you look," he cried, taking her hand and leading her to the mirror.

Shoma stared at Farhaan in the mirror. He had never looked as handsome as he did in that moment. And she realized that she would always love him. It didn't matter what he did. It would not shake her love.

The next morning, Farhaan held Shoma close to him, hugging her fiercely before leaving for work. She hugged him back, with all the love she had for yesterday, today, and tomorrow. After he left, she methodically stacked the twenty-seven boxes into an overnight bag. She took nothing else; she needed nothing else. Picking up the bag, she went out to the waiting cab, to freedom, and a new life.

And in the house, by Farhaan's bed, Shoma had left a note under the diamond and emerald choker trying to explain her love, which grew by the day, and her decision to leave while she still had the strength to do so.

About the Author:

Zia Marshall is a Learning Designer and Communication Specialist skilled in performance and competency development for personal and professional growth. She designs and writes context-sensitive, solution-oriented e-learning, blended learning and mobile learning courses for corporate houses like Wipro, Infosys, HCL, DHL and also for the education sector. Her articles have been published in
http://www.selfgrowth.com/,
https://elearningindustry.com/,
http://havingtime.com/,
https://overcomingms.org/community/.
Her short story 'The Choice' was published in the May 2018 issue of Adelaide Literary magazine.

A GIRL DIED HERE

by Kyle Labe

The cross is white. Her portrait embellishes the center, as if she's crucified. As if she died so we can live. It's on the side of the road, near where they found her body. It's posted there to remind us. I think her boyfriend placed it strategically. To inform drivers: "My innocent girlfriend died here!" But she didn't die. Not exactly. She was murdered.

I don't observe it for long. It gives me the creeps. Actually, no one in town likes to be reminded, but nobody has the gall to remove it. Anyways it'll always be there, lodged somewhere in our collective unconscious, lingering, simmering, waiting to pounce. I keep walking.

Parties like tonight, where everybody and their cousin is drunk, are the ones I hate. It becomes too sloppy if you're there too long. There's an obvious line to cross and no one acknowledges it. Soon it becomes a mesh of human flesh and body odor. People make out with strangers. Enough girls reject a guy, so he locates another boy to hook up with. Liquor spills on the floor and your Chuck Taylors stick. The deejay blasts the same beat and nobody realizes. They just came to dance. They came to get their mind off life, but just like life, it grows terribly claustrophobic.

On nights like these, there's a dampness in the atmosphere. No matter how dry the sky, no matter how luminescent the moon, everything underneath is wet. It's the dew in the grass and the puddles on the asphalt. It's the sensation of drowning when you're not supposed to be outside. For the springtime it's impressively humid. My clothes stick to me. I can't discern if it's fog or mist ahead, but I can't see the street. I wonder if the weather is beckoning me indoors.

A car pulls over. The window rolls down. My anxiety vanishes when I see it's a woman.

"It's awfully late, hon," she beckons. "Do you want a ride home?"

I smile. "No, I'm fine. Thank you. I like to walk."

"Do you live around here?"

"A few blocks south."

"Well... all right. Don't let me see you on the news tomorrow, you hear?"

I nod, and she drives away. Normally I'd accept a ride, but I'm craving a smoke. Typically, I don't carry cigarettes. If I ever purchased a pack, my dad would have a hoot. He'd find them regardless the hiding spot. So I stole a few from a boy at the party. Drunk, he went off somewhere and should've known better than to leave his Camels on the kitchen table. I swiped his matchbox too.

As I strike the match, I see a car. Half of it's on the street, the other in the grass. It's too dark to see anything else. A lamppost flickers in the distance, so I use the match as light. When I approach it, I realize it struck a tree.

No one is nearby to help. I wonder why the lady stopped her car for me, but not this. I hope to God there's nobody dead. I don't think I have the guts to see a dead body in real life.

In the movies it's different, but right in front of you? No way.

"H-hello?" I call, but there's no response. Creeping closer, I peer in the window. The glass is shattered on the leather seat. The prindle is still at *D*. Nobody is in the driver's seat. It's completely empty. I sigh of relief.

Suddenly, there's a shrill scream from the woods. I study the area but nothing is visible. Using my phone as a flashlight, I shine it into the trees. There's nothing but military green and camouflage. My phone dies even though I swear I charged it earlier.

Ambling forward, I hear another rustle in the forest. Then something charges at me, grabbing my shoulders and shoving me to the ground. When I open my eyes I immediately recognize her.

"Ambrose? Is that you?" I say.

She's in shambles. Her hair is disheveled with twigs and mud, and her clothes are ripped to shreds. Her legs bleed down the insides, and her pale skin appears purple.

"They're coming," she says. "They're almost here!" She sounds like a banshee.

"Ambrose, are you okay?" I ask, rising to my feet. There's a brush burn on my knee, and blood trickles onto my pants.

She holds me and glares wildly into my eyes. "They'll be here soon. We have to hide!"

I shake my head. "Your memorial is back there," I mutter, pointing to the white cross. "You're supposed to be dead..."

Glancing at the vehicle, she says, "Is this yours?"

I try to say no, but words don't come out. Darting into the car, she digs in the glove compartment and finds a key. "I have to go, I have to go," she repeats, revving the engine and reversing onto the street. She sits on the broken glass. "I have to go. They're coming," she says and floors it. I watch her drive into the night and disappear.

I piece together what I recall of Ambrose's case. She was seventeen and walking home alone after a graveyard shift. Some out-of-town hooligans jumped her and dragged her unconscious body into the woods. The coroner theorized that her attackers tried to burn her, and when that didn't work, dumped her into a lake. Her linebacker boyfriend found her body three days later. During a halftime, he kick-started a charity campaign in her name. I think, when a boy is killed, he's stabbed. Yet when a girl is murdered, she's beaten, raped, strangled, kicked, smothered, stabbed, dismembered, and burned.

I hear voices. Groveling, they overlap one another and emit the distinct odor of chewing tobacco. At first, it seems in my head. But up ahead I spot three men at the curb. I sprint towards them.

"Did any of you see that car?" I splutter, catching my breath.

If I didn't look closely, the men would seem identical. They don the same greasy wife-beater and have shiny bald heads. Their faces are cut from shaving. Two have unibrows, and the other wears a single shoe.

"Lookie here," one says, "Don't y'know it's dangerous for a girl to be out this late?"

"Yeah," another growls, "Ain't everybody nice as us."

I stand my ground. "Did you see that car or not?"

The other spits his tobacco at my feet. "Barely legal, huh?"

"You never know these days," the one-shoed man says. "I see some of 'em 13-year-olds, and Christ, if they don't make me question myself..."

I back up away from them. My palm grips my dead phone. Watching them, I reassure they don't follow me.

"Bet youse trimmed as a slut down there, ay?" a unibrowed man shouts. "All fresh and wet."

The one-shoed man whistles. "C'mere, girly. Lemme pet your kitty…"

"We'll make you *purr*," the other says. He holds the last syllable on his tongue.

I trip over a rock and stumble onto the asphalt. My head crashes on the blacktop. When I gain my senses, I realize the men disappeared. There's a tiny, delicate *mew* beside me. Startled, I almost roll onto a kitten. It *mew*s again, stretching its mouth into a yawn.

Black, the cat has yellow eyes and a white spot on one of its paws. It's missing half an ear. It wears no leash, so I scan the area for an owner.

While I investigate, I usher the animal under a bush. There's no one around, and it's so dark I'm lucky to see the feet below me. I rap on a neighbor's door, and a light switches on upstairs. Knocking again, I wait to no avail. Repeating this on another house, I receive the same response.

When I return to the cat it remains under the shrub. It purrs a soft *mew*. Just then, as I'm yards away, a snake slithers beside it. My eyes widen as I dash over, but I'm too late. The serpent opens its jaw and clasps its teeth around the kitten's neck, consuming it in one gulp.

When I scream, the door of a household slams open. A woman points a pistol into the night. "You thug!" she hollers. "Don't you know us decent folk are trying to sleep?"

I reach my hand out for help, but she shoots the gun and it rings in my ear. I scramble behind the bush until she reenters the home with the click of a lock.

Standing, I know my house isn't far. If I run, maybe I'll be safe. Then I can call the police. So I speed down the alley, and the woods whip by my periphery. I pay no attention to the stars or the moon or the whispers of the leaves.

The shape of my house appears like the light at the end of a tunnel. Its two stories and green shutters, colorful garden and freshly mowed lawn. As I run, the street stretches further into infinity. The distance increases as I move closer, as if taunting me. I pause to catch my breath, and it seems miles away.

I think, this must be a nightmare. That's it. What do they say about dreams? You can't look at the same spot twice. I try it out. Focusing on a sewer grate, I turn away, then back, and it's still there. I hear that bald man's warning: *Don't y'know it's dangerous for a girl to be out this late?* I recall every film and every true crime show where a girl like me dies, because she believed the place she lived was safe. If I had accepted that car ride, none of this would be happening. All I want is my bed. Pinching myself, I stay in the nightmare.

Maybe the world itself is a nightmare, and girls like me are never meant to dream.

I'm too focused on my thoughts to realize a silhouette under the lamppost ahead. It positions itself like a shadow. Cocking my head, I squint, trying to study its image. Except it's impossible. It's darker than the night. It may as well not be human. I call out to it.

"Excuse me, do you have a car?" I say. "I live just down the street, and I don't like walking at night…"

The voice of my father answers. "You went out wearing *that*?" it barks. "Jesus, you look like a hussy. My daughter! Dressed like one of those trash women. You're asking for it, asking for it, asking for it…"

By this point I've had enough. His voice is enough to crush me but I won't let it. Stealing a rock, I storm at the silhouette, ready to bash its skull in. Yet there's no opportunity before the shadow teeters to me and collapses into my arms. We're spotlighted under the lamp, and every house on the block disappeared. It's as if we're alone in our own black infinity.

I realize, it's Ambrose I'm holding.

She stares into my eyes, petrified as all hell. Weirdly enough, it's as if *she* is the one who witnessed a ghost. The more I gape at her, the more her pupils dilate until her corneas are pools of black.

"He's coming," she says. "I have to hide."

I want to reply but I don't have the energy. As I hold her, a samara floats onto her nose. When she notices it she screams, and the noise shakes us back to reality, and all our surroundings reappear.

"He's going to *kill me*," Ambrose shouts. She scrambles to her feet and, daring to peer behind her, flees into the forest.

More maple seeds fall from the sky like rain. I remember these. My grandpa used to pay me a penny for every one I cleaned off his lawn. He compared them to miniature helicopters spiraling down from the clouds.

The seeds fill the atmosphere around me like a sandstorm. Covering my face, I fight through them. The *tap tap tap* when they hit the ground is maddening. It won't cease. My only solace is when the sound of drumming vibrates the seeds to ashes. The booming music brandishes the area and quakes the ground. I stop picking maple seeds from my hair in order to block my ears.

When I get a good look, I notice a marching band. It consists of at least fifty students—some I recognize, some I don't—with all sorts of woodwind and brass and percussion instruments. A color guard leads them my direction. They have no conductor, but some boy crowd surfs above. Cheering for him, the musicians lift him into the heavens. They hoot and holler and play some triumphant fight song. I push, shove, and weave through, trying to catch a glimpse. I think, this must be the man Ambrose was rambling about. Whoever it is they're lauding is the culprit.

Then he and I lock eyes. He winks at me. It takes moments to register, as his fists pump the air and the students scream for him.

It's the linebacker. It's Ambrose's boyfriend.

I think, oh my God, this is Ambrose's doing. She's telling me something. Of course—nothing else makes sense. She coerced me into some nightmare world so I could feel what she did that night. Her fear, her terror, her hopelessness. She wanted me to know. She wanted me to find out that her boyfriend murdered her in cold blood. Even in death, she didn't want to be alone…

The moment that clicks, everything evanesces. The maple seeds, the marching band, the linebacker. It all evaporates into thin air, and I'm utterly alone. It's like I was jettisoned into reality. I scan around for any hint, any remnant, but there's nothing.

Hazards on, a car pulls beside me and its windows roll down. It's the same lady from before.

"It's awfully late, hon," she says. "Do you want a ride home?"

I nod. "Yes. Yes, please."

She drives me safely to my home, and I thank her. She waits to leave until I'm inside. I watch her from the peephole. All the lights in my house are off. My parents are fast asleep, so I sneak up the stairs. My heart trembles. I pour myself water, but my hands are so shaky they drop the glass. I ignore the mess and climb into bed, locking my door and window. It's strange I should slip into unconsciousness now, when I've been there and back.

The whole night is enough to coax me asleep.

About the Author:

Kyle Labe is an undergrad at Emerson College. His debut book, Butterflies Behind Glass & Other Stories, was released last year. He's had multiple works published around the country.

UNDER THE FLOORS OF CHURCHES

by Libby Copa

She had not wanted him to come with her to the wedding in the first place. That morning as Maren lay naked from the waist up and in a pair of his pajama pants, he sat on the edge of their bed getting dressed, and he told her he would not be going with her now because he had to work. He said he wouldn't have known anyone at the reception anyway. If Maren had hopes, Gerek would have been letting her down.

She dumped out the large suitcase they had packed together the night before and left Gerek's clothes in a mess on the bed. She began to collect her things around the apartment. She went back and forth between the hall and the room gathering all of her belongings that she could before she had to leave for the three-day celebration.

She hated their apartment. It had been Gerek's place first, so most of the furnishings were his and anything that she left she did not think she would miss. The apartment had originally been built to be twice as large, but the Communists had made everything smaller and less convenient and so the apartments had been cut in half. Now the place was all hall and kitchen with one room that acted as everything else. It was a horseshoe and a hassle to move around in when another person was present. She missed her old building next to the market on Ducha Świętego, but she hadn't wanted to live there with Gerek and have him mix with her old memories of those rooms. The only thing she liked in this apartment was the wood floor and the high ceilings in the old tradition.

When her cousin Lukasz had called to tell Maren he had met the girl he was going to marry, she thought he was just being fanciful, for he had also once assumed he was going to marry her—though they had been only five and believed the whole world revolved around their mothers and the days they'd take them to the islands to feed the swans. Now when he called some twenty years later, she still assumed he was acting on impulses that came with not expecting anything to ever change. Lukasz had told Maren that he had proposed to Irena a week after meeting her. Maren thought that this one too would pass like all his other women, but here she was six months later in the middle of the warmest summer in years, getting ready to make her way to his wedding.

She locked up the apartment and quietly went down the stairs, dragging two large suitcases hoping to not be confronted by her neighbor. Maren worked predominantly out of their apartment and as a distraction she caught the city's stray cats in a trap she made and brought them to the shelter to have them euthanized. She had been doing this for many years. There had been an outbreak in Wrocław City of strays and viral infections in the felines from the citizens' lack of responsibility for their animals. They infected what was healthy and pure. For Maren it was more humane to kill them than to watch them suffer. She also felt a slight power over people with each cat she caught; she would take their mistakes and make them right.

She had recently captured a dirty orange tabby that must have weighed twenty-five pounds and whose fur was so matted it had dreadlocks. Just as she was throwing it into her car, a blue Maluch she'd had for years, an old man came running out of her building yelling, "That is my cat! That is my Tiger!" She tried to play innocent and sincere. "Oh, he is? Could I take him in to be fixed? It's free." And the old man looked her over. She knew he saw her only as this petite punk girl with long black hair in high lace up boots who lived in the apartment above him, the girl who played her music loud out the open window, the girl who had moved in with a quiet man who wore suits to work. The old man shrugged, "Alright." Maren had taken her neighbor's cat and never brought it back. She was glad this would be the last time she would have to avoid him.

When she was safely out of her building, she walked down the block to where she had found a parking spot the night before when she got back from the pub. Maren stuffed one suitcase in the trunk and the other in the backseat. She sped off in her Maluch, hoping it wouldn't take her as long to get out of Wrocław as it would to cover the distance to the Highlands.

Maren was in fact not really Lukasz's cousin. Their families had been so interconnected through marriage, they were not exactly sure what the name was for how they were related. They had been nine together at the fall of the Berlin Wall, and ten together at the end of the Soviet Union; they had learned to drive together; they had graduated from secondary school in the same class. They just thought of each other as close family because they didn't know how it could be any other way.

As Maren went farther from the cities, she passed through all the small towns that still looked so ready for war. When she arrived in the Highlands it was very late. The bride's family's grand house was dark, and Maren considered sleeping in the small backseat of her car so as not to have to wake everyone. Although she knew two people could uncomfortably sleep in the back of her dependable transport, and that with her suitcase moved to the front seats, her own body would have just enough room for a rough night, she couldn't imagine waking up in the morning alone back there. It was so black in the country at night and since no one left a light on for her outside she was just feeling her way along the path toward the porch steps when someone spoke, "You're late," and Maren gasped.

"Sorry," he said.

She composed herself quickly. "You should be."

Lukasz was seated on the porch dangling his legs over the side into the shrubs.

"I am not late."

"I needed you here earlier."

"Need and want are different things." Maren sat down next to her old friend and they smoked a cigarette together.

"When Irena's grandmother speaks to me, I can hardly understand a word she says, her accent is so thick."

They looked out across the property, which Maren could only assume was a large rolling field. In the distance she could see a few lamps still on inside a house on a hill.

"Where's your fellow?" Lukasz asked.

"He couldn't make it," she told him.

"Lawyers."

"He's in marketing."

"Same thing."

In the morning Maren ate fresh bagels that the women in Irena's family had risen early to make. She smoked on the porch, drank tea and played Frisbee with the little ones as everyone else got ready for the ceremony and what would follow. Gerek called her cell phone just before she left for the church but since she was rejecting him, she refused to answer. In the car she checked the message he had left; he explained that he was at a bookstore in their city where he was waiting for the next bus to take him to their apartment and wanted to know if she would like anything. She thought it was a sweet gesture, and yet did not call him back because she had left him and he hadn't noticed.

The silence in churches, the ones that echo with history of war, with all that request for forgiveness built up for centuries, always made her feel as if she had done something wrong, as if religion was not about worship, but only about guilt. That is no way to praise God, she thought.

Lukasz had shaved off his mohawk for this day. He was wearing a grey suit with a black tie. He appeared a different man than the one Maren had known all her life. Looking him over the only thing that reminded her of the rebel kid that snuck her in clubs and stole liquor from the convenience store around the corner from her old apartment was his heavy military boots that thudded against the limestone.

Lukasz and Maren stood at the entryway of the old church and waited to greet the witnesses as they arrived. It reminded both of them a bit too much of Lukasz's mother's funeral three years earlier. They had worn jeans and Iggy Pop and The Stooges concert tee shirts to the service because in their mourning, they hadn't changed their clothes in days.

Lukasz was now in this church, dressed in attire that Gerek wore every day to the office, and she didn't like the comparison. She was wearing a lightweight peach dress that she had made many years ago; it fastened with small buttons all the way down the front. She wore her hair tied into a braid down her back. Lukasz was nervous and drank from a flask he kept in his inside coat pocket.

"If Gerek arrived right now and asked you to marry him— this could be a double wedding." Lukasz reached over and unclasped the top button of Maren's dress. Then took another drink from the tin. His cheeks were flushed and becoming too obvious, so Maren took a tip of the drink and then slipped it away into her purse.

"I would not do something with so much haste."

"I never knew you to be so unspontaneous."

"Haste and spontaneity are different things."

Lukasz bent down to retie the laces of his boots. "What if I asked you to run away right now to the Ukraine? We could start a gypsy rock band." Lukasz reached up and unfastened the last two buttons at the hem of her summer dress.

Maren turned her knee outward. "Neither of us speaks Ukrainian."

"Not spontaneous and not romantic."

"We are at *your wedding*," Maren crowed. Lukasz stood and straightened himself.

"A thousand years from now when they find your bones buried under the floors of a church just like this one, do you want them to be able to say 'See, her heart was made of stone and the cold ground has kept it still so perfectly intact'?"

During the nuptials Maren sat between the members of Lukasz's band who had their rightful spots in the wedding replaced with cousins of Irena's. The last time they had been together, many months ago, Maren had attempted to make a nice dinner for them after they had been on tour for so long. Nothing had worked out as planned. Everything either burned or was undercooked. Maren had been lax on her measurements. She had guessed. She was careless. But they had all eaten it, tried to smile, and told her it was good. Lukasz had slipped his arm around the lower part of her back as she washed the dishes and declared that he believed it was about the act of trying to fill your family that mattered and not necessarily the quality of the food.

"Our money is still on you," Honok whispered so the other wedding guests would not hear.

"You mustn't say things like that anymore," Maren responded. She did not take her eyes off the couple in front of the priest.

"I don't think he even likes her," Olés chimed in.

"Boys," Maren scolded and with that the men went silent.

Maren thought Irena was beautiful in a normal kind of way. She also saw how very young she was: smelling of lavender, wearing white without shame, agreeing to marry a man she only slightly knew. Maren had taken no interest in her particulars. She had hardly considered Irena. None of it mattered other than she was the one who would be blessed beside Lukasz for the rest of his life.

Lukasz' father Andros had come over to Maren's apartment a few days after Lukasz had called and informed her that Irena had accepted his proposal. She had just moved in with Gerek, and Andros brought her a very small green cabinet as a house-warming gift. She had placed it in her kitchen and used it to keep her teas in. It was something Maren now knew she would regret not taking with her yesterday when she left.

"She's a pleasant girl," Andros had told her of Irena. "Very quiet and unexpected, but she will make a nice house for him." He tried to fix the water temperature in her kitchen sink that no matter how long it ran, never flowed hot. "Do you think that it's too soon for them to get married?"

"Do you?" she asked.

"I think you either know about someone or you don't."

Maren looked for Andros seated in the front pew of the church. She could see the side of his face and that his eyes were wet.

Lukasz's grandfather sang on his behalf during the ceremony, the traditional song that argued with Irena's family to make her his bride. Lukasz and Irena knelt on the marriage cloth and prayed. Irena placed the embroidered headscarf over her hair, symbolizing the old custom of a woman's union to a man. When the guests threw the coins for the new bride and groom to collect, prophesizing their prosperity, Maren slid a zloty under her shoe and kept it there until everyone walked away.

That night Lukasz's younger cousin, Elzbieta, made out with Irena's fifty year old uncle Josef, Lukasz's father became sick from eating too much smoked sheep cheese, and the second cousins decided to start a band and replaced the musical entertainment for the evening. As expected, everyone drank too much. Olés stayed in the kitchen with Irena's grandmother who kept crying over the beauty of the day and the war over half a century before. They threaded a garland of dried mushrooms. "The only way soldiers can hurt you is if you have something they can take away," Maren heard the old woman tell Olés, or that is what it sounded like to her.

Irena tore her gown on the dance floor and asked Maren if she could fix it for her before tomorrow. Lukasz brought Maren upstairs to the bedroom where his bride had hung her dress when she had changed into a more versatile outfit.

"What is the urgency in getting this fixed tonight? Is she planning on marrying someone else tomorrow?"

Lukasz opened the window and leaned on the sill and smoked a cigarette as Maren sat on the floor against the bed and saw to the white gown. "The photographer is coming again tomorrow."

"Well aren't you lucky that you happen to have a seamstress right on hand."

"I am very lucky."

Maren and Lukasz were used to being in the quietest of rooms together. Maren recalled one night in particular when they sat around her apartment and he played guitar and she sewed patches on his jacket and together they watched a Danish soft-core dwarf porn thriller.

"I know what you are thinking about," Lukasz said looking over at her on the floor.

"No you don't. You couldn't possibly."

"But I do."

Maren snuggled down on the basement floor between Honok and Olés; the air mattress hissed and shifted under their joint weight. After having slept so many consecutive nights beside Gerek, she realized that it was such a unique thing to have to adjust to the sound of someone different asleep beside her. She had to remind herself she liked only the idea of him.

Maren did not sleep long and at dawn, she rose and went up to the kitchen to help with breakfast. The only ones awake were Irena's grandmother and Lukasz. Neither had been to bed that night and on the kitchen table were many loaves of bread. They were adding flour to a new mixture in the bowl.

"May I help?" she asked.

"Oh, but my love, your dough never rises," Lukasz said.

Maren watched the two of them knead the mixture of ingredients and then begin to twist it into pretzel designs on the pan. The old woman buttered the tops and Lukasz began to dust the tray with salt. It reminded Maren of how it had snowed on that one New Year's Eve. Lukasz and his band had made it back from Budapest in time for him to meet her near the square to watch the fireworks. As they walked together toward the islands, the lights exploding in the sky around them, the first of that winter's snow began to fall in large flakes that never touched the ground. Lukasz had

called them "wishing flakes" and they just seemed to stay afloat in the air, in a dance that wasn't ending. They made love on the balcony wearing their winter coats.

Maren went to the stove and stirred the sauerkraut soup that those who still remained at the house would use to cure their hangovers. A white shorthaired cat entered the kitchen and rubbed against the old lady's leg. Maren glanced down at it.

"Maren," Lukasz said firmly. And she looked to him. He shook his head. "Not that one." She hated how he could read her thoughts. "Are you still doing that?"

This was a July heat like no other and no one had complained during the ceremony in the church but now everyone had removed their wedding wear for the least amount of clothing. Maren sat around in the yard with Lukasz's father. The sun beat down. They drank lemonade and tequila. Lukasz and Irena returned from being photographed at the church for the second time. Maren could tell he was tired. Irena's family buzzed around him, vying for his attention.

"It is strange that my wife is not here for this. It almost doesn't seem real," Andros said, resting his drink between his bare knees, letting the perspiration the ice made on the glass run off onto his skin. "It's not how I pictured it, if a father can really imagine the day his son starts his own family. I never thought Lukasz's day would be like this—so luxurious. It's not his style." Maren put her hand atop his.

"I saw you yesterday with tears in your eyes."

"I remembered what it was like when I found his mother," Andros told her.

"How did it feel?"

"Like nothing I will ever be able to put into words." Andros brought her hand up to his lips and kissed her fingers. "You and Lukasz were always getting into trouble together. But you made each other happy. There was no crime in that. Do you remember what it was like?"

"It was just like this, except now he is married."

Andros laughed. "Tell me, is there still a man in your life?"

Maren smiled at the innocence or the cunning in the question. She told him, "There is always a man in my life."

After she ate a large lunch of barszcz with meat pancakes she went down to the cool and damp of the basement and lay on the air mattress. Lukasz soon came and crawled in next to her. He was the most familiar beside her.

"I want to come home," he told her.

"I don't live in that apartment anymore. You know that," She said, turning away on her side.

"That's not what I mean."

"I know what you mean."

He curled his body around hers. "No one will ever be you."

"You're drunk."

"I'm being sweet."

"I am too tired for sweet."

"You know, I'm really getting sick of you rejecting me Maren." They lay there together. Lukasz ran his hands through her hair. He attempted to make a few small braids with her long locks.

When they were teenagers Lukasz had been with Maren when she found the litter of kittens behind Saint Marie-Magdalene Church. He watched her stuff them into a bag and throw them into the waters of the Odra.

"That was really cruel," Lukasz had said with a dark sadness, dragging his feet behind Maren on the way back to his house.

"Yes, well, it is for the best," she had told him.

Maren thought of how it never felt as if Lukasz judged her for anything that she had ever

done. He observed the actions of her life and reflected them. Maren pulled her hair from his hands and moved it over her shoulder.

"The only reason you have been with any of those other men is because they will not love you exactly as you want," Lukasz told her, as he rolled away so their backs faced one another. "Then you leave them using it as an excuse."

"Don't you start to say hurtful things to me," Maren warned.

"I'll mean every word of it," Lukasz said, and he sighed deeply. "But don't be mad for keeps.

Maren decided to call Gerek. Usually she left without much explanation, but she was curious to see if he could convince her to come back to him.

"Have you noticed?" she asked. She was sitting on the front steps of the house. There was a continual flow of people around her, the twenty or so guests still celebrating, going in and out of doors, kids chasing each other around the yard.

"I've noticed but I don't understand." Gerek sounded sad.

"I can't explain it to you." It wasn't that she couldn't, it was that she didn't want to.

"Please try."

She imagined Gerek sitting in the apartment looking at the things she left behind. Reminders of her. She wondered how long he would keep them.

"It's like you don't know how to talk to me," she told him.

"We are talking now." She could tell he already missed her.

She said, "Not like this."

"I don't understand."

"I know."

When Maren hung up the phone she watched as Irena left the picnic area where her family gathered together and walked toward her. She hoped the bride was just going into the house. She didn't know what they would say to one another.

"Lukasz said you liked cats," was what Irena spoke when she stopped in front of Maren, and she knew that Lukasz was watching the interaction between them and smirking. "There is something I should show you."

Maren followed Irena across the grassy knolls away from the house. She saw how untested she really was. How little she suspected anything about the man she married. She saw Irena's ignorance and her kindness. In time she would become more self-serving. After being with Lukasz for a while she'd learn his sense of adventure was always at someone else's expense.

The rundown house was shaded by a wooded area in the hills. It was small like the cottages made of spruce trees that were once so popular. The panes from the windows had long been knocked out by salvagers, or weather, or little kids with rocks. They stepped inside the empty structure and a few cats immediately darted out in all directions. When they entered the hollowed area that would have been someone's main living quarters once, they saw other cats that stayed on their perches, six or seven of them, a few kittens. The purring was astonishing.

"When I was a little girl my grandfather took me here to get a kitten of my own," Irena told Maren. "Maybe it would be nice for me to get one for Lukasz." She looked around. "That one there." She pointed to a grey kitten hardly old enough to leave its mother on the railingless stairs that led up to a high open loft. The feline darted up into the second story of the old house when Irena moved toward it. Maren wondered what diseases they were being exposed to by just being there. Irena started to climb the stairs to go after the kitten. She walked carefully up the steps, trying not to touch the walls covered with grit. The cat Irena

wanted eyed both of them now from the loft. Its coat was almost silver.

Irena went down on her hands and knees when she reached the last step. She called softly to the kitten trying to coax it to her. She was twenty feet off the ground. The loft floor had been partially eaten away. The dust and grime from years fell through the cracks and holes as the wood creaked and groaned under Irena's movements across the old panels.

When the floorboard broke under her, Irena was able to catch herself with her arms on the awning boards that remained. Her sandals slipped off her feet and landed on the floor below her with a heavy thud that set the cats darting off in all directions. Maren looked at Irena's feet kicking as if she were in water and it would help keep her from going under.

"Maren, do something!"

But she didn't. She just stood there looking at the two halves of the new wife of her oldest lover, anticipating that she would not be able to hold her own weight much longer. Maren thought of it as a mercy killing. She knew what it was like to love Lukasz and this would be better for her.

Maren watched the rest of Irena come through the hole in the floor. Her neck hit ground first and the remainder of her body followed. She landed on her back. Her legs were perfectly straight out; one of her arms was crooked and broken under her body. Her eyes were open.

Lukasz was playing cards with Irena's uncles on the patio when Maren came and pulled him away. She could not speak. She did not like that he could be unbearably hurt by what had happened. It wasn't until she had to tell him of his bride's death that she began to worry he may have actually loved Irena. Lukasz put his hands on her elbows and moved in close to her when he realized something was wrong.

"Tell me. What is it?"

"Please don't be angry with me." The thought

that this could make him finally pull away from her was suddenly overwhelming.

"What happened?" Lukasz said. He stared her down.

Maren shook her head.

"What did you *do* Maren?"

They went across the field together.

Lukasz looked at Irena's corpse for a long time. He sat beside her cross-legged on the dirt-layered ground. He closed her eyes and then closed his own and tried to cry. Maren smoked a cigarette in the open doorway. She thought about the whole house burning down. When he finally spoke he said, "Couldn't you have just taken me up on one of my other offers?"

"That's not funny," Maren scolded him.

"I wasn't trying to be funny," Lukasz said sullenly.

"Yes you were."

Maren wondered if there was a way they could get rid of the body and forget about it. Immediately following her thought Lukasz said, "There was a well out front. We could put her in there. It would look like she fell."

"She did fall."

Maren took Irena's arms and Lukasz, her legs, and they carried the body outside. Irena didn't drop into the long tube of the brick well easily. She was crumpled and strange parts of her stuck out of the water that was not deep enough to completely cover her thirty feet below. An elbow. A knee.

They were both hot and sticky as they walked slowly back to the main house together. Maren tied her hair onto the top of her head and hiked her skirt up. Lukasz removed his shirt and lay it over his shoulder. The sun had just begun to think of going down. Before they reached the house Lukasz put his arm out in front of Maren and they stopped in the long grass.

"Something good must come from this," he said softly, almost pleading.

"I believe it will," she told him.

"Do you really?"

"I do."

They paused for just a moment longer to breathe in the open air, and then they continued back to the reception.

About the Author

Libby Copa has degrees from Prescott College and Hamline University. Her work has appeared in publications across the country, including Hanging Loose, Dash, Matter, and Quail Bell Magazine. She loves a good adventure.

APPOINTMENT IN ZANESVILLE
by Don Dussault

Bustling more than usual this morning, Thelma sets the omelet platter down hard before me and deftly slides an omelet into my plate, then one into hers, without looking at me. In the perfect silence the omelets sound as if they'd fallen from the ceiling. It's about me reading the newspaper at breakfast again? I lower the paper halfway. "If the paper irritates you,it gives me a start on the day. Do you mind too much?"

"Your business gives us too little spare time."

Your business she says, true, hers is our home. She's holding back. Deflect. "Excellent omelet again." She's done omelets for years, hard to make bad omelets. At worst, you get scrambled eggs. "Perfect coffee, too."

It ought to be, with a two thousand dollar coffee maker. Something on her mind. She ventures, "Did you sleep well?"

I must look bleary. Not what I want to think about. "Fine. You?"

I recognize her strenuously bland tone. "I slept well, under the circumstances."

Circumstances? The word wakes me up and turns me off at the same time. True? I couldn't tell, with my back to her, instantly asleep. "Midweek,

I need to crash early."

Not the greatest excuse and she doesn't buy it. "Those long days of yours must be dreadful."

I hear a little empathy in the words, less than usual. Irony? She knows the demands of my work. "I'm too busy to notice."

"We both have long days. The boys will be up soon. I'll have to get them ready, drive them to school..." She continues talking while, unhearing, I nod and turn to the business page. Then a slight edge to her tone alerts me she is watching me. She has a rhetorical question I've heard before: "Is this another of our talks where I do all the talking?"

Unusual cutting edge in her voice, start of a rebellion? No way I want heavy talk. Stall, say something. "We'll talk when I get back."

"Today is your Zanesville trip?"

"I'll be back tomorrow night."

"Of course you will. And tired."

Some empathy there. Despite my hopes, she may not forget. This could turn unpleasant. I hate this let's talk. Get it over with now, while I can spare only a few minutes. "What's tiring is I'll be in suspense for two days." If she saves up her anger or whatever it is, she'll cut loose tomorrow evening, let me have it at length. Better defuse her now. She has that waiting look, forcing me to pursue, "So talk."

Serious look, serious voice. "The last few times we made love..." a subtle emphasis on few... "I felt objectified."

She sounds like she wants to continue but she stops and waits. The sex thing again. Objectified! An accusation? Her features have gone blank, meaning she expects a response. I could have done better. Too quick. It's happened before. Avoid that one for sure. Sound convincing: "You made me happy."

Inane. Her tone and demeanor firm up. "I'm glad you were. I mean, we weren't quite together. I mean even when we were, we weren't. Oh, for sex it's no big deal..." She lies. Sex is more to her than she'll admit... "It's a symptom. We don't connect much in other ways. Even when you're home."

"I feel connected with you." My automatic denial. "We men are different..." not a good start... "our pleasure isn't as all-consuming as yours..." I hate this, for her it's about romance while I worry about the plumbing. Division of labor? She looks impatient. I'm awkward at this kind of talk. Must avoid blather. Skip this and go to work. No, get it over with. Soft soap it. She's skeptical. "For us men compartmentalizing works."

Her eyes say she wants to buy in. "I don't know what you mean."

"We can't open the door too early."

"You make it sound so businesslike."

Why the hell are we talking about this? Not like we're sexcrazy kids.

Admit we're getting on. "It can't be like it was at the beginning, can it?"

"We're not that much older."

Some calm has entered her voice. She's coming around. She is still well within child-bearing age. Does she want another? There's a topic to avoid! Delete from my head. Where does romance go? It slips away in the flood of daily chores, hers, mine. She knows that. Never admit our romance slackens. "We've grown less demonstrative. Um, quietly romantic."

She makes a little frown, "Maybe too quiet."

Her revenge. Was that supposed to hurt? I can win this, clinch it, feelings, emphasize feelings, "We've slowed down. At heart we haven't changed." That better be my last ploy. quick glance at my watch, seven-thirty. Still unsettled, she admits, "We have our ups and downs like everybody else."

Is this a talk all couples have? Could be a few out there who just live, happy with each other? She has a full enough social life, reads books, pop psych, women stuff, grand notions of married life and consummate orgasms. She's not as bright as I thought when we were courting. Years of housework   wear down the brain? Shift gears. "Next year I'll take an extended vacation. We'll travel. Send the boys to your mother's."

She doesn't quite concede. "You should go. Your driver's waiting."

He'd better have taken the car to the wash this morning. "He can wait. It's his job to wait." Let her see I'm willing to talk as much as she needs. "I can finish the newspaper on the way in."

If not satisfied, she's mollified. "Go. It's good we can talk."

Free at last. "Yes, Thelma, we'll talk more," and I'm hoping not for another ten years or so...

The best hotel in Zanesville, they call this place. Another dinner in a no-star restaurant, fattening American fare, a steak fresh from Chicago too well done, an over-buttered baked potato, a choice of whipped cream desserts, then to a room with soporific walls boasting color photographs of Middle America. The local landscape is a straight line dividing an endless cornfield from an empty sky. Is any structure more boring than a grain tower? Damn, forgot, call Thelma.

Exchange of hellos. Her voice sounds normal, without residual anxiety from our chat this morning. I tell her, as if she couldn't guess, "I'm in Zanesville."

"How was your trip?"

Same old everything, airport, pilot, sky above, dollops of clouds below, the familiar multi-green midwestern checkerboard. Brevity the soul of wit. "It was good. Clear skies all the way."

"Good. The boys are studying in the livingroom. Want to talk to them?"

"Really studying?"

"Really. And the TV's off, if you can believe that."

"With things running so well, it's best we don't interrupt them. How was your day?"

"Good. I did the laundry. Found some nice filet steaks at the butcher's, so I didn't need to raid the freezer. Picked up some shiitakes, green beans. Think you can make it back for dinner tomorrow?"

"Probably. Pretty late, though."

"By ten?"

"Nine-thirtyish, with luck. I'll call if I get delayed." A moment of silence.

"After that long trip, I'm crashing early tonight."

"You do sound tired."

"Yes, and restless at the same time."

She sounds concerned. "Our conversation this morning, it left me a little on edge. You?"

A hint of apology? "We had a good talk. Travel wipes me out sometimes. Strange rooms. Erratic sleep leaves me feeling ragged in the morning. I'll take a pill and I'll be fine."

I seldom call her on these trips. I'm content with her as a helpmeet. She sees to my comfort, stabilizes my life. The hunter needs a village to return to, and his own warm hut and a ready meal. Isn't romance overrated and rutting like pups undignified? Should have interrupted the boys' studies a moment. No harm in a short break. I don't talk to them enough. They're closer to Thelma.

In daylight from a taxi Zanesville is no more prepossessing than at night. The morning sun darts in and out of my eyes as I ride toward the outskirts to visit the factory expecting a dreary day going over numbers with a manager who might be failing and should get fired. Funny

how shop foremen restrain their ebullient language in my presence. When I encounter a union rep or have a question for a technician at a machine, our chats are technical and terse. My chauffeur concentrates on his driving. Recently married, two kids already. Pilot stays in his cabin. Fifty-something, new grandkid, Red Sox fan. To me, minimal people. The loneliness of power. A cliché, but personal.

The roads are shiny damp. Must have rained last night. Automatically I read, Your driver is Felix Jackson. Full-face photo of a Negro man. Here in Zanesville a black cab driver? Do many whites signaling him on the streets change their minds when they see the driver? Better not ask him about that. The serious mirror face looks at me. He's noticed my interest in the wet road. "Rain's done. We should get sun all day."

Thanks for the weather report. Looking for a bigger tip? I can dispense wisdom, too. "Sun helps the corn grow."

I'm coming off as a farmer now? Unconvincing. He rolls with it. "Rain and sun, they bring life."

Having exhausted my interest in conversation, disinclined to reveal anything about myself, I plunk a period on philosophy. "So true."

Last night I felt better about Thelma after my phone call than I do now, in clear daylight. I can't dismiss a faint unease. Our diminished enthusiasm may be simply what happens after spending years together, every day, every night, which I find reassuring yet sometimes boring, while she feels haphazard dissatisfaction...

The boys have gone to bed and I'm pouring myself two ounces of cognac (this was a week ago) while she watches me in a hiatus from her distracted demeanor all evening. As if to invite trouble I observe, "You sometimes think you made a mistake?"

I'd tuned into her thoughts or she into mine. She gathers herself. "It isn't you. You're who you are. Steady, rational." Compliments not entirely complimentary. Stuffy, uninspiring? "I knew who I was getting."

She didn't say I haven't disappointed her. "We were young then. Full of expectations."

Bluntly, "We still are."

As she looks at me, she is confirming she still resents the forced change in our lives six years ago, when the former grad student envisioned hanging out with academics and their spouses in ceremonies, teas, book clubs sparkling with wit while I'd advance from adjunct college instructor to full professor, my expectation at the time, and she, this grad student, couldn't let go those expectations after I've moved on into my father's business as he long wished, an unplanned career change after my indiscretion in a lumberyard she hasn't quite forgiven me for, most likely saw me as prime laughing stock when, driving home, I detoured to pick up six hardwood planks for garage shelves and in a far corner of the yard decided I couldn't suppress nature any longer and was observed peeing near the fence by a part time employee, the son of a department head, initiating a widespread rumor that reached the dean. In her longsuffering mode, surely embarrassed, Thelma never scolded me.

"You're disappointed over... that."

"Oh, kind of, I guess," she acknowledges with suspect reluctance the shock she hasn't quite recovered from and the loss of a lifestyle she loved perhaps as much as she loved me. Academia's departure from our lives took part of me with it. "The past is past," she concludes without conviction...

The taxi is turning onto a steel bridge with a bend in it. The driver catches my glance. "This is the only Y-bridge in the country. Maybe anywheres."

I spot a second entrance merging onto the single bridge span. Green traffic light. Not desiring a tour guide I say nothing, preferring he con-

centrate on driving. Not much to see anyway, with a concrete barrier just high enough to bar my view of the river below. Bridge walls revive my unease. A wrinkle in my expensive suit? Uneasy about Thelma. Why shouldn't we be happy, when, after our financial struggles while I was a lowly economics instructor, Father brought me into his expanding tool and die business, entrusting to me his midwestern enterprises while he remains, comfortably for me, on the coast, bringing us, Thelma and me, into the arenas of self-made wealth. She should be happier and, come to think of it, also should I...

I swirl my cognac. She has more to say. "Except it's hard to keep the past in its place, sometimes. You know what I mean?" Her unnecessary qualifier, sometimes, tells me she is hedging. I wait. She goes on, "You're less relaxed. Early to work every morning, late for dinner most nights."

"I'm content."

"That isn't the same as happy, though."

Is this discussion now about my failings? "You're picking at tiny scabs and making them bigger." Come off as positive. Sell her on getting used to this new life we have. "We have the good life."

"I'm doing fine. I'm thinking about how your work consumes you." Meaning she worries my work consumes her. Gradually, of course, like a python that swallows its victim whole and takes weeks to digest it. "Are you saying I make you unhappy?"

The instant I say that, I'm sure she'll misunderstand it. She frowns. "Where did that come from? I'm not unhappy and I'm not blaming you for anything. Can't I be concerned about my husband overworking himself?" She's on a roll, "When we talk, you call it picking at scabs. Can't we just say what we feel?"

She has used that before and it always stumps me. I have too many feelings to sort out on a moment's notice. Tell her she's hiding her own feelings. From me, from herself. No, she'll hear that as an accusation. Restraint. Don't push hard. "I hear some doubt that you're happy."

She tries to explain, "Not like I'm hysterically happy. If we're not unhappy, aren't we happy?"

She's asking me. Good. I seize my advantage. As in business, you strike while the iron is hot. "Yes, we are, basically. We're settling down. That's not thrilling. But we're alive and well." Mustn't forget, "And we're together."

She's taking in my words. A long second passes as she flips them over. "We go through these stages, don't we?" I'm not sure what she means. I force a smile...

Leaving downtown we're into more suburbs and trees than I expected. No cornfields. Thankfully no sights for my tourist guide cabbie to point out. Heading southeast into the morning. Lost in my thoughts, I hadn't noticed when my cabbie put on dark sunglasses. Modified aviator style, though more rounded. Almost black. The sun flashes on them. I can't see his eyes. I don't think he's looking at me. Hope he won't try more chitchat. My briefcase waits on the seat beside me. I could review some reports. No, enjoy the morning light, the trees. My eyes glaze. I confront a machine the size of a diesel locomotive, no, a three-story building, with flat unpainted steel panels, thousands of panels, removable so I can oil the machine, and I must, all day every day haul around a quart size oilcan, red with a foot-long spout narrowing to a tiny opening I insert into thousands of places in the machine so it won't fail to do whatever it 's supposed to do. Low single story homes in the suburbs yield to fewer, larger homes surrounded by broad open spaces and clusters of trees. Fresher air. The machine continues running in the back of my mind like a silent movie.

While otherwise faithful to Thelma I'd sought solace from boredom a mere twice compared with other executives I've chatted with, who lacked all scruples in their eagerness for pay to play. Only in this last year have I partaken of the itinerant businessman's prerogative, with bowlsfull of trepidation and a richness of guilt until, over weeks, I could convince myself I'd done nothing unfair to Thelma, for there's no real infidelity in my minimal whoring— ugly word, face it— when I did employ the services of a thirtyish woman made up and dressed as if fresh out of her teens and found the experience diverting yet, afterward, unsatisfying, a weak replacement for some undefinable loss in my life, a pale reward for driving myself hard.

The suburb outside the taxi window blurs. My thoughts wander. Peripatetic adventurisms are natural for the descendants of hunter-gatherer males, not betrayals of the spouse-mother back home tending the hearth. Thelma would never consider having one-nighters. Too staid for soirees with random muff-divers, too protective of her wife-mother status to invite the complications of a second man into her affections, she might yield to a damaged lonely soul seeking a stable berth in a womb-bearer. Nothing to worry about. She feels sorry for me as I leave on these trips, spending nights alone in hotel rooms in cities where I know no one. Never occurs to her my time away may be a blessing, some relief, bring a rare taste of adventure...

At her parents' home after our wedding, noisy and stuffy with guests, the hired photographer, a family friend, takes us aside and stands us, Thelma and me, in front of the fireplace, with a lushness of bright flowers swelling from tall wicker baskets beside us. From the face hidden behind the camera comes the photographer's voice, "Smile, not that I need to tell you. Holding hands, good. So pretty in that white dress, Thelma."

Thelma's mother chimes in, "Face the camera." Her tone pleads, as does Thelma's sometimes. "You'll have plenty of time to gaze into each other's eyes. Face the world." We aren't inclined to hear her. Turned inward, we are, from the beginning, as we'll always be in that photo. Enough that we have ourselves and time. I tell Thelma, "You fell to me like a trump card in a weak hand."

The notion amuses her. "You look so impressive in the classroom." I'm not tall nor handsome, though not ugly either, was never considered an imposing figure. I appreciate the flattery. "I want to have a part in my students' growth." Sometimes I get sententious, which amuses her. "I like the growth of your manly part better."

She had her prurient moments in those times long bygone, when any day or night could like wildfire flare into an adventure. Like that spontaneous Sunday afternoon when we're side by side sweating on a damp bed, still breathing hard, and she says, "I never knew I married Tarzan," her sincerest, most telling compliment. Tarzan, the primal male who controlled nature, commanded apes and elephants, yet at times found himself embroiled with uncooperative feline species. A mental image brings a wry inward smile, Thelma hugging and kissing her cat. She's always had cats. Now we've mellowed, a subterfuge word to say whatever we're not saying. Last night's pussyfooting. We're saying what? Oh yes, stages. I go on, "Well, I'm nowhere close to my midlife crisis of eyeing red sports cars and chasing trim blondes. I may be a betrayer of male-hood because I'm content, really. Not looking anywhere else."

A chill infiltrates her voice. "Why should you, anyway?"

Amazing how little she knows of men or biology, remarkable ignorance for a college grad. A secretive mistrust of the male where temptation lurks? Long-distance telephone isn't the best medium for debate, if that's what this call is turning into. Irritation creeps into my voice. "Well, that's my point."

Her irritation aroused, she snipes, "It isn't much of a point."

I shouldn't push back now, at this moment, this distance, yet I hear my voice: "I don't understand menopause, either."

"Is that some kind of accusation— that I'm pre-menopausal, a male code for goofy?"

I recall how smartly we communicated in our early years, how we grasped with ease the nuances of each other's casual words and gestures, every faintest shift in the shading or brightening of our eyes. Times long gone. Now annoyed, obliged to explain the obvious, I suppress my stern maleness to win a truce. "I wasn't clear. I simply meant we're heading toward middle age in a proper way."

She sounds mollified, "It's my fault for leaping to conclusions."

So I surrender and now we're apologizing to each other. I tell her I'll see her at dinner and she wishes me a safe trip home. Pro forma. An emergency landing we can walk away from. What were we mobilizing for, and what got resolved, if anything?

The taxi driver cuts in, "Looks like they got more rain out here."

I'm yanked too abruptly out of my ruminations to respond. A strange enervation persists. I'm elsewhere. On edge over banal talks that portend dreaded destinies. The taxi turns into a street of low apartment and industrial buildings. Sunlight strikes the driver at a new angle. His face brightens in the windshield mirror. Pockets of dark shadows appear. Under his cap a skull grins at me! A death's head, brownish as if dug from the earth! Is that a tiny light in the eye sockets? Death conveying me to my work. The taxi slowing— why? An instant of fear... Relax. It's nothing, simply that we've arrived. The skull disappears from the mirror as the driver removes his sunglasses and turns toward me. I focus on the meter. Twenty-six fifty. In conspicuous black-on-yellow the meter warns, "Cash Only." I fish in my billfold. Total cash content: a fifty and a twenty. Blame my distraction for poor planning. Let him keep the change, he gets a tip almost equal to the fare. Thirty feet from the two-story building with tiers of windows like a school, I can't be seen haggling for dollars with a taxi driver. I resign myself to overpaying for my social prestige. "Keep the change."

A broad smile. Large white teeth. "Thank you, sir."

I open the door anxious to end this damnable ride. He reminds me, "Don't forget your brief-case."

Of course. I half-turn, reach for it, clutch it, launch myself out the door, and my feet slide in the wet grassy road-verge on the outer edge of the sidewalk. I make a futile grab at the door before I'm sprawled on my back in a puddle I hadn't noticed, a slather across the sidewalk too shallow   to drown a spider, neverthe-less wet enough. I hear the front door of the taxi creak open. Queasy, quick to rise to my feet, I'm brushing water off my suit with my hands as the driver arrives. I'm muttering to him, "I'm fine. I'm fine."

The taxi is gone. My suit is water-stained, prob-ably grass-stained. Trousers soggy. Socks damp. Erect, trying not to trudge, I advance toward the building and its many windows. Every window must have people in it watching my inelegant arrival.

About the Author:

Don Dussault lives in the San Francisco Bay Area. His history includes a BA and MA in Eng-lish literature and postgrad study in linguistics. He's placed several pieces in literary publica-tions and is wrapping up a multivoiced saga of a dysfunctional family.

A ROOM FOR TWO

by Cristina Oramas

Sweat made her tight white dress cling to her curvy figure. "Why do you always make me meet you in such dingy motels?" asked Rose. The bed had a thin layer of dust on it that flew into the air when she sat down. "Uck. Even the carpets smell like piss," she said, twirling her hair. Her face contorted in disgust.

"You know why," said Rick. He took his jacket off. "Besides, it's not *that* bad. Do you want a drink?"

"Really? You never spend time on drinks. You usually just get right to business. Time is money for me, after all. But I guess I can spare a few extra minutes for a regular. Especially, if that regular is you, Ricky," said Rose. She smiled at Rick.

Rick turned around, rolling his eyes and began making drinks on the barren bathroom counter. *One should do it.* The pill dropped into one of the cranberry vodkas with a splash. The drink bubbled.

"I just wanted to take a minute to thank you for the last few months. I know I may just be another client, but you've been a wonderful distraction while I've been preparing for the campaign," said Rick. He didn't take his eyes off her, watching her reflection in the bathroom mirror as she made herself comfortable on the bed.

I can do this... I can do this. He took as deep breath and turned to face Rose. His hands shook as he handed her the glass, its contents finally settled. "A toast to new beginnings."

Rose grabbed the cold glass. "You sure are sweating a lot Ricky. You okay?" she asked.

"Yeah. I-I'm okay. It's just r-real hot in here." He loosened his tie with his free hand. Sweat dripped down the sides of his forehead.

Rose placed her glass on the small night stand next to the bed. "Here, let me turn on the A/C," she said.

Rick swallowed hard. "I just need to sit down." He put his glass down next to hers.

"The patio actually doesn't look like a complete dump. Sit outside and get some fresh air while I turn this ancient thing on. The room should cool down in a few minutes," said Rose.

"Yeah, good idea." Rick trudged to the sliding glass door. The track was rusted, making it difficult to open. *Damn door. Fuck it's hot.*

The patio was enclosed by a tall dark fence. A large tree on its other side provided nice shade. Rick picked the lawn chair that appeared less broken from the mix-matched set surrounding the small table and sat down. *Not a complete dump.*

"This damn thing is on its last leg. On the bright side, it's loud enough to help muffle out any sounds of *business* being conducted," said Rose. She walked to the sliding glass door. Her large breasts exposed in the sunlight shined, catching drops of sweat that rolled down her neck.

Why does she have to be so beautiful? "Take a seat," Rick said, pulling a chair for her. It was rusted and covered in leaves and dirt from the low hanging tree.

"Um, no. Why don't I take a seat here instead? I think we'll both be much more comfortable," Rose said, taking a seat on his lap.

"Y-yeah," Rick said. "So, as I was saying, I just wanted to say thanks. It has been a really stressful time and Marge has been a pain in my ass the entire time. It's been nice to get away with you every week, even if it's costing me a fortune." He grinned and kissed her cheek.

"Haha. Well, everything in life has a price. And I'm what some might call a high-end piece. I don't come cheap," Rose said. "And you know the rules, no kissing."

"Yeah, sorry. I forgot. Marge has been a bitch the last few months. I just miss the intimacy. She wants to be the politician's wife, but never wants to put out for it in the bedroom. Anyway, that's why I wanted to talk a little before getting to it."

"My clients don't normally want to talk about their failing marriages before our visits," said Rose.

"That's just it, I'm not going to be a client any longer. After today, I have to cut ties with anything that may hinder my political career. I can't afford to be spotted at dingy motels with a woman that's not my wife."

"Oh."

"Yeah."

"Well then, let's drink and get to it. I can probably make another appointment by the end of the night."

"Don't be like that."

"It's fine. Shit, we left the drinks inside. I'll get them." Rose got up, smoothing her dress out over her large behind and stomped inside.

This mother fucker thinks he can just stop seeing me. He promised me Rome, and Hawaii. Jewels. Everything.

"Mine's on the desk," said Rick from outside.

"Yea, I see it. Just a second, going to add more vodka to them. They've watered down a bit," Rose said. She pulled a small plastic bag out from her purse containing two pills. *Fuck you.*

Rose grabbed their drinks and walked to the bathroom counter. She took a sip from hers before adding more vodka to it. She then dropped the two pills into his glass and covered them in vodka. *You think you can just cut me out like that.*

"You okay in there?" Rick asked, peeking his head into the room.

Rose adjusted herself in front of the mirror. "Yep, coming." She walked to the patio, almost spilling the drinks. She handed Rick his glass.

"A toast to my future success in politics," Rick said. They clinked their glasses and took a sip from their drinks.

Ricks hands were still shaking. *That's it, take a sip. Just a si...*

About the Author:

Cristina Oramas is currently working on her B.F.A. degree from Full Sail University. She loves to share stories that are close to her heart, as well as share her love of fantasy through her writing. On her free time, she enjoys going on adventures with her boyfriend, and curling up with a good book and her dog. Linkedin: www.linkedin.com/in/cristithewriter Facebook: https://www.facebook.com/cristina.m.oramas

LAST NIGHT

by Cassie Lawson

"Do you want to get high tonight?"

I nearly dropped the receiver and choked on my Dorritos. "Wha- wait. What?"

"I can come pick you up in like half an hour. What are you doing tonight?"

I could hear Benjamin fumbling with something glass or ceramic as he spoke rapidly over the phone.

"My family's at my brother's soccer game. But I don't know, Be-"

"Okay, I'm on my way." Click. And that was that.

I left a note by the phone for my mom explaining I was studying for a test with Benjamin and would be home by nine. I knew she wouldn't really care if I hung out with him. We'd been friends since sixth grade and had the most inexplicably comfortable girl-boy friendship I had ever known. We had different circles of friends, but we could count on each other when it really mattered – talking him through battles with his stepmom and him driving me to school on days I couldn't bear the nasty girls on the bus. My mom loved him; my dad was indifferent. It was strange that my mom approved of the boys who were in actuality the worst of influences. Deviants are the best liars.

Twenty-seven minutes later I locked the front door and hopped into Ben's white Corolla. Some weird, rhythmic trance music was throbbing out of the car and into the dusk.

"Hey."

"Hey." I hoped I sounded nonchalant.

We drove and parked about eight blocks away near the freeway onramp. Benjamin was nearly giddy with excitement. He loved getting people high for the first time. Like notches in his belt or headboard or bong, or whatever.

He lowered the music and rummaged through his satchel and pulled out a bong. "This is Serendipity," he introduced. I smiled thinly.

I nervously watched a car drive past us, hoping it wasn't some neighbor or God forbid my parents. The sun was sinking fast in the sky, creating a remarkably vibrant splatter of pinks and oranges over a sheet of pure honey. I was about to comment on this but-

"Oh shit. I left the canister on my dresser. We have to go to my house," Ben announced, starting the engine, turning up the volume and pulling onto the freeway. As I could not think of a reasonable reason to protest this new turn of events, I silently assented as we sped under the most beautiful earthly ceiling in a quest for another altered state.

We quickly fell into familiar banter, making fun of our pervy chemistry teacher and Ben's ex-girlfriend, Psycho Princess. They dated for only a few months but she would occasionally follow him around campus and once left a poorly produced mix tape on his windshield. We were now convinced she would soon be in a rubber room, beside the neo-hippie transfer student I gave a hand job to in the back of the library last fall. It was our go-to conversation: a dissection of our previous relationships and unknowing

We pulled up at Ben's house — his mother's house since the divorce — and I pulled my drooping thrift store purse close to my chest. His mom's house was a huge gray building with two massive turrets alongside each side. It was nearly dark and tiny lanterns led the way to the stained glass door. When we stepped inside, the jaunty cackle of laughter was punctuated by Ben's mother humming to herself, carrying a bottle of wine past the foyer to a lively table of guests in the dining room. Jazz music was coming from somewhere.

"Ben, we can't stay here," I whispered and backed into the front door.

"No, it's fine. Come on."

He steered us into the dining room where we announced our presence to adults who barely registered our hellos, then quickly headed up the staircase. Inside Ben's extremely cluttered room, he immediately grabbed an orange prescription bottle and pocketed it. He rummaged through some seemingly useless debris while I lingered in the doorway. Boys' bedrooms always fascinated me: almost universally messy, nearly unhygienic, but somehow charming in the details. Ben's school notebooks were stacked on top of his green Jansport backpack, towers of quarters on the dresser, discarded clothes all over the bed and floor — It was a case study in teenage disorganization. I had to restrain myself from picking up the fast food trash.

I had only been inside his bedroom once before at the end of sophomore year when we studied for a chemistry final. We had been alone in the house and it had been the only time I wondered if our relationship was more than platonic. I had waited to see if he would make a move while we memorized the periodic table, but nothing happened. I had been too shy to vocalize my curiosity and now that possibility seemed nonexistent.

His beeper went off. "It's Nate. We should go meet up with him."

"Uh, I don't really know Nate. It'll be weird."

"No, no, it's cool. I promise. I *promise*. It'll be cool."

No, I thought, it's fun with just us. Once again without a defense or alternative, I agreed to this latest change in plans. Luckily, Nate was holed up in his car just a few blocks away in the parking lot of an independent movie theater.

We somehow escaped the house without further interception or inquiry and were soon pulled up next to Nate in the practically barren movie theater parking lot. It was now completely dark, the neighborhood and evening soaked in inky tranquility. Nate slammed the backseat door, hanging off our headrests and already changing the tape to something decidedly more melodic.

"Check it. This is some dope shit," Nate declared, revealing a black film canister filled with what, by the smell, could only be the ground remains of an ancient and profoundly unwell skunk. Ben readily agreed and began neatly packing the bong. I suddenly wanted to go home. This was stupid. It was after eight o'clock and I was already imagining the interrogation when I returned home by my typically despotic mother.

"Here," Ben said simply.

I gripped the bong by its mouthpiece and just stared at it. "I don't even know how to use a lighter," I quietly admitted. This, of course, was hilarious to them and they proceeded to make fun of this for a full minute while I contemplated throwing the bong out the car window.

After the laughter sufficiently subsided, Ben showed me the finer art of lighter maneuvering and bong usage. It was once again offered to me; I took it gingerly and pressed my mouth to the glass opening and lit up.

After a couple pass-arounds, the car was pretty cozy with smoke and the house music back on the stereo. The conversation turned to school gossip and then to some seniors who I didn't really know. Nate was graduating in a few months and had no apparent plans beyond tonight, let alone June. Even as a junior, I had a laundry list of schools and majors to consider. I fleetingly wondered what decisions I'll have made in a year, if I could raise my SAT scores another fifty points before applications were due.

A security guard meandered through the lot, headed in our direction. It was nearly nine and I reminded Ben of my curfew. Nate reluctantly disengaged from his backseat activities, snatched back his cassette tape and slammed the door with a nod to us. I hazily wondered if this was the last time I would spend time with Nate in this fashion. Was this the beginning of a habit or a solitary incident? It's difficult to articulate the exact formation of a relationship or pattern or obsession -- it becomes blurred and soon washes away with the beating back of memory. The middle details and certainly the end can be easy to summon -- but the start? The commencement of something im-portant, in reflection, seems to unfold like a dream. You're already enmeshed in the pattern or obsession before there's an awareness that there is something important happening.

While I puzzled over what exactly occurred during the evening, Ben and I drove in an easy silence. When we pulled in front of my house, he prepped me for what to do if my parents discovered I was high: to tell them that some-one else had the weed, not him. Deny, deny, deny. I just prayed I didn't smell as bad I imag-ined I did.

I heard the Corolla zoom away as my mom barely said good night to me, and I went to get ready for bed. In the bathroom brushing my teeth, I stared at my clear reflection and tried to force myself to remember every detail of the night. It seemed so important at the time.

About the Author:

Cassie Lawson is a middle school teacher by night and writer by late night. She lives in San Diego, CA with her family.

SOLO ACT

by Malcolm Garcia

She holds a yellow feather.

--Do you know anything about birds? she asks.

He shakes his head, no, and moves over to make room for her on a bench in the bus shelter at the corner of 10 A Avenida and 24 Calle. Fog rolls in and weights this lethargic morning in Guatemala City with a kind of blahness that hinders his motivation. He closes his jacket against the lingering mist and waits.

A quiet settles between him and the woman. She brushes a lank strand of gray hair from her face and cups the feather in her hand. She wants to talk, he thinks,. Why else would she have asked him about a feather? He hopes the bus arrives soon. The silence and his conviction she wants to speak leave him uneasy. He's used to his own company. Well, what do you think we should do this afternoon? he'll ask himself. Or, Well, it looks like a nice day for a walk, don't you think? The sound of his voice breaks the solitude of his apartment and the ears of his dog perk up and then relax, like an undertow the silence that follows the unanswered question pulls everything with it until all that is left is his hope that something in the ether—spirits, energy, he has heard various notions—is listening.

--Well, the woman says.

He stares at his feet. Out of the corner of his left eye, he can see her looking straight ahead but she might as well be looking at him because of the way he feels her next to him and her desire to talk. He does not mean to be rude but he doesn't know how to respond. He has grown so used to his own company that what social skills he had have all but disappeared. What would he say? Where would the conversation go? His wife, Martina, was the social one. He left this sort of thing to her.

A taxi passes them, the damp pavement hissing beneath its tires. He listens to the noise of its battered muffler until he can't hear it. He doesn't know what to think. A woman alone sitting in a bus shelter a little after seven on a Saturday morning? Well, he just doesn't know. He's going downtown to Sophos, a bookstore. He started three different books recently but none of them held his interest. This morning, he decided to buy another one. Sophos won't open until nine. He'll stop for a cup of coffee nearby. He couldn't sleep. Laying in bed staring at the ceiling seemed less appealing than just getting up and doing something.

He's read that reading helps keep the mind active and wards off senility. That and exercise so he makes a point to read each day and take his dog out. His neighbors dub him el *paseador de perros* because they see him three to four times a day with his dog in Zone 10 strolling near the National Equestrian Association of Guatemala. The moniker makes him feel terribly self conscious. His neighbors must think he has nothing better to do. He is retired, yes, but the idea that people, complete strangers no less, presume he has time on his hands bothers him deeply. He doesn't think of himself as retired any more than he does a widower. How would he describe himself? He can't say. He gets up in the morning. He sees the day through. He occupies his time until he sleeps. Is that not what we all do in one fashion or another? he wonders. What difference does it make that what I do now is different from what I did before? Can't help what other people think, right? He doesn't want pity. He wishes people would leave him alone and mind their own lives without jumping to conclusions about his.

--Well, the woman says again.

He had almost forgotten about her. He forces a smile to be polite. She lives in a small apartment, he presumes, possibly on 13 Calle, near a shopping mall. Maybe she has a roommate or lives with a friend. She's not wearing a ring so he supposes she's not married although who knows these days, right? She probably made coffee this morning and ate fried plantains, cream and tortillas. He had fruit. He doesn't drink coffee, never has, but he wakes up early unable to break years of routine when from this very corner he caught the eight o'clock bus to his office at Azteca Bank. Sometimes, he walks his dog past the bank and peers through the windows but he recognizes no one there now. However, his dog is old, has arthritis, and more often than not he takes it for much shorter walks than would be required to reach the bank. He gives him all sorts of pills to loosen his joints and ease the pain, about as many pills as he now takes for blood pressure, cholesterol and God knows what else. The dog was already old when he picked him up at United For Animals in Antigua after Martina died. He had wanted a puppy. A woman behind the front desk told him to complete a questionnaire. Among other things, it asked his age. He wrote his birthdate and the woman looked at it and frowned She explained that dogs can live up to fifteen years. Judging by your birthdate, you'll be eighty in fifteen years, she said. Was he in-

tending to make plans if, you know,—she became flustered at this point— something should happen to you. Who would take the dog then?

--You think I might die? he asked.

Her faced turned red. She opened her mouth but sounded like someone choking. She didn't know what to say and he enjoyed her discomfort. He didn't think of his age as a sign of impending doom any more than he did his retirement. He gave the woman the name of his niece. She'll take the dog, he said, and then added, if I die before it does, just to see her squirm but she didn't. She had resigned herself to the candor such a discussion required and looked at him without flinching so that faced with his own mortality in the blunt, steadiness of her gaze, he turned away mumbling that perhaps an older dog would be preferably.

Martina would have handled the situation differently. She would have said, Here is the name of my niece. You can confirm with her that she will take the dog if I pass away before it does. Pass away. Such a ridiculous expression, he thinks. People don't just float off somewhere like dissembling strands of smoke. They die. Yet, when Martina died, he could not say that she'd died. He could not fathom applying that word to her. If he mentioned her death at all, he said she was gone. Like, she'd gone shopping and would be back in an hour. He avoided friends, the sorrowful, commiserating looks they gave him, and he stopped answering the phone and eventually they stopped calling and dropping by. He found the solitary, empty quiet of his now still apartment comforting in that its silence became a kind of companion that also left him alone. He rationalized the absence of people in his life as a long sought effort to have some time to himself.

After he brought the dog home, he gave it a bed of blankets, a water bowl and sat across from it in his living room waiting to see what would happen, anticipating how this addition to his life would change things. He waited, watching the dog as it stared back at him until he grew bored. After an hour he took it out. Then he resumed his position in the living room and waited until the next time the dog needed to relieve itself. He didn't name it so as to maintain an appropriate, almost formal, distance between the two of them. The dog would always be dependent on him but he did not want to be dependent on it. Now, Sin Nombre , as he has come to think of the dog, is fifteen and still here. So is he.

--Do you know the bike trail through Plaza Mayor de la Constitucion? the woman asks.

He doesn't. He hears himself answer, No, his voice sounding hoarse and far away. He has not spoken to anyone this morning. With Sin Nombre, he does not need to speak. He just shows the dog its leash and he responds. After their walk, he washed some clothes. Martina always complained that he didn't separate whites from colors. She never stayed angry with him for long. They'd always end up laughing at the absurdity of something he'd ruined in the wash. He still throws everything together. This morning, his right hand shook when he poured the soap. He doesn't know what to think of that.

--It was so wet out when I started walking this morning to the park, the woman says.

She goes on about how fog had settled just above the coconut trees and how water hung off the leaves of the trees and splashed her face. Turning a corner, she saw a young man kneeling in the grass. He asked her if she had seen any Hooded Grosbeaks. She hadn't. She knew they were some kind of bird but not much more than that. He said he collected their yellow feathers. He took off his glasses and breathed on the lenses, rubbing them against the sleeve of his jacket. Putting them back on he said, "There," as if he had accomplished something significant. He rubbed his nose and smiled and at that moment, for some reason, she fell in love with him.

--That's just ridiculous, isn't? the woman said.

She started walking again going no more than a few feet when she saw a yellow feather in a puddle. She picked it up. Water ran down her hand and into her sleeve. She smelled orchids, avocado and pine and she turned around but the man had moved on and she saw only the spot where he had knelt in the grass.

--You really don't know anything about birds? she asks showing him the feather again.

He shakes his head.

--I thought maybe it was what he was looking for.

She drops the feather. It spins in a circle landing on the wet, sticky pavement just as a bus turns a corner and comes toward them. The woman stands. He stands too although it's not his bus but it feels good to get up. He stretches and feels joints crack between his shoulders. He should have something to do, he thinks, some task that needs to be completed other than buying a book.

The bus stop and its doors open. The woman steps in and he thinks of following her and sitting beside her but then a tired feeling he gets when he considers making an effort that would make him aware of vacancies in his life overwhelms him, and he decides, No. Just buy a book. Even if he joined her, what then? Follow her off the bus to wherever she was going? Then what? Spend the day with her? But the day would end and he'd never see her again just as he won't see her again now by staying put. Or, would he? Would he ask for her phone number? Would she ask for his? He watches her walk down the aisle and take a seat. The bus pulls away. She looks out the window at him or through him, he can't decide, and maybe, just maybe, she looks disappointed. Maybe not. Maybe he sees disappointment in the reflection of his own face in the window of her seat. He waves his hands chasing away these thoughts as if they were flies. He must not have slept well last night.

--Here we are, right? he tells himself.

He watches the bus leave. He notices a group of young people across the street reading a map and waiting for the light to change. They talk excitedly. One of them points to the bus shelter and back at the map and then at the bus shelter again and they all nod in agreement. The light turns green. Sliding to a corner of the bench, he waits for them to approach appreciating the few seconds he has left to himself.

DUST

by Maggie Slepian

I was at a stoplight, the one that never seems to be green no matter which direction you come from. It was the part of town where the radio comes in clear, and the air was the kind of hot that feels heavy in your throat. I missed that stoplight every day, going east to work with the sun flashing off my bug-streaked windshield, and heading west at night, the glare level with my eyes, throwing yellow-white blurs where the road should be.

She was waiting at the crosswalk, looking at a piece of paper creased in her hand. The dust-blown breeze caught the side of her skirt and lifted it in a slow wave.

The light flicked green. The song ended. She stepped down from the curb.

My heart felt like it was going to jackhammer out of my chest and my palms got a burning sweat spreading from my gut like a sick buzz. I pulled into the dirt lot across the road and turned the key, listening to the tired tick of the engine.

***

Her garden had died the summer before; the first one either of us had tried to grow. We were just renting the house, but the landlord gave me permission to build a garden bed as long as it didn't attract rabbits. *Radishes, chives, and zucchini do well in the Northern Rockies,* she told me. *The best time to plant is the end of May, after the last frost.* She bent over the kitchen table and dug her thumbnail into the chipped groove from that time I didn't use a cutting board. She flipped open the library book and pointed to the chart marking what plants do best in our region. There weren't many. Short growing season, unforgiving. We didn't know what we were doing, so it never really stood a chance.

She had been doing it more and more. She thought I didn't see when she stopped in a doorway or the middle of the room and looked ahead like she was seeing something through the wall. A hole opened in my chest every time I saw her standing like that. Growing a garden would give her something to think about, and it was a project I would do well helping with. I built the box, and she shoveled out the two yards of dirt sagging the bed of my pickup. We planted it together, stretched string to mark the sections. Zucchini needed the most room, chives didn't need much at all. She had dirt smudged on her nose and she smiled as she dug her hands into the crumbly soil. I felt a lightness in my chest, like a burst of stale air from a breath I didn't know I'd been holding.

By late August, her garden had sprouted, then died without giving up a single radish or zucchini. *A bug,* I told her as we looked down at the sprouts, all dead or dying, the soil littered with small leaves. *Mites must have eaten the roots.* She stood looking down at the shriveled radish leaves and a tiny bulge that might have been the start of a blossom on a snap pea vine.

I didn't see her in the house when I got home from work the next day. I checked each room until I found her standing on the back porch, looking down at the garden box. I tried to keep my breath quiet so she wouldn't hear the nervousness that made my throat dry, imagining things that sent black spots blocking my eyes. I cleared my throat. "Would you want to go dancing tonight? At the Old Faithful?"

"No. I need to wake up early to dig up my garden. Everything is dead." She was still facing the yard, the 5:30 shadows crawling diagonally down the side of the house, slicing her back almost perfectly in half.

"I can take the day off tomorrow and help pull everything up. I think we're supposed to cover the soil with a tarp so it's ok for next season." I pushed down a hot coal in my stomach as she tensed and shifted away. I wanted to grab her shoulders and shake her, pull her around so she wouldn't have a choice but to face me. It felt like an empty contest with no winner—she wouldn't turn around until I left, and I wouldn't leave. I stood looking at the back of her neck for so long that the shadows moved down her spine, and it suddenly became real important that I didn't stay to watch them hit the ground. I went into the house.

I found her in the bedroom later, a closed book next to her hand, curtains pulled down to block the last yellow shreds of light scraping through the window.

"I'm still thinking about going to the Old Faithful. That band you like is playing—we don't have to dance if you don't want to."

"I have a headache. You should go though." Her voice was half hidden by her arm flung over her face.

"Alright, you need anything?" *Please look at me.* No answer, head shake so small the hair splashed out on the pillow didn't move.

***

The Old Faithful was busy for a Wednesday and I had to pay my dues before the bartender sloshed my beer across the counter. I pushed a five at him. "No tab."

The bar was three-deep with girls in summer dresses, hair hanging down like curtains. I grabbed my beer and kept my head down, edging towards a table in the back, open because of its proximity to the swinging kitchen door. Waitresses flitted in and out, holding trays high above their heads, weaving back and forth around the tables. Most had worked there since high school; one had a kid who came to work with her some nights. He sat on a bar stool with a pack of crayons, hunched over the pages of a dinosaur coloring book. The noise of the bar didn't seem to bother him, and the bartender passed him sticky red cherries every time he passed the boy's bent shoulders.

The band took their final slugs of beer and climbed back onto the small stage, ducking their heads under guitar straps and adjusting the mic stands. The song they played was one I recognized, as did most everyone else. Before the first chorus, every table near me sat empty and the dance floor was a blur of bodies, girls getting spun out and pulled back in time to the music. A guy I recognized from town bumped my chair as he followed a girl towards the dance floor.

"Hey sorry man—didn't spill your beer, did I?" He clapped my shoulder and winked, following the girl onto the crowded dance floor. I was the only person left in the section. Scattered pint glasses and dirty napkins left an uneven landscape on the tables, the chairs around me crooked and empty.

I ducked my head as a waitress turned the corner. The music rose like an oncoming train and I felt like I was taking up too much space sitting alone at the table. I kept my eyes on the floor as I pushed my seat in and headed towards the front porch. Nobody said anything to me but I felt my face get hot as I crossed the bar.

The days were still hot as hell, but the spike of fall hung in the air after the sun went down. Late August is when the West goes up in flames, and a breeze from the north brought the sharp smell of burning plains from a hundred miles away. Smoke must have been in the air when we first met, because it made my heart hurt in a way nothing else could.

This wasn't the first time she didn't want to go dancing, but it was the last time I asked.

***

We met at the Old Faithful. I was there with my buddies from work, she was there with another guy. I'd seen her around town and thought she was real pretty. She smiled at me from across the bar, the guy she was with ignoring her and waving his sloshing beer in the air. I didn't smile back but felt my face turn red; I must have been staring without noticing.

I ran into her all over town after that. In line at the grocery store, filling up at the gas station. Maybe I'd always seen her around, just hadn't noticed.

I never could think of anything to say to her. I saw her a few more times at the Old Faithful with that same guy, and then one night she was there alone. She sat at the bar, talking with the bartender and ignoring the guys who tried to buy her a drink. I was getting heckled pretty bad by my work buddies at that point, and when I saw her there alone, I switched from beer to whiskey. There was no band that night, but the jukebox was pretty good, so I waited until song came on I wouldn't embarrass myself dancing to, and shoved my chair back.

My voice left me as soon as I reached her barstool. I hadn't thought about the fact that I didn't know her name.

"Uh," I cleared my throat and almost choked. She turned around and pushed her hair behind her ear, she was half smiling and probably laughing at me in her head.

"Will... would you... I know this song I can dance to it." It wasn't really a sentence, but she'd been waiting for it and hopped off her stool.

***

I didn't bring her to my parents until after I'd given her a ring, after I knew her favorite order at all the diners, how she took her coffee, that she had a baby brother who didn't live to see a year old. She wanted to be a teacher, wanted to help kids, wanted a family of her own. Wanted to move out of town and live on a farm with chickens and a swing set in the yard. I promised she'd have everything that she wanted and it made my heart hurt.

My dad was a drunk and my mom spent her days sad and quiet. They lived barely an hour away but I hadn't seen them since the last branding.

Her eyes were blurry with joy and the flash of light reflecting off the diamond chip on her hand. She'd met my parents once before in passing, before we even held hands in public and I didn't know how to introduce her.

She spent the branding day on the porch with the other women, fitting into their group like she'd been going to brandings for years. I pushed calves, grinning up at her and giving her a wave every time I caught her eye. She brought me a beer and kissed my cheek.

My dad waited till the afternoon to shake her hand, then stood in stiff silence until a rowdy yell from the fire pit gave him a reason to hurry off and join the ranchers watching the air ripple around the glowing irons.

At night, we passed around a plate of Rocky Mountain oysters. We told her she'd be part of the club if she ate one. Eyes squeezed shut, she nearly swallowed it whole, reaching right away for the nearest can of beer abandoned at our feet. The whoops and cheers made her laugh so hard she had tears running down her cheeks. I wanted to marry her right then and there.

The fire burned late into the night, mingled with drunken guffaws and calves bawling for their mothers.The day had been long but she was still fresh as anything. A smudge of dirt streaked across her high-boned cheek, a wisp of hair that had come untucked stuck to the corner of her lip. I clinked cans with whoever was standing next to me and tried to head her off as she walked to where my dad stood at the edge of fire, mustache drooping over a lip packed fat with tobacco.

She stood next to him for a moment, brought her beer to her lips without taking a drink. She didn't seem sure whether she should speak, or let him talk first. When he finally said something, like a can of gravel being shaken in your ear, she seemed startled. I stood close to her, taking a pull of flat beer and trying to relax my shoulders. He was already talking and I had to work hard to hear him.

"You know he ain't right, don't you?" my dad growled, not taking his eyes off the fire.

The beer turned in my stomach.

"Sorry?" She kept a smile on and leaned in closer.

"He ain't right. Not put together right." Her smile faltered but she held it, nodding without understanding.

"That's enough dad," I said, trying to keep my voice low and quiet. He didn't look at me, but turned his head and spat into the fire.

"Come on, we're going home." I held her hand tight to stop mine from shaking. My dad's voice pounded in my ears.

***

The bang of the door snapped me back to the Old Faithful's front porch, tapping the Copenhagen can I didn't remember pulling out of my pocket. With a flurry of high voices and flash of skin, three women clattered down the stairs, hands fluttering, blowing kisses, straightening dresses. They went in three different directions like the wind had blown them apart, voices dissolving into the distant screech of a train and the background of crickets.

A car door slammed and one of them came back into focus through the dark parking lot, crunching over the gravel with the wobbly but determined gait of someone who's had a few drinks and is wearing uncomfortable shoes. She strode up the porch steps and leaned against the railing, facing me and crossed her ankles.

"Got a light?"

"No ma'am I don't smoke." She raised up an eyebrow and looked at the Copenhagen can still flipping through my fingers.

"You don't want this stuff. It's the devil. Wish to god I'd never started."

"I can handle it," she said, eyebrow raised and a with a smile that made my stomach tie in a knot. I put a pinch in my lip and held the can out, but she grinned and waved it away.

"I just wanted to see if you'd give it over." I pulled the can back and stuck it in my pocket, face burning.

"Well ok, I don't know what you're getting at but if you want some it's alright with me." She laced her fingers through her hair and pulled it high on her head, twisting a hair tie around and flipping the hair from side to side until it was secured in place, a dark brown rope falling past her shoulders.

"You going inside?" She asked, pushing herself off the railing. I hooked a finger into my lip and flicked out the chew.

"Yes ma'am."

The band was in the middle of a song and the dance floor was shoulder-to-shoulder, people swaying in place, two-step stunted by the packed floor. The beer-heavy air hit me and it was hard to breathe. Her fingers were laced through my right hand, and I followed the curve of her hip into the crowd. The music flooded me and I felt like laughing or crying or maybe both. She spun in a half circle and faced me, crooked grin, hair swinging. One more spin and I pulled her in, grasped her other hand and started a two-step. As I closed my hand around hers, she pulled back, eyes wide.

"You're married?" She mouthed over the music, lifting my hand up to show me my own gold band snugged around my finger. I tried to pull away, bust through the crowd, and go home before I could feel worse, but she tugged it back and grinned, lifting a shoulder in a careless shrug. I folded my hand into the curve of her lower back, felt the swell of her moving under the thin dress.

***

I tried to close the door quietly but the latch stuck, rattling the knob that I could never get to tighten right. The rhythm of her breathing shuddered out of syncsynch. My pillow was still on the couch from the night before, but I would have to take a blanket from the bed.

I stood at the edge of the bed and held my breath, waiting for her to say something.

"You awake?" I finally whispered. The fan whirred and I thought I heard her sit up, but the tiny swell of blanket never moved. I knew better than to touch her, every time I did— near her, in the bed, close to her at all—made her think about what we couldn't have. It would send that dead look to her eyes, her mouth set in a thin line, shadows creasing her forehead. She didn't answer. I grabbed a plaid blanket from the end of the bed and sank onto the couch.

***

She was gone by the end of the summer, the real end. After the fires have burned out, but the trees have turned the colors of the flames so the hills still look on fire. The elk scream in the canyon, the air is sharp.

I don't want to paint her badly. She never did anything like throw a plate into a wall, slam doors, yell at me. She just slowly turned inside out until one day she sat in a kitchen chair, smaller than I'd ever seen her. She spoke into her lap, said she didn't want to try anymore. There was something wrong with us, and she felt broken whenever she looked at me. I told her I understood, that I wasn't going to fight her. I'd told her I was sorry so many times the words came out like powdered rust. She knew it wasn't my fault, that it was just the way I was made. I'd done the best I could. Sometimes you just lose.

I spend most of my days alone now; I think that breaking someone else would do me in for good. I still go dancing at the Old Faithful but I don't want to start anything new. Don't want to tell someone else that I'm not all complete.

I thought about what would happen if I came up behind her in the pharmacy, touched her shoulder. She might walking down an aisle, or waiting in line at the checkout. She would be surprised, recognize me in the time it took to finish turning her head. She'd take my face in and I'd be smiling, making sure of it. That's where my movie reel froze and I knew I wasn't getting out of the truck.

The door to the pharmacy opened and my heart hit the back of my throat. I waited for her thin wrist to hold the door open, for the flare of a skirt caught by the wind. I let my breath out as a stooped man stepped slowly outside, putting his weight on a cane before easing down the step. Unable to hold the door and steady himself at the same time, it hit his shoulder as he took an unsteady step. He tripped, caught himself, and shuffled towards the crosswalk. The door stayed closed behind him.

The engine had cooled, but the hot air in the cab was dry in my throat, settling like a weight on my shoulders. I rolled the window down, the crank sticking at the top of every turn. I turned the key, heard the clatter as the engine came back to life. I pulled out slow enough I didn't kick any dust up, and drove west.

About the Author:

Maggie Slepian is a freelance writer and editor who lives in Bozeman, Montana with her cat Heisenberg. She spends her summers climbing, mountain biking, and backpacking, and her winters catching up on work and teaching her cat how to walk on a leash.

THE HITCHHIKER

by Joseph Washburn

I sat it in the passenger seat of the pickup, the August heat already making the outside unbearable. Slowly, I slid my hand under my coat, touching the cold steel of my pistol. The plan was in motion, and I have done this many times. Looking over at Steve the man who would die soon as he shifted the truck into gear. I stared at him like I did every mark etching their faces into my brain. His short brown hair, his rough skin and that 1980 style mustache, it's the least I can do to remember the people I kill.

The plan is simple, find a big enough truck, hitch a ride, and kill the driver leaving no evidence I was ever here. I wrapped my hand around the grip taking in the rough cool texture.

When Steve looked over at me and said, "Hey man I forgot to mention it when I picked you up, but I need to make a quick stop at the next exit. My sister has a farm and I need to drop something off."

I nodded as I eased my hand off the pistol. "Hey, not a problem I'm just happy you picked me up. It was way too hot to be walking." I replied.

I leaned my head against the window trying to look bored as I thought, "Ok his sister is expecting him I must wait until after he's done. I'll stay in the truck, so she doesn't see me with him."

I watched as we turned off the interstate, after several twists and turns I had no clue where I was and decided just to lean my head back and close my eyes.

I was jerked awake by my head slamming into the dash.

"Ouch!"

"Sorry man. I didn't even see that rock in the road."

The coppery taste of blood filled my mouth as I grabbed my nose. "I think my nose is broke!"

The truck came to a stop as Steve said. "I am sorry again I think I have napkins behind your seat give me a minute and I'll grab them."

Holding my head back trying to keep the torrent of blood from flowing everywhere I stiffened as I felt Steve reaching behind me rummaging around.

"Just one more moment I almost got it." He said.

I closed my eyes thinking how this could get any worse. When I felt something cold slide across my neck. Steve breathed onto my face now only inches from me his stinking rotten breath snaking its way through my broken nose.

"I usually have to hunt from my next meal but you my little gazelle, walked right up to me."

I tried to speak but there was too much blood in my mouth. "Was my nose bleeding that much?" I thought. Pain blossomed on my neck as my mind drifted. I opened my eyes one last time to see his rotten teeth smiling a huge grin as he said.

"You look Delicious.

About the Author:

I am 33 from Alabama. I am married with four kids, and after my wife finished with her masters in elementary education I decided to enroll at Full Sail university for creative writing. I am currently working on my BS in Creative writing for entertainment.

HOMECOMING

by Emelyn Grace Jaros

The radio was less staticy that I remembered. Jason Aldean's twang had only to compete with the whir of the AC and the rumble of tires against broken-up asphalt. One vent was pointed up at my face and drying out my eyes. I turned off the AC with a hit of a button on the rental car's freshly windexed dashboard. I rolled down the window instead and let the hot wind sweep in the smell of manure and drown out the air-freshener tang. I saw motion out of the corner of my eye and knew that James had raised his hand to shield his nose and mouth. I put my hand out the window and carved the rush of air into waves with twists of my wrist.

I felt my muscle memory kicking in as I turning off the main road onto a side street whose sign was still bent from when Sam had taken it out with a John Deere our senior year. Back at the airport, James had asked me if we should program in the address. I said no. He said it had been a while. And he was right but I still knew every turn and could probably do these last 500 yards with my eyes closed—I could certainly do it drunk.

I signaled and steered the compact Honda onto the gravel driveway. The house was set back from the road, so that you couldn't see anything more than the peak of the roof over the maples and oaks. The rocks churned under the tires and clinked off the car's metal underbelly.

I pulled up in front of the porch and shifted into park. I put my finger on the button to shut off the engine but paused. "Don't take any of it personally."

James nodded and I pressed the button. The engine fell silent but we still didn't get out. "We don't have to stay the whole time if you don't want to," he said.

I opened the door and stepped into the blaring heat. James followed and walked up the sagging front porch steps by my side.

I stopped at the white front door. The paint was still scratched away, exposing the yellowed wood underneath, from where Lacy used to jump at it to be let back in. She had to be dead by now. I did the math in my head to be sure. She would be eighteen and I didn't think that was possible. I know that that should make me sad but I didn't feel it. I would later, maybe.

I tried the door even though I wasn't sure if that was still okay. It was locked anyway. I knocked and the wood felt soft enough under my knuckles that I checked if the raps had left indents. They didn't—none that I could see at least.

The door swung open and Mason stared at me. He had gained weight, his stomach swelling out against a stained white T-shirt. He stepped aside and said, "You find the place okay?"

We stepped into the living room. All of the furniture was the same, through a little lumpier and more scratched up. The floral curtains were drawn against the sun's heat and the ceiling fan fixture threw yellow light over everything. The blades revolved slowly as if out of habit. Mason stared at me, challenging me to answer his question. His face was puffy. Maybe he was drinking more now.

"This is James," I said, putting my hand on James' arm. I leaned into him slightly as he extending his other arm to shake Mason's hand. Mason glanced down but his arms remained static at his sides.

"How's mom?" I asked as James shoved his hand into the pocket of his jeans.

"At the hospice place. Been better."

I already knew she was at the hospice center. That was one of the few things I had gotten out of Mason when he had called two days ago to tell me that I needed to come home. He didn't want to make that call. That was obvious as soon as I had answered. But I guess mom had been asking for me. I'm not sure which surprised me more. That she had been asking for me, or that Mason had actually made that call.

"I go see her in the mornings. She's the most lucid then. You can come tomorrow it you can find the time."

"I'll go get the luggage," James said, his hand brushing my lower back as he turned to leave. I wanted him to stay, to keep his hands on my body and to let me lean into him. My body felt heavy and my thoughts a thousand miles away from my pounding heart.

"I've missed you," I said, as the front door creaked shut. I knew it was a mistake to say it but it was true. Or at least it felt true as I stared at him in the waxy light.

"Save it," he said, turning to go into the kitchen.

I followed him. Pill bottles were clustered next to the toaster and a medicine time table was stuck to the fridge with a Disneyland magnet. It was the one we had bought when we went together the summer after I had finished middle school. Mickey Mouse holding a fly fishing

rod. It was made of clay and the tip of the rod had broken off sometime since I had last seen it.

"What can I do to help?" I asked.

"We're selling the house. You can pack up the attic," he said as he opened the fridge. White condensation billowed out into the humid air as he took a beer out of the door. I tried not to see it as an accusation as he smashed the top off against the counter.

"You're selling it?"

"Medical bills," he said and took a sip.

"We can help with those," I said before I could consider how to word it. Another mistake. Maybe I should have shouldn't have called James and me "we." Maybe I shouldn't have said "help." Maybe there was no way that it was going to go over well.

"We're fine. We've been fine. Box up the fucking attic if you want to feel good about yourself. That's why you're here, ain't it?"

"That's not fair." I felt my throat tightening and pressure starting to build behind my eyes. I swallowed and blinked hard a few times. I wasn't going to cry.

"Don't you go talking about fair."

The front door's hinges announced James' entrance. The wheels of my suitcase clicked over the tile grout as he came to stand next to me. He hitched his duffle bag higher up on his shoulder as he quietly asked, "Where should I put this?"

I looked to Mason. "My room?" I started.

"Does it look like we've remodeled." He walked out the back door that was situated awkwardly between the stove and sink. This time I thought better of following him.

I thought they would have taken it over, made it into bland guest room or something, but it was all how I left it. James stayed at the doorway as I walked first to the bed—a twin draped in a purple polka dot quilt—and then to the desk. I put my hand on the back of the wooden chair, a little surprised that it was real and solid under my palm. I had a cork board stuck on the wall over my desk, covered in movie ticket stubs, sketches and photos. I ran my fingers over a strip of pictures from the photo booth at junior prom. Izzy and me laughing and sticking out our tongues and trying on prop hats. I had almost packed it when I was leaving that night but couldn't bring myself to touch it. I had regretted not bringing it. I had pictures of us on my phone and computer but this one felt more real. I could put it somewhere I couldn't avoid seeing it. I could let it hurt like she deserved.

James walked properly into the room and put the luggage next to the bed. We hadn't shared a twin since college. He sat down on the bed which creaked under his weight. "How you holding up?"

"I knew he was going to be like this," I said, forcing myself to shrug.

"That doesn't make it easier. Or okay."

"He deserves to be mad at me," I said, pulling the chair out from the desk and sitting down.

"You saved your life. He shouldn't be mad about that."

"He doesn't see it that way," I stood up again, my body craving motion to combat the mess of thoughts competing to drag me under. "I'm going to go box up the attic."

"Okay," he said, standing up.

"Can I be alone?" I asked. "You look tired. Maybe try to take a nap." He did look tired but then I am sure that I did too. We had been up until one in the morning packing and then had to be at the airport at six.

He searched my face for a moment before sitting back down. "Come get me if you want help."

I closed the door behind me, keeping my hand on the doorknob for a moment before I could coordinate my body to walk. I could just barely reach the cord that hung down from the hatch

in the ceiling but could manage if I lifted myself up onto my toes. I pulled it hard, using my weight as I dropped back down to flat feet. Then ducked out of the way as the hatch fell. I unfolded the splintery, dusty ladder and climbed up.

It was noticeably hotter, the air stale and dense. The roof was slanted so that I could only stand up if I was right in the middle of the space. Light filtered in through two windows, one on each of the triangular-cut walls. Boxes and broken things crowded the space. I sat cross legged near the open hatch not sure what Mason wanted from me. It looked as if everything that could fit in a box was already in one. Probably he just wanted me as far away from him as possible.

Sweat dampened the bridge of my nose and the back of my neck, soaking into the nape of my pony tail. The air seemed useless to my lungs and I felt my head begin to ache. I stood up, which made me dizzy for a moment. I stepped away from the open hatch. One of the closest boxes was labeled "X-mas" in sharpie scrawl. I flip one of the flaps cardboard up. Newspaper wrapped around and wedged between ornaments. The acidic smell of ink rose on the heat. I let the flap fall.

I walked to the window that overlooked the front yard and knelt down in front of it. Our sleek little rental car looked out of place in the patchy dead grass and dirt. I had thought of that at the dealership but getting something else—a pick-up or jeep maybe—might look like a mockery. I had hesitated at the desk until James answered instead. I twisted away from the glass, sinking down so my hip rested against the floor boards. I rested my head back against the window frame. The paint was peeling and sticky.

I saw a bottle in the corner, wedged behind a wicker rocking chair with a hole in the seat. Wine. With the label peeled off. There were about three inches of translucent yellow liquid still in it. I had forgotten I had stashed it there. I used to sneak up here to drink after my mom started to get stricter about alcohol in the house, once it had officially become a "problem". I had even greased up the hinges with WD-40 to lessen their creak. I had taken it from the auto shop Mason had been working at back then. It was probably still up here too somewhere.

Izzy and I used to play up here sometimes, re-arranging the boxes and furniture into forts. We weren't tall enough then to reach the cord so I always had to convince Mason to help. Once, he had closed the door with us still up here. I had fallen trying to open it from the inside and broken my arm. Mom locked herself in her room and cried for an hour after we got home from the hospital. He won't open the door again after that. He said mom and I were always locking ourselves places. He did that a lot, compare me and mom. I never really locked myself away much until after we got the news about Izzy's accident. Then I hardly left my room for a week. I had heard my mom talking on the phone through the wall, telling some friends that she was thinking she was going to have some sort of doctor out to the house. I thought that was just about the stupidest thing I had ever heard as I laid under the sweaty sheets. It wasn't like she didn't know what was wrong with me. Izzy had died on the pavement after her sister's Kia was T-boned by a truck at the intersection out front of the CVS. There wasn't much of a mystery about it. At least, it didn't feel like one then. She had died and I wasn't going to ever be okay again. But I was okay. Air kept filling my lungs and slowly, I was able to make it through a day without crying. And then the mystery of it all began to set in. She shouldn't have even been in that car. She only was because I had been too far gone to drive us home from Johnny's. I had slept over on the sofa and Izzy's sister came to pick her up. That was the last time I had ever gotten drunk.

After about a week and a half of not leaving the house, I had packed up and left. I had lived in a motel. I had worked there too for a while. I thought that I would come back after I had

proven myself, whatever that meant. But then I got into college, and graduated and got married, and I still didn't come back. It took all of this to get me back here. I let that sting for a moment. I let myself think about what it must have been like here after they realized I had left. Mom must have been a wreck and Mason had to deal with that day in and day out. I always made excuses. That I had to leave. That I would never have gone to college or meet James—Hell, I might be dead by now—if I had stayed. But not this time, no excuses. Just the image of Mason listening to our mother crying through her bedroom wall while he should have been at work. I didn't think I could fix it, not after this much time had passed. But maybe, this silent penitence could count for something, even if only something internal.

About the Author:

I am a Mechanical Engineering student at the University of Pittsburgh and am pursuing a minor in Creative Writing. My work has previously appeared in Flash Fiction Magazine.

SOME OTHER SIDE

by Leslie Johnson

Yesterday I attended my grandson's "Baby Is Brewing" party at a new beer garden in St. Paul, where male and female guests of all ages were invited to drop a pack of diapers by the bar before sampling IPAs and oatmeal stouts. My grandson's fiancé – yes, they're having the baby before the wedding – wrapped her skinny arms around me and kissed me on the cheek, bending down to reach me where I'd sunken into the cushion of a low canvas sofa, one of several placed around the outdoor patio.

"Gammie-Gam!" That's what she calls me, for some reason. But she's a sweet girl – smooth brown hair swept back over her shoulders, a quick smile, leanly muscled arms and legs. She's a marketing director and marathon runner, and for the party she wore black leggings, sneakers, and a stretchy white top that clung to the hard ball of her pregnant stomach. How very comfortable she looked. Why couldn't it have been like that in my day?

"In my day," I told her, "only ladies could attend a baby shower. This is much better."

She sat down beside me and took my hand. "Did you have one, Gammie? Before Josh's dad was born?"

I nodded. In my day, you usually had a shower only for your firstborn, so I had one, but not when I was pregnant with David, my grandson's father. It was for my first baby, the one I lost, and I was going to tell her about it, my future granddaughter-in-law, but her friends

were calling her from the lawn of the brewery to join them in their game of corn hole. I gave her shoulder blade a little shove. "Go! Have fun!" And she kissed me again and skipped away, so light on her feet for a pregnant girl that it made my heart pang.

It was late autumn, 1958 it must have been, when my best friend Eileen gave me my baby shower. Well, it was Eileen's mother, Mrs. Larson, who said it wouldn't be Christian to let such a young mother-to-be bring her firstborn into the world without one. I was a teenage pregnant newlywed, and according to my mother, I should have thanked God daily that the boy's parents made him marry me. According to my mother-in-law, Marietta Swenson, I'd ruined her son's life. That was Norman, my first husband, and I moved into his room where they set up a foldout bed for me underneath a shelf of his high school baseball trophies. My mother, a widow, moved to Iowa to live with her second cousin Fern, once I was "squared away," as she put it, in my new home.

Anyway, Mrs. Larson hosted the shower in her living room on a Wednesday afternoon, immediately after Eileen got home from high school, which was soon enough for the ladies to have adequate time to return home and cook dinner for their menfolk.

In those days, even for an afternoon tea in a working class home, it went without saying that ladies would wear dresses and heels, hats and gloves, pearls or perhaps a decorative broach. To my surprise, Marietta sewed a dress for me to wear from a quite decent fabric of mustard-gold and kelly green checks, with a Peter Pan collar, empire waistline, ample room for my round stomach, and green rickrack circling the hemline.

Old Mrs. Swanson picked us up in her station wagon, and after fitting myself into the backseat, I felt quite thrilled to be dressed up in a new garment on my way to a shower in my honor. For months now all I'd been wearing were Norman's old T-shirts over unzipped dungarees cinched with yarn or a couple of horrid muumuus from the Sears bargain bin. Maybe Marietta had sewn the dress so she wouldn't be embarrassed of me at the shower in front of the ladies from Abiding Savior Lutheran Church, but I didn't care. Marietta herself looked unusually buoyant in her powder blue skirt-suit with her best silver *solje* pinned on the collar. I held the Jell-O mold she'd made on my lap, the pimento olives and celery slices suspended in the wiggling yellow gelatin, as she and Mrs. Swanson gossiped lightly in the front seat. I'd never been to a baby shower before. I was the first of any of my friends at school to get married and have a baby, and I felt a sudden swell of pride to be the center of attention in such womanly endeavors.

My enthusiasm dampened a bit when we stepped inside the Larson house and I saw a much smaller gathering than I'd imagined – just the three of us coming in the door and Mrs. Larson along with two other Abiding Savior ladies, Mrs. Holm and Mrs. Iversen, who had once been my Sunday school teacher. They were waiting for us, seated on folding chairs facing the sofa.

Mrs. Larson must have noticed the flicker of disappointment on my face. "Eileen and the girls will be here any minute now!" she reassured me, beckoning me to the seat of honor on in the middle of the floral sofa. "Any minute."

As if on cue Eileen clamored in the door, the thud of her book bag hitting the floor in the foyer. "Willa!" she squealed, bursting into the room in her big plaid dress and matching headband. She'd made me promise when we younger never to tell a soul, not a single soul, that her mother ordered her wardrobe from Chubettes – *"Your chubby lass can be the belle of her class!"* – and I never did. I clutched her shoulders a bit too tightly when she rushed to the sofa to give me a hug. I'd missed her.

But there was only one girl following behind her, prim Becky Sundlist in her everyday sweater set, simpering as usual with her pursed-lip smile that she thought covered her overbite. She wiggled her fingers at me in greeting.

"Joyce and Nancy were going to come," Eileen said. "They *wanted* to, but there was an emergency meeting after school today for the Harvest Hoedown committee."

"Which is important," Becky interjected, which made me hate her a little bit. Still to this day.

"The fire chief," Eileen said, widening her eyes, "all of a sudden says we can't use hay bales in the gymnasium this year even though that's the foundation of practically all the decorations. So *now* what?"

I lifted an eyebrow, nodding in mock concern, as if humoring children. "Look!" I framed the mound of my belly sheathed in my beautiful new maternity dress with my open hands, smiling, my fingers stretched wide. "Can you believe it? Look how big I've gotten!"

Mrs. Larson hadn't made much of an effort to decorate – just a vase of yellow carnations on the coffee table – but at least she served iced lemonade and finger sandwiches, egg salad and deviled ham on Wonder bread with the crusts cut off. They tasted heavenly to me. "Eating for two!" I said as I pinched second helpings from the platter, along with a small slice of Marietta's Jell-O mold to be polite. There were games, starting with Scrambled

Words which Eileen had copied herself on pieces of school paper. I gripped my pencil in utter confusion as the others quickly translated the nonsense – *eantlbk, ifearpc, eiradp,* and *teisbans* – into blanket, pacifier, diaper, and bassinet. The prize was a wax paper pouch of pastel mints.

Next, as I recall, was some kind of memory game with objects on a tray, and then Mrs. Larson placed on the coffee table a naked plastic baby doll, a box of Kleenex, and a few silver safety pins. As the mother-to-be, I was the first one blindfolded with a big cloth dinner napkin that Mrs. Iverson tied so tightly onto my head that I could feel my temples throb. "No peeking!" she screeched with sudden hilarity, but the cloth was so dense I couldn't if I'd tried. The ladies laughed as I fumbled, trying to diaper the slippery doll with the flimsy tissue, and downright howled with merriment each time I pricked my fingers with the pin and bleated in pain, stabbing hopelessly at the doll's torso.

Next Mrs. Larson clapped her hands, telling Eileen to clear away the games. Time for gifts! The church ladies helped carry the presents to the coffee table, and trusty Eileen sat beside me with her steno pad and pencil, ready to transcribe each gift and its giver for the record.

Baby gifts back then were rarely extravagant; nothing like the all-terrain jogging strollers and pop-up infant gyms you see nowadays. I received a hand-embroidered bib from Mrs. Swanson and a small variety of useful items, as I recall, from Darvell's Pharmacy. A few onesies in white and yellow (no one knew the gender of the baby beforehand, of course, in those days), some baby bottles, and a small stuffed teddy bear from Eileen, which Becky informed me was from the both of them.

"My turn," said Marietta. She clasped her hands in front of her flat chest, which was her habit before making an announcement or declaration of any kind. Then she held up one finger. "I'll be right back."

She disappeared down the hallway.

"She brought her gift over on Sunday, Willa," Mrs. Larson said with conspiratorial glee, "so you'd be surprised!"

Marietta reentered carrying a huge rectangular box wrapped in baby blue paper that almost matched her outfit. With dramatic flair she lowered it onto the coffee table before me as everyone leaned in. Eileen snipped off the shiny white ribbon and added it to the paper plate hat she was making. I ripped off the paper and opened the lid to see a beautiful layette of blue with mint-green accents, all knitted by hand, of course, by Marietta. The Abiding Savior ladies oohed and aahed, their hands in a flurry to spread out the items on the table before me: two blankets, one large and one small, two little sweaters with hats and booties to match, one set in blue and one in green. She had her heart set, my mother-in-law, on a grandson.

"Those little teeny tiny stiches!" chirped Mrs. Larson. "Look at all those jillions of teeny tiny little stiches! How did you ever *do* all that?"

"Perseverance, dear," Marietta said, with a satisfied tilt of her chin. "Just one row after another."

Eileen and Becky started stuffing crumpled wrapping paper in a trash bag while the church ladies refolded the layette; Mrs. Larson excused herself to see to the coffee service in the kitchen.

Within minutes, it seemed, the gifts were swept away, replaced by coffee service and cake, a Duncan Hines angel food glazed with pink icing on one side and blue on the other. Eileen put the crown of bows on my head, securing it with a ribbon tied under my chin, and served me the first slice. Pink frosting only, I requested. Everybody clapped as I took the first bite, my taste buds overcome with sweetness. That was when Mrs. Iverson said, "There's nothing in the world like having your first baby."

With that the room suddenly stilled, a sort of a preparatory hush; side conversations ceased and the ladies shifted in their seats with a communal inhale, like the congregation in their pews at Abiding Savior Lutheran right before the recitation of Apostle's Creed.

"It was the dark of night," Mrs. Iverson began, and the ladies exhaled. "In the middle of a blizzard. February eighteenth, 1924. It wasn't supposed to be my time, oh no, not till April, that's what my doctor said, and I was supposed to go to the hospital in advance. My father's farm was successful, and no daughter of his was going to give birth in a barn, so to speak, like the common folk. But I'll never forget it. That *pain* that grabs you from the inside and just *pulls* like some kind of devil – no, a thousand tiny devils all with their own pitchforks, stabbing you all over your belly from the inside."

"Stabbing and stabbing," echoed old Mrs. Swanson.

The ladies seemed to have heard it before, all nodding and exclaiming in unsurprised voices as Mrs. Iverson continued her tale. She and her young husband had lived on the edge of her parents' farm in a cute little bungalow her father had made for them out of a former hen house. *"Run for my Mama! Run for my Mama!"*

Eileen clutched her knees on the sofa beside me and gasped as Mrs. Iverson flailed her arms in the air, reenacting her drama. Her poor husband was so frantic he forgot to put shoes on as he ran in his socks across the snow-covered fields to the main farmhouse for help, and for weeks after Mrs. Iverson's first daughter was born right there on her living room floor, both of his pinky toes stayed black from frostbite.

"Weeks and weeks," Marietta affirmed, as if she'd witnessed the discolored pinkies with her very own eyes.

Then Mrs. Swanson lifted one of her liver-spotted hands, holding it in the air as if for benediction, and all eyes turned to her. "In my day," she began.

Her voice started out waveringly but gained stamina and speed as she continued – in her day, nobody went to the hospital, no, if you were lucky you had your mother or grandmother or a neighbor in the bedroom with you who knew a little something about how to help you through. In her day, mothers died, babies died, it happened all the time, and the fact that she herself was sitting before us today, sixty-four years after birthing her first son, was indeed a miracle. She'd bled and bled, the blood gushing out of her body like a river, a river with no other source than her heart – her very heart and soul were flowing away, away from her with her very life. All of the ladies' heads were nodding together now, pumping like cylinders in one machine that urged along old Mrs. Swanson's voice to the end of her story: "And I said, just as clear as a silver bell even as I was losing consciousness, I said, *Let me go, let me go if you must, but save my baby...save my baby!*"

With a dramatic pause, she pointed her bony finger at me and Eileen and Becky, who had both shifted closer to me on the sofa without me noticing till now. I felt their shoulders pressing against mine on either side of me, heard their quickened breathing in the air by my face. I think we knew in that moment, the three of us, that I was really leaving them. Their world, that is. Crossing over to some other side of womanhood.

"You girls," said old Mrs. Swanson, shaking her finger. "Do you know how lucky you are? To live in this age of modern medicine? You'll never have to know that kind of torture."

Mrs. Larson pranced around the coffee table in elfin-like steps to pat Eileen on the shoulder. "That's true! I don't remember a thing. Not a blessed thing!" She smiled and sliced the remaining wedge of angel cake into slivers for the ladies' seconds.

"I felt nothing but joy," concurred Marietta, "when I finally opened my eyes and they brought him to me. My Norman. My sweet son! They removed him by Caesarean, just one neat incision, and they lifted him right out, easy as pie from the oven. The doctor couldn't believe that a woman of such narrow frame" – here my mother-in-law paused to fold her hands and place them neatly on her lap between her slim hips – "could bring such a big, strapping baby boy into the world."

Becky Sundlist said, "I've got to get home. We've got a math test tomorrow, and my mom is helping me do flashcards."

"Flashcards!" exclaimed Mrs. Iverson, as if this was something new-fangled and marvelous.

"I'll walk you, " Eileen said, and I felt my neck heat up because I knew they were going to talk about me, once they headed down the sidewalk together. The party was breaking up, the church ladies also taking their leave, and I suddenly felt like I might start to cry. Mrs. Larson was at the door saying her hostess goodbyes.

I sat on the sofa as long as I could, still wearing my paper plate crown.

Yesterday, I remembered, sitting on that canvas sofa at the brewery, waving to my grandson on the lawn with his friends as they threw giant sponge darts at a Velcro target, sweet and beautiful and perhaps terrified. I took a breath, readying to push myself up from the low-slung sofa with as much grace as I could muster at my age, and just in that instant, I remembered:

How I'd steadied myself with my hands on the hugeness of my stomach, feeling my baby suddenly take a turn inside. The front door was wide open. I could see old Mrs. Swanson stepping slowly down the driveway to her station wagon with her car keys clutched in one hand, and Marietta following behind carrying her Tupperware with the leftover Jell-O. There was nothing else for me to do then. I took a last slow breath, getting ready, and followed them through.

About the Author:

Leslie Johnson's fiction has been broadcast on NPR, selected for anthologies, and published in numerous literary magazines including The Threepenny Review, Glimmer Train, Colorado Review, Third Coast, december, Cimarron Review and the current issue of The Flexible Persona. Winner of the 2017 Pushcart Prize, her work appears in the "best of Pushcart prose" anthology, Love Stories for Turbulent Times (Pushcart Press, Jan. 2018). Leslie teaches at the University of Hartford and conducts workshops for the Connecticut Office of the Arts. She is a recipient of the CT State 2018 Literary Arts Fellowship Grant.

THE GATS CLUB

by Kedrick Nettleton

The sun was in that awkward, end-of-summer stage, where it refused to completely set at the end of the day and hung just slightly above the horizon, getting in people's eyes and causing intense reflections of light off glass and steel. Albert sat next to a window about three stories up – at a two seat table in the corner of the Gats Club downtown, his friend Stephen in the seat across from him – and was almost blinded by the sunlight coming at him off the windows across the street. He peered through squinted eyes down at the pavement below.

"I don't think it's her."

Stephen shrugged, a glass in his hand. "Maybe not. Looks it, all I'm saying."

Across the street from the Gats Club was the Austere Hotel, and it was in this direction that they were staring. Most of the people who milled about the parking lot and by the lobby doors were the richer types, suits and dresses, definitely not local. They hailed taxis, waited for valets to come. The more intrepid of them chose to walk, their well-polished shoes making brisk *clacking* noises on the pavement. He knew their life. They travelled to dinner reservations, to anniversaries. To clubs with pulsing neon lights and the promise of easy, sweating bodies. Wherever they went, city lights awaited them, city lights and an ending to the day that wasn't already written. That was appealing to Albert, at the Gats Club.

Most nights, nights when he and Stephen were deep enough into drinks that their own lives didn't seem quite so bad, the people down on the pavement represented nothing more than a well-dressed ant farm. He could study the creatures, see the tunnels that they dug in their strivings, and then go back home. Tonight that had been complicated; they were now staring more intensely than usual, trying to determine if perhaps they might just know one of those ants down there on the farm.

"Could be..." Stephen mused, his breath creating fog on the glass that he held to his lips. The liquid in the glass was cherry red, but Albert had been in the bathroom when the order was taken, so he wasn't sure what it was.

Albert shrugged, softly pursing his lips together into a *shhh*. To talk seemed wrong, somehow, watching what they were watching. It took out the illusion of voyeurism, of spectating. It involved them as active agents in the dramas beneath, a role that Albert didn't want.

"I think it *is* her, though," Stephen said, ignoring Albert's previous shush. "I mean it doesn't look exactly like her, but I think it might be."

Albert shrugged.

"And so if it is, there's something to behold, right? Anna Fitz? Looking like that?"

Albert didn't say anything. He cupped a hand over his eyes to watch the girl that he and Stephen were staring at down on the sidewalk. She wore a long red dress, tight to her form like a sheath to a knife, with a slit in the thigh and a low cut to showcase all that she had to showcase. Her feet were displayed in strappy silver heels, and even from where Albert sat he could see the bright red nail polish on her toes.

"Anna Fitz," Stephen said, letting out a soft whistle. It wouldn't have mattered if it had been a loud one; the Gats club was mostly empty. Too late for the day drinkers and too early for the nighttime crowd. They'd have to leave before those folks came, if they wanted to stay in the quiet.

"Close your mouth," Albert finally said, seeing his friend's expression in the glass. "You're drooling."

"Sorry," Stephen said.

"Might not be her."

"Looks like it."

They'd been going back and forth for too long, now. Albert pinched the bridge of his nose, feigning a headache. "It most certainly does *not* look like Anna Fitz."

And that was true, almost. It didn't look like the Anna Fitz that they had known in high school, the pretty quiet girl who'd rather have spent a day in sweats and a tee reading than in anything resembling formal wear. That Anna Fitz had been popular, in a kind of detached way. She attended social events – the dances, the parties, the movie nights with projectors and bed sheets on lawns – perfunctorily, like she simply wanted to avoid the hassle that would accompany her absence. Albert had been, at least a few times, desperately in love with her, but even her modestly positive social standing was far above his own circle.

Still, even though the clothing and the hairstyle didn't match... well, it *did* look like Anna Fitz. And it gave Albert a queer feeling in his stomach, something akin to stage fright. Not even the champagne that he had now had two and a half glasses of was putting him at ease, though he could begin to feel the glass slicken in his hand as his palms began to sweat.

At that moment, it wasn't hard to see the reason that Stephen was staring, and it wasn't because he was remembering the bookish girl that Anna had been in high school. She had bent over, down the sidewalk, and the view down to her breasts was unimpeded as they hung low. She was retying a sandal, one of the strappy heels. Retying? Was that the right word? For some reason, Albert blushed at this. He blushed as he saw the rise and fall of her mostly uncovered breasts, and then he felt angry. He wanted to push Stephen over, to tip his chair.

The real reason they had been staring for what must have been nearing half an hour, beyond the fact that the woman was leaving little to the imagination and looked vaguely familiar, was that Anna Fitz – or whoever she was; Albert was pretty much operating on the assumption that it really *was* her – was drunk off her ass, and she was stumbling around the parking lot trying to make contact with the wealthy passersby. Albert and Stephen had been trying to guess exactly what it was she was saying when they'd caught a glimpse of her face and recognized her.

"I really do think so. Like ninety-eight percent," Stephen finally said, his breath reaching a normal pace as probably-Anna stood up to her full height.

Albert felt dirty, but it was just an uncertain flash of feeling. Being there at the Gats Club had always seemed somewhat empty to him. He had always been reminded of the zoo, of the thick panes of glass that separated the contented visitors from the teeth of the predators. People wanted to see action, wanted to see power, but they wanted it from a safe distance. Only with a barrier separating.

"She's asking them something," Stephen said. He nodded down at Anna, who was engaged in conversation with somebody going out the lobby of the hotel. The man was dressed in bright white pants and a blue polo, and his hair was arranged like the subject of a cologne commercial. When Anna got his attention, she stumbled over and wrapped her hands around his wrists. For a few moments, she spoke, her head facing the opposite direction as Stephen and Albert's. Finally, the man shook his head no – not before glancing down and helping himself to a look – and walked on, the same as everyone else had done. There was the hint of a smile on his face. Anna Fitz stumbled over to the elevated flower bed that framed the front door of the hotel and sat on the concrete, her face broadcasting drunken defeat.

"Maybe she wants to use their phone?" Albert shrugged. "Waiting for her ride?"

"Why wouldn't she just ask the front desk?"

"Maybe she doesn't know what a landline is."

That got Stephen chuckling. Chuckling a little too much, actually, and it caused Albert to wonder how many glasses of the cherry colored liquid he'd had.

"We should go before too long," Albert said. That dirty feeling was only intensifying, settling in the dregs of his body. A kind of casual, unfocused sadness, not foreign to these nights he spent drinking with Stephen. The sun was setting, now. Soon the city lights would turn on, the ones that held so much promise for the Austere people.

Stephen nodded. "Taxi, though." He smoothed out the front of his slacks and sighed. "I don't want to drive."

Albert nodded, thinking. Which was the worse prison, in the end? Solitary confinement in a windowless room, or a glass cage open to the world going by? It was an image that always seemed to spring to Albert's head when he was here. The walls of the Gats Club, at least in his estimation, served effectively as prison bars.

The place was decorated in the style of a fifties Bond movie – stark white tablecloths, varnished wooden floors, and a lounge to the side of the room with sofas of crushed velvet. The bar itself was framed by large-bulb lights, almost like a makeup vanity. The man behind the bar in the slim shirt and vest had his head

buried in his hands. Albert wondered if his shift was ending or beginning.

"Did you know her?" Stephen said.

"Pardon?"

He inclined his head down to the girl, who still sat on the flowerbed. "Back in school, you knew her, right? You liked her."

"Just a crush." Albert shrugged.

"Well, congrats." Stephen grinned – almost leered. "Never would have guessed she'd turn out this sexy. Kudos on the judgement."

Albert shrugged again. She *was*. Sexy, that is. Back in high school, he'd probably have paid cash to see Anna Fitz dress like a high society slut. He still remembered the fantasies, actually, the ones he used to have. He imagined her under him, he behind… imagined her smooth skin, her soft breaths. Later, of course, after the hallway and the janitor's bucket, those fantasies turned rough, tinged with the bitterness that had ended up clouding Albert's last few years in school. Seeing her now only made the sadness settling in his gut that much heavier.

"Asking for directions?" Stephen mused, raising the glass to his lips. "Waiting for someone? Getting worried?"

"Let's go," Albert said.

"I changed my mind. I want to see what happens."

They were close friends, these two. Albert couldn't think of anyone that he trusted more than Stephen. Couldn't think of anyone that he'd been through more with than him. Still, he felt his collar tighten around his throat and he felt his blood pulse. The beginning of a sweat sheen was beading under his hairline, and he imagined shoving Stephen's face hard against the table.

"Well I want to go," Albert said. "Place'll fill up soon."

Stephen turned towards him with red-flushed cheeks and a look that was partly combative, partly confused. "What else do you possibly have to do tonight?"

It was too saddening to answer the question truthfully, so Albert rolled his eyes, laughed in a kind of haughty way that he would hate coming from anyone else, and stayed put.

"How close were you two?" Stephen pressed. He and Albert hadn't really gotten close until college, until the admissions department put them together by chance. The fact they'd gone to high school together was just so much trivia. "You guys ever talk?"

"Not much, honestly."

"No?"

"No."

Stephen shrugged. "Thought I remembered you saying something about her."

"Just a crush."

"Yeah," Stephen said, the word a lament. Both, probably, still wished for a world where something as innocent as a crush could exist.

"She was a nice girl."

"Looks it." Stephen snorted. "I mean it. Kind of a nerd, honestly."

"Yeah, I'm just messing. I remember her. Could have sworn you said you guys talked."

Albert had lied about that. It made it easier to forget about the day in the hallway with Anna and Paul Sanders, easier to forget about the day that he'd slipped a note into Anna Fitz's locker in between classes, casting furtive glances around the gray hallways and about to burst with the feeling in his heart.

"Oh, no," Stephen said, though his tone was one of glee. "Look."

Anna Fitz had abandoned her seated position by the flower beds; she was now hunched over, on her knees, heaving into the bushes. The slit on her dress rode high enough where Albert could almost see butt-cheek, but not quite. One of the strappy heels was stretched tight and looked about to break.

"Someone's had a bit too much," his friend continued, chortling.

The people passing by her from the hotel lobby didn't stop. They cast their own glances, judgmental looks that said *Oh, here we go, another one.* The women's faces got smug, but the men's gazes were directed downward, to the rear bulging in the dress. Nobody asked her if she was okay, nobody offered to hold her hair. Albert kept expecting someone to do *something.*

"She needs somebody to take her home," Albert said, finally.

"If she's not careful, that's exactly what's going to happen."

"You know what I mean."

"You know that I'm right."

Paul and Anna weren't dating when Albert had slipped his note into Anna's locker. *Talking,* that's what it was known as, to the kids who engaged in it. Albert understood it now as a kind of pre-dating. But maybe even that was too strong a word; Anna didn't even really like Paul. They never did end up together, if he remembered. He was exactly the kind of person that she didn't belong with, the kind of brash high school boy who'd end up a cynic in college when he finally discovered that the world doesn't bend over for him. Albert should look him up, sometime, to see. Would it make him feel better, to see that Paul had failed?

It didn't matter that they weren't dating, or that Anna didn't even have feelings for Paul. Paul *thought* it was leading somewhere, arrogant ass, he *thought* he was wearing her down, and he took exception to the note that Anna Fitz found in her locker – stupidly signed, by the way. Albert had sometimes wondered how different his outlook on life would be now if he had just scribbled something generic like *Cyrano* or *from a secret Admirer.* That was more romantic, anyways.

Paul had beaten Albert. No, not beaten. That was the worst part. Slapped him. Found him walking towards his last class at the end of the day, pushed him into a corner of the school, and shoved the note in his face. Anna Fitz had followed behind him, for reasons that Albert never really found out. Maybe she was trying to stop him. He'd have liked to believe that.

Paul slapped him, twice, on the cheek. Hurt less than a punch would have, probably, but there was something condescending in the action. Like Albert wasn't even worthy of a beating, that he wasn't even threatening enough to expend the energy on. It was a humiliating slap, and thinking of it now still made Albert's collar hot.

He'd taken a step back, then, to avoid whatever was coming next from Paul, and he'd slipped. Of course, of all the possibilities, there'd been a janitor's cart behind him. His foot didn't quite land in the soapy water, but it hit the edge and tipped the whole procession over, and him with it. Again, it didn't hurt physically. The water wasn't even cold. But he found himself soaked, slapped, and on his backside in some apparent form of supplication in front of Paul.

And Anna? The bitch had laughed. The worst kind of laugh, the kind that she tried to stifle, but couldn't, so it just came out louder. Like she knew that she shouldn't, that it was cruel, but just couldn't help it. When she slapped Paul on his shoulder, it was almost playful. *"Leave him alone,"* she'd said, hooking her arm through Paul's shoulder and tugging him away from where Albert sat dripping. *"Let's go."* They didn't even end up dating. Albert heard through the grapevine that she'd let him down easy after that. Paul never got to get her in his car, never got to slip her panties off and watch the windows fog up.

Every time Anna saw him after that, she smiled at him. Not a mocking smile, not a friendly smile. It was a pity smile, the kind of smile that said she was embarrassed to see him and remember what she had seen. Of course Albert was embarrassed, too. He turned red right along with her.

Albert's face was deep red, now, and he was glad for the Gats Club's lighting, glad that Stephen couldn't see him. Albert had always had this strange fear that his thoughts were transparent. He feared that, somehow, people could read what was passing through his mind as easily as one of those electronic banners in Times Square. It's why he found it difficult to talk to the women that he met at work and occasionally here at the Gats Club. They'd see through him, see the images that his mind would create. They'd be disgusted. It was enough to shut him down.

"She's really down now," Stephen said.

She was. Anna Fitz had abandoned her four-on-the-floor position by the flowerbed and was now sprawled out on the concrete, her long legs pressing against the sheath dress. One arm was thrown over her forehead – dramatic, it would have looked, if the expression and hue of her face didn't speak so clearly to sickness.

"This isn't as good as I was hoping," Stephen sighed. "Kind of just sad now, really."

Albert nodded. He envied Stephen. He wished that he could look with casual disdain at Anna Fitz below and laugh and smile and think that she got exactly what she deserved, that that's what hanging out with guys like Paul Sanders does to you – turns you into a drunken, high society slut, waiting to get picked up by some other douchebag and probably raped. He should have felt vindicated, felt that he got the better end of the deal after all. He couldn't.

He suddenly wondered why it hadn't popped into his head to get up and go to her. There were only three flights of stairs separating him and this woman. She needed someone, clearly. There was a phrase that Albert's mother used to use, though he didn't know where it came from. Wherever she'd gotten it, it leapt into his mind, now: *Heap burning coals of shame on their heads.*

And there was more to it than that, Albert knew. He hated to admit it, but the thought of walking those flights, of bending down on the sidewalk and reaching out a hand to Anna Fitz... it brought the same kind of butterflies to his stomach that he'd had the moments before he'd dropped that ill-fated missive into her locker. He couldn't stop his mind from creating the narrative: he'd help her up, direct her to his car – maybe carry her, if she was too unsteady on her feet – and they'd go to his little apartment. Not in a pushy way; only because Anna was too drunk to tell him her address. He'd ask, of course. Of course he'd ask. He'd lay her down on the ratty little couch in his living room, cover her with blankets, maybe help her out of that dress. And the rest...

Would he tell her who he was? Would he mention that day back in the hallway, the janitor's mop bucket? Paul? Albert wasn't sure. He hadn't had this feeling of lightness – *buoyancy* – in him for some time, now, and he couldn't shake the feeling that the feeling alone was worth acting on. It was worth it.

"Where are you going?"

Albert hadn't realized that he was standing. His friend was staring at him, eyebrow raised, a confused and pleasant expression on his face that made Albert feel slightly guilty about leaving. Hopefully Stephen would have the sense not to drive home.

"I'm going to help her," he said. He was sweating freely, now.

"Help her?" Stephen pointed down to where Anna was now attempting to crawl into the hotel lobby. Judging by the progress she'd made and the distance of the lobby's automatic doors, Albert had time.

"She needs somebody."

Stephen leaned back in his chair, clearly searching in his addled mind for something funny to say, some double entendre, but Albert was already off. He dipped his chin at the little bartender in the shirt and vest, throwing his jacket around him as he walked out the doors.

His steps were light on the stairs, though his breathing was heavy. When he hit the ground

floor he strode out the door with purpose, not bothering to cut across to the crosswalk. There were no cars.

Anna was still crawling, her dress visibly dirty and tearing at the seam down the leg. Albert got a brief glimpse of her panties, red ones.

But then he stopped. He was across the street now, just a few hundred yards from the lobby. He had stopped to look up to the window he had just been sitting at, expecting Stephen to raise a glass, but the sun's reflection made the window a mirror of the buildings around it.

When he turned back, there was someone next to Anna. Two someones, actually. Two men, both dressed in shirts and ties. They had come out of the hotel, probably; Albert could see there was an SUV waiting for them by the lobby doors, a driver staring at them expectantly. Both men had smiles on their faces, and one of them had stopped and knelt down to where Anna was splayed out on the ground.

Albert stopped walking, feeling for the first time how hot it was.

Anna was saying something to the men, and the men's smiles grew wider. The one who was down next to her reached hands out, one under her and one over, and they rose together. Albert saw the other man wink at his friend.

And it would have probably been easy to stop it, he realized. He could tell them that he knew the girl. That he was late and that she'd had too much to drink. He could thank them for helping her but assure them that he'd take it from here. He could make sure they didn't try anything; he could make sure that Anna Fitz didn't disappear into their SUV and wake up in bed with one or both of them tomorrow, remembering nothing, regretting everything. He could stop it.

But he didn't. The two men awkwardly walked Anna Fitz to the SUV, and together they worked her into the backseat, like two parents with their child. Then they started laughing. One of them – the one who'd knelt down to

Anna – took the keys from the valet and got in the driver's seat. The other climbed in back.

Maybe they'd just take her home, Albert thought. Hoped, maybe. Did he hope? He watched the SUV drive away.

End

About the Author:

Kedrick Nettleton is an undergraduate student, currently pursuing a degree in Creative Writing from Oklahoma Baptist University. He has had stories published in The Route Seven Review and Dragon Poet Review, and has been a finalist in the Scissortail Annual Writing Contest at East Central University. He is the two time recipient of the Mitchell English Scholarship for Creative Writing at Oklahoma Baptist University.

LINGER

by Jessica Olivos

Linger

Until one day I heard it. I heard the song. I heard the beautiful orchestra in the beginning then her voice bringing me to life. I felt relieved and hurt at the same time. At first I told myself this song is beautiful, till I realized I knew that song! It just all happened so fast. All these images popping into my head, it was like a flipbook. I was in my high school English class listening to my mp3 player, trying to tune out all the loud voices. I wasn't even aware of the fact that I had that song, so I left it on repeat and tried to do my assignment. I didn't even do my assignment that day; instead I got out a blank piece of paper and started to write down the lyrics. The class was rowdy and some of the people in class kept on trying to talk to me but I just ignored them. I was in shock; I had no idea that song had such an impact on me. My eyes got watery and I wanted to hold it in, but I couldn't. That song broke me; I felt four again. My English teacher sat next to me and asked what was wrong. He took me outside and said I could take a breather. Even though I felt a little bit better, I took his offer. It was cold, the air smelled fresh since it was raining earlier. I walked around not knowing where I was headed. I didn't know how to feel: sad, angry or even happy at the thought that my mother once deeply cared about me. Believe me I felt all three. I always had a slight memory of when I was four, but "Linger," by The Cranberries, just painted a clear image of everything.

It's my mom standing in the kitchen just cooking and crying. I was playing with my dolls in my room having the time of my life because I had a Barbie dream house that was as tall as me. That was almost every little girl's dream. My two older brothers were playing outside; they were always running around driving my mom crazy. While I was playing, my mom was cooking in the kitchen and listening to the Cranberries. I could smell the soup, the smell of garlic lingering all over the house. I couldn't wait to eat the garlic soup. It always tasted so good, my auntie's famous recipe. I could also hear her beautiful voice as she was singing along to the words, till I heard her voice crack. I thought to myself that I was going to go make a joke about her singing. It sounded like a duck ran over by a car. I started to walk out of my room and stopped under the doorway when I saw her face down on the cutting board. She wiped her nose and that's when I realized she was crying. My mom was crying, the person who always held me when I needed her. The one who would tickle me, the one who would tell me there was no such thing as the boogieman, was crying. I had never seen her cry before. It was all new to me. She had stopped cooking but she was still singing and crying. I went to hug her.

"It's okay. Go back to your room. The food is almost done," she said.

I just wanted to hug her, just like she always hugged me. But she didn't even let me do that. I didn't know why she was crying but now I know. It was around the time my father died. I guess it wasn't only the thought of her losing the man she loved but the thought of having to raise three kids all on her own. That was the day The Cranberries first got stuck in my head, the day I saw my mother cry. I didn't know it at the time, but it was the day my mother decided to stop being a 'real mother'. The day I started to feel alone.

I was still her princess; however after that I wasn't raised in a safe or stable environment. As the years passed matters got worse. When my mother started doing drugs more than usual and staying out late. She would come home early the next morning and fall asleep. I was supposed to be up and ready for school, but missed school constantly. As she slept, I would watch Telletubbies while eating my cereal. I use to love staring at her while she slept. I'm sure to others she looked like Cruella de Vil, but not to me. She looked peaceful and absolutely stunning. Because of all the missed days, I was held back a year.

In all 6 years of elementary, I attended 5 different schools. This was when I started to feel self -conscious and like I didn't belong. Everyone would look at me like a weirdo. Then again I had short hair like a boy, clothes that were a little too big, and even mismatching socks. In third-grade, one freckled-face girl, with red curly hair and blue eyes, finally spoke to me. I remember her because she was my first 'friend', but in reality her mom worked in the front office and told her she had to. She let everyone know that she was forced to talk to me. The kids started whispering and looking at me. There was an incident when I farted and everyone looked around.

"It's the weird girl, and it smells!" a boy said.

Nobody wanted to sit next to me or even talk to me. Not even the girl who was forced to be my friend. Every time I went to school, I became nervous. I'd bite the sleeve of my sweater and keep quiet.

My biggest fear in life was that I was going to be left alone. Luckily, my brother and I were always together. He looked after me and always made sure I was safe no matter what. He

was there for me when my mother wasn't. He was even there when I didn't want his help. I liked to call him Booger because he has a mole on his nose that looks like a booger. He's about two years older than me, and three years younger than my oldest brother. When my mom went to work or to party, we were left alone; Booger made sure I was with him. He was there when we were riding our bikes, breaking into hospitals to skate, or running away from the cops because we were trespassing.

Once I broke a car window that belonged to mom's new boyfriend. My brother pissed me off by locking me out and teasing me, so I threw a huge rock and the window shattered. When my brother saw the look on my face and how scared I was, he opened the door of this ugly blue van.

"Yeah you better run! If I see you again im'a kick your ass!" My brother yelled at some imaginary person.

Why? Didn't take me long to realize he was covering for me. I had lost count on what number boyfriend my mom was on, but she finally came down and saw the broken glass and was hysterical.

"It was a bunch of kids that ran by here. I tried to get them but I didn't want to leave mamas alone," my brother said looking right at her.

She looked worried and confused; she looks at me then back at him. I'm her spoiled brat, so if I cry she'll believe everything. I start to sob and tell her how scary it was. As I'm crying, I manage to look at my brother and he winks at me. I smile at him and try not to blow my cover.

I was nine years old when I was taken away from my mother and not to long after my brothers were also removed from her custody. My God Mother took all three of us in, but things were not exactly better living with her. She had five kids of her own and she had rules. Rules were different to my brothers and I. We did not have a curfew, we went out whenever we wanted and we never really went straight home after school. My oldest brother was the first one to take off which led me and my brother booger, the one I was closest to. He promised he would always stay with me, that I would not be left alone. Until one day I was showering and I hear him going at it with my godmother again. "You're not even my mom so leave me alone, mind your own business," my brother is yelling at her.

Shut up get the fuck out of my face I hate you," my brother sobs as he yells.

I start to cry and cover my ears. My God mother tells him she's done with him, he's ungrateful. He's crying now and hitting the wall. He knocks on the bathroom door.

"Mamas I'm sorry I have to leave," he tells me.

I get up from the shower floor, a little too fast and I get dizzy, but I manage to get out of the steamy shower and get my towel. I open the door and he's crying.

"I can't do this anymore. I can't stay with these people. I didn't want to leave you but I just can't", he's crying so much as he speaks that I barely understand him.

When he walks away, I go back into the shower. I make the water go hotter. I step into the shower, fall onto my knees and replay everything that just happened in my head... not to long after I break down. I start to cry because my world just got torn apart.

After that, I didn't try anymore to make friends at school. I was talking back to my teachers and I went through this rocker phase. I would wear black nail polish and all sorts of black bracelets. Marilyn Manson was my go-to artist because I could get lost in his music. I also cut my wrist around that time but that didn't last very long. I quickly figured why add more pain when I was already in pain.

Just because I didn't talk, didn't mean I wouldn't stand up for myself. I would give attitude to anyone who even looked at me funny. I would tell them to stop staring and get the fuck out of my face. There was this one guy who

made a smart remark about my mom and I slapped him across the face. He asked what was my problem if I didn't even like my mom. He's lucky I didn't knock his teeth out; I was just being nice by simply slapping him. Just because my mom caused so much damage and pain didn't mean I didn't love her. I do love her. I was tired of walking around mad. I wanted to be better, but I still had a deep feeling of being alone.

I finally started writing poems about how I felt. My English teacher in high school had us write in a journal everyday. He said he wouldn't read it unless we wanted him to. I didn't let him read anything! It was too personal and embarrassing. But when I heard The Cranberries song in class, I started to let him read my journal. Yes, that same teacher who always helped me out. I think I got along with him because he reminded me of Booger. He always gave me my space in class and didn't look at me like I was crazy. He made me feel comfortable. When he finally read my journal and saw all my poems, he was astonished. He told me how much potential I had as a writer and understood all the pain I felt.

The song gave me confidence to do better in school, and motivated me to become a writer. I would put it on my playlist and listen every morning; I would wake up with a smile on my face singing along to the words with my terrible voice. I would walk the halls at school feeling brought to life, feeling like nothing and no one could stop me. It reminded me that I wasn't alone.

I mostly wrote about how terrified I was of becoming like my mother. Scared of doing drugs, scared of sleeping around. I was scared of being a disappointment, not to others, but to myself. It's not that I hated my mother, but I just didn't want to be anything like her. I wanted to be proud of myself, but I had nobody to look up to. I was always surrounded by heartache. My poetry allowed me to open up. When I would read it back, I would just end up crying. I felt like I was reading something written by someone else and I felt sorry for them. It was hard to believe it was actually me who felt so broken. Reading the truth about me convinced me to change. I didn't want to feel sorry for myself. I wanted to be proud. I continued to write and I made sure I was making the right choices in school. Things like making sure I didn't go around and sleep with random guys or smoke bud. It was quite tempting, but it wasn't what I wanted. I made my own choices, and I chose not to do anything that I would regret later in life.

Just like it was my mother's choice to give up, it is my choice to do the exact opposite. I was just four when my dad died of a brain aneurysm. I faced so much and yet I'm accomplishing so much because I don't want to give up like my mother. I know it sounds as if I hate her, but I don't. I probably should hate her, but as the song says, *"You got me wrapped around your finger."* Despite everything, I love her and I don't blame her. She didn't provide me with the best childhood, but she did give me what means the world to me. She gave me the little boy I call my son. The little boy that makes me smile every day. My mom got pregnant and just like before, she wasn't stable enough to keep her son. However, she signed her rights to him over to me. I had miscarried twice before, so getting him made me absolutely happy.

My mother and I were pregnant around the same time in 2011, but I didn't find out about my mother's pregnancy until after I miscarried. I was just 19 years old, but I was going to take responsibility for my actions. My boyfriend stepped up within seconds and said he would be there for me no matter what. I fell in love with my unborn child so quick, and when I lost it I was devastated. Therefore, I was so freaking angry when my mother told me she was pregnant. Our kids would have been the same age. I resented her for it. How could someone so unhealthy and someone who had lost custody of all her other kids be pregnant? I didn't understand how my unhealthy and unsuitable mother was given the chance to have a child

when mine had been taken from me. It's sad to say but I hated her for it. In time I was happy and excited but it took me some time to be okay with the fact that she was going to have a child.

The night before her c-section I asked her if I should be prepared, if there would be drugs in her system. I wanted to know if I should be prepared to take a child home. I also told my boyfriend that we might end up with a little boy. I told him either he was in or out because that little boy would be my number one priority.

"I wouldn't expect anything else from you," he told me.

She didn't test for anything the next day. Everything went well and she was going to be allowed the keep the baby. I figured I would end up with the baby in a several years, but didn't expect it as soon as it happened. I was at work when I got the call that changed it all.

"Jessica I am calling regarding Jacob. We will be removing him from your mother's care and you once told me under any circumstances you would take him in," the social worker asked and paused waiting for me to answer.

"Yes of course," I told her trying not to cry.

"Okay. He is being removed as soon as we arrive to her home Mrs..." before she could even finish I told her I would pick him up right away. She said that's fine.

I called my husband and had him pick up Jacob since I was at work. It wasn't planned, but that day I became a mom. A few months later I got pregnant again, and lost it again. I came to the conclusion that the reason I kept losing my babies was because I was meant to be my baby brother's mother. I was meant to be Jacob's mom.

"I had him for you," is what my mother started to say.

I wasn't mad at that, and I agreed. If I had to choose, I wouldn't change anything because

Jacob was now my life. It wasn't easy. I was working and going to school. but I managed to do that and take care of Jake.

I always have these random moments when Jake is playing with his cars and I think to myself, that is my son. My world. I stare at him and my eyes start to get watery. They get watery and I get stuck in that very moment. It's as if time stops, just like when I first heard the song 'Linger'. Staring at him puts me in awh. I feel happy and heartbroken at the same time. Happy because that beautiful creature is mine. Heart broken because I see that beautiful boy and I ask myself how in the world my mother would let him slip through her fingers. How could she lose him too? I really thought things would be different this time with him. I figured she would do better for him. No one was surprise when she lost him but me. I was shocked because I was a fool, "You know I'm such a fool for you. You got me wrapped around your finger", Dolores O'Riordan said it best. My mother always had me wrapped around her finger so I saw no faults. I no longer resent her, I'm absolutely grateful for giving me such a beautiful gift. I will put linger by the cranberries on full blast and allow my son to hear me sing and let him have nothing but happy memories of me. I'll sing while he continues to play with his cars and wait till that one day he starts to sing with me. We will dance, sing and we will laugh at the fact that we are not very good singers; but we will sing our heart out anyways.

MISS NOMER

by Ross Dreiblatt

"A true Queen of the Valley always carries herself with the utmost grace, style and speaks clearly with the occasional well placed vulgarity."

This phrase, the one so royally pronounced weekly to eager drag contestants every Sunday at the Queen Mary Bar in Los Angeles's iconic San Fernando Valley, so long ago, ran through David Goldstein's mind as he stood at his father's grave site.

He sighed deeply, not because he missed his father, but because he missed an opportunity to come to the funeral in full Alexis Carrington black widow mode. A floppy black hat, sunglasses and high stink eye behind the sunglasses would have felt just right. The outfit might not be appropriate for the humid outdoor Florida burial site, but it would fit his mood. There weren't more than a dozen mourners gathered around the burial site and David only knew Aunt Ruthy. She wouldn't have cared, probably would have gotten a kick out of it.

The Rabbi officiating over the ceremony cleared his throat and asked if anyone would like to say a few words before they proceed with the burial. Aunt Ruthy nudged him in the ribs, but David just shook his head. Maybe I should throw myself in the grave and scream 'No, take me instead!' he thought. Ah, but he didn't have the wardrobe to pull it off. He'd probably get a rise out of the others gathered here, his dad's last remaining friends he supposed.

Aunt Ruthy stepped up to the Rabbi, "Yes, I'd like to say a few words."

David rolled his eyes at her. Ruthy was a spunky little firecracker for a 75 year old woman who weighed about 80 pounds and most of that was tits and ash blond wig.

"My brother Max was a loving brother, a loving husband and...a good father." She threw her chin up towards David.

She's admonishing me to keep quiet, he thought. But even I have some sense of protocol. After all, I'm a true Queen of the Valley, carrying myself with the utmost grace.

"He wasn't perfect, none of us are, but he was a good man. A man we all came to appreciate. He was a war veteran and defended his country bravely during world war 2."

David wondered if Ruthy would get through her spiel without saying 'fuck.' The older she got, the less she seemed to be able to control her language. He loved that about her. He loved everything about her. She was the mother and father he wished he had.

"I remember when Irene died, god rest her soul, and he moved down here to Sunny Vistas right next door to me. He looked so sad. I realized he'd never lived alone a day in his life and he didn't have a clue. Couldn't even figure out the microwave. I would cook for him sometimes and then we would talk about the old days."

The Rabbi took out his phone and began swiping at the screen.

"What are you doing there?" Ruthy stopped to squawk at the Rabbi, "Put the fucking phone down! This is a goddamned funeral! This maybe just a job for you, but this is my big brother, this is someone's father, a little respect for chrissakes!"

The rabbi put his phone back in his pocket and apologized.

David smiled, oh how he loved Ruthy. He remembered spending a summer with her in Las Vegas when he was a teenager. She was working as the box office manager for the Silver Slipper Jubilee Topless Dancing Revue. That's when he knew. He knew that staring at tits did nothing for him, but the costumes sure did. And God bless her, Ruthy did all she could to wake up his burgeoning inner drag queen.

"And please, come by the apartment, I have some cake and coffee. Thank you." As Ruthy finished, she was tearing up, leaving her mascara to run into the well-worn crevices of her face. She put her arm through David's arm, "Come, take us home."

Home.

David inherited a one-bedroom condo from his father. So odd, he thought. He hadn't had a real conversation with his father since his mom died. He hadn't seen any purpose for it. After his father moved here, Ruthy had kept him apprised of his father's failing health, always begging him to get in touch. David had told her had no interest in the idea. If his dad wanted a relationship with his only child, it was up to him. Not a word from him after that. In fact, the will bequeathing him the condo was the closest his father had come to acknowledging him. No legal terms, just a short note, 'I want David to have this apartment and be happy here' signed off by a lawyer.

Sunny Vistas Retirement Village and Resort in Boca Raton, Florida, would now become his home.

Maybe he would stay here. He simply had no place else to go. He was out of work, had less than a thousand dollars to his name and was living with 2 roommates in LA and they were past their expiration date. He was not involved with anyone, in fact, may never again be involved with anyone, he thought as he drove into the main gate of Sunny Vistas. He needed a change of scenery, although this wasn't the change he was hoping for, this may have to do.

Since he left home in Great Neck, New York to run off to Hollywood when he was 19, he'd never really had his own home, never felt like he belonged anywhere. His parent's home had felt like his parent's home, alien to him. He and his father had never gotten along, so he never felt welcomed there. The only place he'd ever felt at home was the stage, specifically the stage of the Queen Mary in Studio City so many years ago. That's where Miss Nomer was born. Miss Nomer was a true Queen of The Valley. He owned that stage for a good 10 years and then it all ended so abruptly, so cruelly. No warning, just a sold sign on the front door. He tried taking his act to a few other bars, but it was never the same. Instead of being the main act, the reason for the bar, he became at best a sideshow, a filler between muscled up go go dancers.

The father who had chased him out of his own home years ago owed him a home. The circle of life is complete, he thought.

He parked in front of his new home and helped Ruthy, his new next door neighbor, up to her apartment for the funeral 'after party.'

David looked around Ruthy's spotless chrome and mirrored apartment. She'd decorated it years ago and now it looked like well-kept time capsule. In fact, it looked like the lounge of The Queen Mary. David's new home looked more like a thrift shop, all of the stuff his mom had bought and never thrown out still haunting him, following him.

"Where are those little boxes you're supposed to sit on?" He vaguely remembered the Jewish ritual from his grandmother's funeral years ago.

"You mean for sitting shiva? Ucch." Ruthy waved him away." I got no patience for that anymore. What do you kids say, I have no fucks anymore? Look, this is Sunny Vistas, someone goes every week, who has the time for all that tsuris? Some coffee and cake is fine. I got Entenmanns in the fridge, help me put it out."

David smiled. "The kids say, I have no fucks to give, Ruthy." She still thinks of him as a kid. He was 48 and could probably pass for a retiree here at Sunny Vistas. He caught a glimpse of himself in one of Ruthy's mirrored walls. Without his drag, he was plain. The very definition of plain, he thought. He was balding and becoming pot-bellied. He was losing his jawline to middle age. With some make up and the right wardrobe, he could still pull off a fabulous Miss Nomer, but out of drag he looked like an accounts payable clerk from the valley. Even worse, he felt like an accounts payable clerk from the valley. Maybe that's why he was morphing into one. It had been months since he 'donned the tiara' and he felt like all of that wit, the fabulousness he'd cultivated was draining out of him. Miss Nomer, where have you gone?

"I have no fucks to give!" Ruthy proclaimed with a laugh. "Also can you get the white table cloth from the top shelf in the hall closet for me?"

David fetched the table cloth to cover the glass topped Dining room table. A table cloth had been Miss Nomer's very first outfit way back when he was just a boy in Great Neck wondering what it would feel like if he had a cape and a crown. It felt good. Too good, he thought. That table cloth had ruined him, had opened up a life in him that he began to nurture and develop from that day forward. The future Miss Nomer would overpower David Goldstein and guide all of his thinking, all of his decisions until she finally pushed her way on to that stage in Studio City. And where was she now? Was she also buried with his father?

"You look so sad, hon." Ruthy rubbed his back. "Maybe you do miss him some, huh?"

He looked at Ruthy and sighed. He wasn't mourning his father.

"Listen, tomorrow we'll go down to the café in the center and have a nice breakfast. They have all kinds of classes and shows, it'll take your mind off."

The next morning David sat with Ruthy at the Vista Café in the huge clubhouse that anchored the Sunny Vistas complex. Ruthy studied the grease stained paper menu while David passed judgement.

The place looked more like an after-thought at an airport than any kind of café, he thought. Such a far cry from Dupars, the famous Los Angeles diner that was his go to for breakfasts in the valley, just down the street from the Queen Mary. The tons of eggs and bread he must have consumed there over the course of a decade, all between 2 and 8 in the morning, while trying not to smear make up and white gloves. The Queens of the Valley all packed into their usual booth, refusing to let the night die.

"The stuffed French toast is really good here, but I can never finish it." Ruth took off her reading glasses for a second to advise him.

David would just order an omelet. They could fill it with cheese and bacon and whatever else they had, he didn't much care. He could not stop thinking about the past, maybe because there was no future? He would fit right in here at Sunny Vistas. Well almost. His reminiscences would undoubtedly be very different than the average Sunny Vista resident.

They gave the waitress their order and sipped coffee while waiting for the food to arrive. David watched as people who struggled to walk, struggled to breath came and went inside the lobby of the building. They looked miserable, faces all hardened by age and disease, or whatever other bad news that comes with growing old.

"So, how long do you think you can stay down here?" Ruthy asked.

David snapped out of his reverie. "Maybe forever, I don't know. I don't have any plans, nothing going on in LA." Maybe this inheritance was his father's idea of a cruel punishment. 'I want David to have this apartment and be happy here.' Was his father laughing at him from the grave?

"No job, no shows? Not a boyfriend or anything? What about that French guy, Pierre, right?"

David finally smiled. Pierre was actually Peter, David had dubbed him Pierre during a show and it just stuck. "We broke up a while back." Peter was in the audience of one of his shows, right before the place was sold. David decided he would badger him and charm him from the stage that night. He usually picked some random housewife or someone who looked generally clueless from the audience to pick on. Peter was handsome, the sort of unattainable handsome that had haunted David's fantasies, but as Miss Nomer, anything was possible.

"Oh, that's too bad, you looked like such a happy couple in the pictures you sent."

Couple? No. It was all wrong for so many reasons. Peter fell in love with Miss Nomer. The more David tried to be David, the less Peter was interested in him. Eventually they just drifted apart. Last he had heard, Peter had married a woman and moved down to San Diego. The bottom line: Miss Nomer had game, David didn't.

"David, you're not even fifty yet, no? You shouldn't stay here, although I would love to have you next door, but you should be with young people." Ruthy leaned over the table, "This place will kill you. Between the yentas and the altacockahs and their always moaning about this and that." She waved her hand,

"Ucch."

"Alter..what? I don't think I've heard of that one." David loved Yiddish slang, schmuck, schlong, goy all of that background noise from his youth.

"Oy vey ismere, how can you not know alter cocker? It's an old fart who just whines all day. Are you mispocheh or what?"

David laughed. Mispocheh, family. Also his favorite Jewish Queen of the Valley, Bruce Ratner aka Miss Pocheh one of the five famous Miss's. Miss Pocheh, Miss Nomer, Miss Spoke, Miss Ah Ginny, and Miss Take. Not to mention the grande dame, who ran the show every night, the Queen herself, Ida Slaptor.

"So finally I get a smile out of you!"

"You did, I'll give you that. It made me remember one of the old...queens from the act. A true Jewess on stage."

"I loved your show, you were really the best. You made me laugh so much, that's why I hate to see you so sad. But I understand, your father passed and it's complicated. Maybe we could go see one of the drag shows down in Miami, that may cheer you up."

The waitress stepped up to deliver their food. David was grateful for the interruption. He hoped that she'd forget about the idea. He couldn't bring himself to see a drag show right now. It would be like water torture, reminding him that Miss Nomer is effectively dead and the huge empty space in his life.

Ruthy began cutting her French toast as she continued, "We could make a night of it, maybe stay down there. Maybe you could even see if there's a place for you to perform?"

"Let me think about it, okay?" No way would he think about it. He couldn't explain to her that his drag was a relic, an antique, an old vaudeville act. It's a very different world out there now. He'd seen the change in LA over the years, with the rise in stature of the trans movement and of course, Rupaul, drag became something different, no longer the fun it once was. The young queens were dismissive of those that had pioneered the way forward for them. The attitude, so necessary for a real queen, seemed to be a cheap imitation, a Chinese knock off, not born out of experience but out of You tube. It was no longer about entertaining people who came to see you, but as a weapon to bludgeon your audience with.

And without Miss Nomer, who was he? Without an audience did he not exist?

"I know this is hard for you to believe," Ruthy put down her fork, "But he did love you, in his own way. He would ask about you all the time. You have to realize, for someone from his generation and background it was difficult..."

"Ruthy," David looked in her eyes. "I don't have to realize anything anymore." He was done trying to rationalize why a father would reject his own son. He'd spent too many years waiting for some kind of acceptance. Instead he'd gotten a condo in an old folk's home.

After breakfast, Ruthy gave him a tour of the clubhouse, with all the amenities that were now included as an owner of a condo at Sunny Vistas. They had a gym, pools, tennis courts even bocce courts. David thought for a minute about signing up for the gym, but he felt his waist was beyond control, beyond the help of a workout. Besides he no longer had to squeeze into a gown every night, so what was the point?

As they went through each facility he was confronted by the zombie stares of his fellow residents, the dead eyed look of going through the motions just to keep their hearts beating for a little while longer. Why? Just because. This is me, this is who I am now, he thought.

As they strolled down a hallway, they heard some yelling and a voice over a microphone telling everyone to settle down coming from one of the rooms.

"Bingo" Ruthy informed him. "It gets rowdy in there sometimes. Do you play? It's a lot of fun.

I won about thirty bucks last week. Come, let me show you."

The huge bingo room was packed. At least 20 big tables full of people. On stage, a man in an old army hat and a plaid shirt filled with medals and pins was talking into the mic.

"You have to be orderly here. When you have Bingo, just yell out and raise your hand okay? Don't come running up to the stage with your card. A card checker will come to you. If you can't follow the rules we have to stop the game, okay?"

"That's Jerry," Ruthy confided to him. "A real schmuck. He's always holding up the game just to hear his own voice, that son of a bitch."

"Just get on with the fucking game!" A voice from the audience.

"There's no cursing, okay?" Jerry addressed the side of the room where the comment came from. "We got ladies here and there's no reason for it."

"Fuck the ladies, Jerry, just call the goddamned number already!" A woman's voice from another part of the room.

David smiled to himself. These oldsters had a little moxie, a little life left in them. This is actually a great audience. Too bad Jerry just can't work the room.

"Okay that's it. I'm just going to stop until there's some quiet. It's up to you guys." Jerry folded his arms across his chest.

"Oh fer chrissakes!"

"Listen," Jerry spoke into the Mic again, "You think doing this stuff is so easy? There's a lot going on and if you guys are screaming and cussing like maniacs I can't keep track of everything. There's a lot to have to do up here."

David agreed with Ruthy, this guy was up there just to hear himself talk into the Mic. If Ida Slaptor had that mic, this crowd would never get out of here alive.

"C'mon let's get out of here before I strangle the SOB," Ruthy tugged on David's arm.

David was fascinated., "Not yet, Ruthy."

"If there's a lot to do, then do it already!" Another voice from the peanut gallery and some mild clapping.

Touche, David thought.

"Okay would one of you like to do this up here? It's not just reading numbers, it's making sure cards are checked, making sure payouts add up, making sure everyone hears the numbers. If anyone thinks they can do this…"

This was a plea for help. A bright Bat Signal lighting up the sky in the middle of the night from the poor downtrodden citizens of Gotham City. David looked at Ruthy for a second and cocked his head. He raised his hand. "I can do this. I'm an expert Bingo caller, years and years of experience."

Silence as everyone looked towards the back of the room.

Jerry stood on his toes and looked over to David. "Who are you?

"This is my nephew, David," Ruthy yelled beaming with pride. "You know Max Goldstein? This is his son. He's staying on at Max's place right now."

"Well I'm very sorry about your father, David. He was a fine man and a veteran. Now I can't have you come up here and start calling numbers in the middle of the game though."

"Is there a bingo game tonight?" David thought he always did better work at night anyway.

"8-10pm."

"Sign me up. And I'd like to urge everyone here to come and bring your friends." David looked down at Ruthy. "We have some work to do."

∞

At 7:55 pm Ruthy opened the entrance to the Clubhouse doors so Miss Nomer could make her entrance. She was a brazen red head tonight, hair piled a good foot above her head. The make-up was a little over the top, but that would be offset by the soft lighting of the Bingo room. She had her trademark white gloves and black stilettos. The gown was…not her best, but it would work. She and Ruthy had spent hours taking out the waist of an old Dolly Parton number David had bought at an estate sale over a decade ago, and it still didn't quite fit, but with a glittery shawl draped over the back, no one would see that it didn't close. And if they did, so much the better. Miss Nomer would work it, no matter what.

The cleavage pulled it all together and would pull the eyes up front instead of any of the flaws in the fit of the gown. She was a double C Cup tonight. Usually this would be great for tip money, but she had her doubts whether this crowd would be tipping. Still, she rehearsed Ruthy on how to prime the pump. "Just walk up and shove a sawbuck into my cleavage when I hit a punchline."

"Can I see your ID, please?" The guard at the front door to the clubhouse could not take his eyes off of Miss Nomer's flaming red hair.

Ruthy pulled her ID out of her purse. "This is my guest tonight, Miss Nomer, she's running the bingo game."

The guard's eyes moved down to Miss Nomer's chest. "Huh?"

Miss Nomer wrapped her shawl in a dramatic upsweep. "Eyes up here cupcake. I'd swear you'd never seen a bingo caller before. Come Ruthy, we don't want to be late. Well, not too late."

All eyes turned towards Ruthy and Miss Nomer as they crossed the clubhouse lobby. Miss Nomer ate up the attention, like a starving man at a buffet in Las Vegas. She slowed her gait down a touch to make sure everyone had a good look. As they waited for the elevator she tilted her head and gave a polite queen's wave to the oglers.

When they were in front of the Bingo room, Ruthy pulled a cassette deck out of her shopping bag. "I don't have my glasses on, which button is the play button?"

"The second button. Red button is stop. Watch for my signal. Ready?" Miss Nomer checked her hair and gathered her shawl.

"Ready." Ruthy hit 'play' as Miss Nomer entered the room.

Bad Girls from Donna's Summer's 1979 album blasted out of the speakers. The room was packed and any trace of conversation stopped. Miss Nomer heard a gasp.

She sashayed up to the stage and grabbed the mic and gave Ruthy the signal to stop the music.

There were some giggles and some murmurs as Miss Nomer raised a white gloved hand. "I am Miss Nomer, Sunny Vista's resident bad girl and this is the part where you clap, ladies and gentlemen."

The room responded immediately with applause.

Miss Nomer exhaled. I have them, she thought. For the next two hours I will not let a single one of them go. They are mine.

There was some talking in the audience. She could not allow that, not yet.

"Hello Yentas! Keep the yenting to a minimum for the moment. And Hello Altercockers!" She looked directly at an old man sitting at the very front. "You know, no one knows more about altering their cocker than I do, so let's begin!"

More people began filing into the room as word of mouth spread throughout the club house. Standing room only.

"Do I need to explain the rules?" Miss Nomer stood by the bingo number basket.

Jerry, in his old army hat and shirt full of medals and pins, stood up from the side of the room. "What are you wearing? This is..a crazy thing!"

Miss Nomer shot a laser stink eye straight at Jerry and moved towards him.

"Jerry? Cupcake?" Miss Nomer put her hand on his shoulder. "This is not your stage tonight, sweety." She lifted his hat off his head and put it on top of her red hair. "Crazy thing? I suppose we all have our own drag, don't we?"

The audience loved it. They loved her.

"Now, the rules. When I yell out a letter, like B for...bitch or I for I'm so fabulous, if you're able to take your eyes off of me, make a mark on your card with those cheap markers on the table. By the way, I need one of those for a touch up on my eyebrows if you have an extra. If you get a Bingo, I want you to yell this out and only this, otherwise we will not hear you, ready? Fuck me, I have Bingo."

There was a split second of silence and then the crowd erupted in laughter.

"Can we all practice now for a second? One... two...three.."

"Fuck me, I have Bingo!"

Miss Nomer saw a few people leaving, she understood. They could always come back when Jerry took over. She'd have to work out which shifts he would have with him.

Chin up David, Miss Nomer thought, this isn't so bad is it? We'll make our way here. Life needn't be so grim after all. You and I will make this work.

The words from the will swirled in David's mind again, 'I want David to have this apartment and be happy here.'

Ruthy ran up to the stage and stuffed a dollar in her cleavage. Maybe Ruthy was right, maybe his father did love him in his own crazy way.

About the Author:

I have a background in journalism and business. The first chapter of my novel, 'I Am Not Brad Pitt,' was published in the August 2018 edition of The Write Launch and I had a short story appear in La Chaleur Magazine this past August.

DEALING WITH DAPHNE
by Henry Simpson

Daphne had already worked her way into Vergie's confidence, displaced Lily in her life. Now she was pushing her out of the house. Soon she would convince Vergie to have her lawyer rescind her employment contract. In a few more weeks, Lily would be homeless, jobless, and cast out of Montecito society. She laughed.

She had to discredit Daphne, but how?

She closed her bedroom door, opened her laptop, searched the Internet to find LSD effects: physiological, predicable and benign; main effects, emotional and sensory, disorienting, might mimic psychosis.

How to administer to Daphne? Easy: add a few drops to her silver flask. Mrs. Steele filled it with gin each morning.

No, too risky. If Daphne went nuts with the flask nearby, someone might test its contents and ask who spiked it with LSD. Not Daphne or Vergie, obviously, and Mrs. Steele was neither cunning or bright enough. Who else lived in the same house? Lily, obviously.

She lay back on her bed, closed her eyes, daydreamed, thought back to the session with Selena, the fortune teller. "Gold," she had said. "It's powerful. It may be the key to something else." It came to her in a flash.

#

She waited until Vergie and Daphne had gone to the country club, then pulled on a pair of latex gloves, then collected Daphne's gold cigarette lighter from her room, wiped it down to remove fingerprints, took it to the wine cellar, set it on a dish, eyedroppered liquid LSD on each face. After it dried, she wrapped it in tissue, took it to the garage, unwrapped it, put it in the Alfa's glovebox.

She went back in the house, poured a scotch, and imagined the scenario: Daphne would drive somewhere, open the glovebox, spot her missing lighter, and grab it. Her perspiration would liquify the LSD and she would experience a psychotic episode. Observers would think she was nuts, the news would get back to Vergie, and she would have second thoughts about cousin Daphne.

#

Saturday morning, she met with Vergie and Daphne for breakfast on the veranda. The mood today was somber, victors pouring champagne and doing most of the talking.

After Vergie and Daphne chatted Friday night's follies at the club, Vergie said, "Lily's leaving us."

Daphne glanced at Lily. "Whatever will she do now?"

Vergie said, "Speak up, Lily. You're like a bump on a log, silent, stewing in your own juices."

"I've applied for a position in Dallas," Lily said.

"She'll have to get a horse and a Cadillac," Daphne said.

"And become a Baptist," Vergie said.

"What sort of position is it?" Daphne said. "Do you get to sit, or must you stand on your feet all day behind a counter?"

"Most of us work for a living," Lily said. "Vergie, You asked me to work for you, begged me. You have a short memory, dearheart."

Vergie looked away.

Daphne said, "You can't blame Vergie for wanting me to run the show, sweetie. Family and all that crap."

Lily said, "My work contract with Vergie has one year left to run."

Vergie said, "Perhaps you could stay on in some capacity, love. I suppose I could fire Mrs. Steele and have you take over the housekeeper's duties. She is such a dunce anyway."

"Where would she sleep?" Daphne said. "I think what you're suggesting wouldn't work out. It would be impossibly humiliating for Lily, moving from upstairs to downstairs, and I personally don't relish the thought of living in the same house with her if she'd no longer be part of our social set."

Lily laughed. "Thanks for being so considerate, ladies. Offering me a job instead of throwing me out on the street, and then withdrawing it based on the awkwardness of living in the same house and talking to me."

Vergie smiled, then began laughing. Daphne soon followed.

"See," Vergie said. "She has a sense of humor. We'll all get past this difficulty I'm sure."

Daphne looked at Lily, eyes flashing in triumph.

#

"I'm taking the Alfa out this afternoon," Daphne said.

"Are you sure it will run?" Vergie said.

"I started it up. It purrs like a cat."

"Where are you going?" Lily said.

"I haven't decided yet. I don't know this area well."

"I suggest you stick to the back roads of Montecito. They're twisty enough to give it a workout and the traffic's light. You'll have fewer problems if anything goes wrong with the car."

Daphne laughed. "You're so cautious, Lily. You put a wet blanket on everything. The Alfa's safe enough, and if I run into any difficulties, I can handle them."

Vergie said, "Why not do Santa Ynez? Take a run up there, check out the wineries, and stop in Solvang for lunch at one of those touristy Danish restaurants."

"I like the winery idea, Vee. Come along with me and we'll have a grand old time."

"No thanks, Dee. I hated staying there for rehab and don't want to return to the scene of my degradation. All the same, it's pretty country. San Marcos Pass offers wonderful views of the mountains and ocean."

"How're the roads?"

"Tricky the first time, they wind, and steep cliffs."

"Sounds like a perfect workout for my Alfa. Are you sure you won't come with me, Vee?"

Vergie shook her head.

Daphne did not ask Lily, did not even look at her.

"Drive carefully," Lily said.

Their eyes met briefly, no words.

#

Later that day, Lily found Vergie in the west end library, sitting for once alone on the couch, Old Fashioned glass in hand, open bottle of gin and bucket of ice on a table. She checked her watch. "It's only two o'clock, Vergie. It's early to be getting drunk."

Vergie looked, blinked, noticing her for the first time. "She's gone."

"Daphne?"

"Who else, love? She went to Santa Ynez."

Lily hesitated. "Good riddance."

"What?"

"You heard me."

"You sound angry, Lily. What is it?"

She felt rage rising quickly, overwhelming her. "You are incredible, Vergie." She paused. "I'm leaving."

"Why?"

"It amazes me you'd ask such a stupid question. What's wrong with you?"

"Don't glare at me, Lily. I have no idea what's got under your skin recently, and talking to me like this, it's . . . well, it's almost inexcusable."

"Shut up, and listen to me—for *once*. I put my life on hold for you and you betrayed me. You asked for my friendship and I gave it to you. I saved your life the day you OD'd. I forced you into rehab. I helped you deal with the loss of your husband. I got your house in order and made it safe to live in. I did all of those things for you without being asked or paid. I did them because I'm probably the best friend you've ever had."

"I've done a lot for you, too."

Lily laughed. "I borrowed your car, lived in your house, ate your food. Big sacrifice to you for a full-time caretaker and pal." She shook her head. "Then you asked me, *Lily, please come work for me*, you begged me, and I quit my job to do it, and now you're going back on all of it, acting like it never happened. You didn't keep your word, Vergie. You let me down, all for— her!"

"Are you jealous?"

"Of course I am."

"But she's my cousin, Lily. What else could I do?"

"You talk family, but don't know what it means.

You don't know who loves you and who only makes you feel good. You and Daphne are the same, both rich, lonely, loveless women who don't know who your true friends are. I don't know which one of you is worse. Daphne is honest, at least. She says exactly what she thinks. You lie constantly, even to yourself. Daphne will destroy you. She went through her own fortune and several men. Now she'll go through yours. In a year or so, you'll both be broke. You're well on your way. Look at yourself, drunk in the afternoon, like before. All you need are the pills to complete the picture. Keep it up, you'll die."

Vergie stared at her, wide-eyed. "You took them away. You're leaving, I want them back."

"They're gone."

"At least return my pillbox."

"Buy another. See Bill Secrest and have him fill it with pills. Then get drunk and swallow them. End your misery."

Lily handed her the Mercedes keys. "These are yours. I won't need them now. If you want to go anywhere, please have Roman drive you."

"I don't need anyone to drive me anywhere," Vergie said coldly. "Having the Mexican here was your idea. I'll fire him when you're gone. I'll unhook the cameras too. I don't need security men controlling my life."

"You don't know what you need, dearheart. Good luck."

Vergie looked sad, forlorn. "I'm sorry, love."

"Me, too."

As she left the library, Lily heard the tinkling of ice cubes dropping into a glass.

\#

Lily settled in her boyfriend's living room before the TV, relaxed on a sagging couch, soon fell asleep. She awoke to a ringing old-fashioned dial phone, got up and answered, Danny calling, reminding her to feed the cats, he would be home in an hour with Chinese.

"I said I'd get the food," she objected.

"It's easier for me," he said.

He had a good point. She decided to make a home of the place, even if temporarily, wiped off old dishes and cutlery, set the rickety table in the kitchenette. When she had more time, she would go grocery shopping, equip the kitchen, cook a few meals. What a novel idea. She had never lived with a man for more than a single day and night; such short stays did not count.

Early evening, she went to the back door, a herd of cats, eyes sparkling in reflected light, looking up at her, distant mewing, coming closer as she stepped out onto the slab, scattered the kibbles, milling bodies, tails scraping against her legs seductively, urging her to spread the abundance among them and do it quickly.

Danny soon walked in with bags of Chinese, set them on the table, glanced at the dishes and cutlery, shook his head. She fetched beer. They both sat, opened the bags, sorted The food, set to with plastic utensils, eating from steaming food containers.

"Boy, this is the high life," Lily said.

"Ain't this great?" Dan said. "You like playing the blue collar old lady? Wow, this must be comedown from palace life, princess." He stared at her. "Were you a real princess over there?"

"For a while I felt like one, but then the queen's evil cousin came, saw through my act, persuaded the queen to demote me to commoner, and she expelled me."

"Are they dykes?"

"It was a power play, not sexual."

"I've been curious, Lily. You don't date and you've been living with those two women. Can you swing both ways?"

"Why? Does the idea turn you on?"

"Sure, it turns all men on." He hesitated.

"Straight ones, anyway. I don't know how homos feel."

She smiled. "If I answer the question, you'll stop wondering. What fun is that?"

"For me, or you?"

She laughed. "For both of us, Danny. I enjoy tantalizing you, and you get excited."

"Seriously," he said.

"Only under duress," she said.

"What?"

"How much is enough not to be considered a whore?"

"How much of what?"

"Money, property, lifestyle, everything."

"More than I can afford. High-class hookers get thousands and they're still considered whores. I've known guys, they marry a chick they don't love just to get laid. That's a whole lifetime, big money if you think, which nobody does."

"You do."

"I can usually get what I need for nothing or a few drinks, never for money, I mean, I never pay a chick for a favor—well, mostly never."

"Mostly never?" She laughed. "You're a big liar, Danny."

"I know. All men are liars, but so are women, and women are worse liars." He paused in midbite. "Hey, I answered your question to the best of my limited ability considering my lack of formal education and sophistication. Now it's your turn to give me the correct answer."

"A fortune," Lily said.

"Fair enough. I'd do it too. Hell, I'd even bare my cheeks for a dude or give a blowjob."

"How do I know you haven't already done it with a guy?"

"Because I'm a macho man. Say, I'd like to continue this conversation, but I've got to get a few hours of sleep and then go back to work.

Maybe we can continue it tomorrow. Do you like biking?"

"I did when I was a kid."

"Not the kind you pedal. I mean motorcycles."

"Harley-Davidson?"

"Those are cool, but I like road racers. Let me show you mine."

She laughed. "Is this where you show me something big and impressive to prove how macho you are?"

She followed him out to the garage. He pulled open the door and revealed a shiny red motorcycle resembling a rocket sled on wheels.

"It looks expensive."

He ran his hand along the tank. "It was. It's a Ducati, an Italian racing bike I got from one of my employees, owed me money, and, well, he died."

"Died, in the line of duty?"

"Sort of, but he was off the reservation, crazy, shot a cocaine dealer, and the dealer's bodyguard killed him. It's a long story, not for now."

"And you inherited the bike?"

He nodded "Let's make a run up the pass tomorrow. I can lend you leathers."

"Danny, you're full of surprises."

He grinned at her. "Ain't life fun, princess?"

#

She slept in and Dan worked through the next morning until almost ten o'clock. Back home, he showered, slept for a few hours, and was raring to go riding by one o'clock. He found a set of red and black racing bike leathers cut for a woman somewhere and gave them to her to try on. The were loose in the chest and ass but fit reasonably well. Danny had a matching pair. The two sets probably had an interesting backstory, but she did not ask. All she could conclude from the fit was the girl had been top and bottom heavy the way male bikers seemed to prefer.

He helped her put on a bike helmet, told her to climb aboard and hang on. "How do we communicate?" she said, voice muffled, conversation hopeless. She felt as if she were about to be fired from a cannon, and as soon as Danny took the Ducati out onto a city street and accelerated up to a speed illegal on any California highway, her nascent fear was realized.

Soon they were on U.S. 101, zipping down the coast against a stiff headwind, dodging and passing lazy Sunday afternoon traffic, then a quick right turn up San Marcos Pass Road, two opposing lanes cut into a mountainside, steep fall left, sharp rise right. Cars grouped bumper to bumper in serial packs, delayed by the slowest poking mobile home, truck, bus, or torpid car in front. Danny wended his way through each pack and passed his way to the front, oblivious to oncoming traffic, blind corners, road hazards, other threats to life and limb and, once there, sped on to the next pack, as if racing himself as Lily leaned against him, arms around his midsection, bodies joined at each tilt and turn, like being on a roller-coaster without the guardrails or certainty of a safe landing, happy end.

The intense ride up the pass felt like forever but took less than ten minutes, ending when Dan turned onto a narrow stagecoach road, drove for a mile, and stopped at a weathered clapboard tavern resembling an old ranch house. Dozens of motorcycles were parked in front and bikers of various descriptions were congregating, drinking beer, bullshitting, arguing, joking, sparring. Danny pulled the Ducati in and parked it near a group of European racing bikes apart from the Harleys and Hondas. The bikes were segregated but the bikers were fully integrated and enjoying themselves loudly and with gusto. Danny walked her around, introducing her to friends. They drank beer, hung out for an hour or so, had a good time, then left the throng, went into the tavern, ate dinner inside—dim lights, plank floors, walls covered with ranching tools and western memorabilia.

\#

Driving to work the next day, Lily heard a local news report, a traffic accident in San Marcos Pass. The victim had run off the road at a sharp turn, plunged off a cliff to her death. No witnesses, wreckage undiscovered until Sunday. Driver identified as an Italian tourist, accident cause unknown.

"Shit!" she said, and finished the drive to work.

\#

They went to Vergie's home office after breakfast. "You are now my business manager, Lily. Your duties are as before, managing the household and finances, as well as anything else I decide to add. I also expect you to be my full-time companion and see to my personal needs and happiness as necessary. You don't have to sleep with me, for sex at least. Sometimes I get lonely and like to have companionship in bed, but it's up to you."

"I hope you don't expect me to be at your beck and call twenty-four hours a day, seven days a week."

"No, of course not. We're not married. You have a right to a personal life. Let's work on it as time passes."

"Okay."

"Good, I'm glad we got it out of the way. I want you to handle a few things for me immediately. I've been procrastinating, and you've liberated me from guilt by returning." She smiled.

Lily laughed. "It's wonderful to be useful."

"I want you to go to the city morgue on Monday and identify Daphne's remains. They called last week and asked me, but I simply couldn't go over there. They said she's battered and bloody but recognizable. They did an autopsy, probably suspected drunk driving, or a heart attack or stroke. Found nothing. She drove off the stupid cliff without a seatbelt. We'll never know why. Take a look, say it's her, and have them send her bits and pieces to the same

mortuary that did Tony's cremation. They should give us a discount."

"Monday morning, fine."

"It was damn careless of her to die. Probably mechanical failure. You warned her about the car. She showed poor judgment taking it, and was quite inconsiderate. I know you wanted it. I wonder if she took it to spite you."

"Maybe she was depressed."

"Do you think it was suicide?"

"Who knows?"

"Go to the county impound lot and check the wreck to see if it's repairable and worth fixing, fat chance. If it is, get a cost estimate. If it's a total wreck, send it to a recycler."

"Okay."

"You know, Lily, I'm having serious second thoughts concerning Daphne. I didn't realize until now how I'd misjudged her and allowed her to influence me. You've suffered as a consequence of my bad judgment and pigheadedness. I am truly sorry for all the pain and misery I've caused you."

"It's all in the past, dearheart. Leave it there."

"No, I need to say these things to clear the air between us. Daphne coaxed me out of rehabilitating and back into her live and let live ways. She was a bad influence."

"And I'm perfect?"

Vergie laughed. "Hardly, but you are loosening up a bit, champagne and occasional cocktails."

"I had to be your watchdog for a while, dearheart. You're doing better."

"We both are, love." Vergie's eyes roamed. "I'm her sole heir, unless some bastard comes out of the woodwork or one of her ex's." She giggled. "Not to worry. In such an eventuality, I'll call my Jew, get lawyered up as good as the next man."

"Vergie, please."

"You should've heard my parents speaking."

"What's your attitude toward Gypsies?"

Vergie leveled her eyes on Lily. "What a strange question."

If she only knew, Lily thought.

"They have colorful, cozy wagons, live mostly outdoors, clever people, but untrustworthy, at least it's how they're portrayed in movies." Vergie paused. "I have absolutely no idea regarding Gypsies. Never met one in my life."

Lily smiled.

"I'm not sure what all Daphne has left," Vergie continued. "Squandered money on lovers and other fun. I'll check with her lawyer and find out what her will says. He's Italian, I think. I hope he speaks English so I don't have to hire an interpreter or Italian Jew to get what's coming to me."

Lily laughed. "You're hopeless, dearheart."

"Reminds me, love. I can change my will now that she's gone, add that foundation you wanted. You've met Mr. Sullivan. Schedule a meeting with him next week, some day in the afternoon, we can make the necessary changes." She came to Lily, hugged her. "You are so good at business, and you make everything easier for me."

"Anything else, ma'am?"

"Yes. Call up a vintage car broker and tell him to sell Tony's cars."

"Got it."

#

Monday morning, Lily got up early, selected a blouse and slacks from the wardrobe, flats, wig, gold wire glasses. Mrs. Steel was in the kitchen as she entered to get a glass of juice, gave her a startled look at first, then smiled. "Good morning, Mrs. Hove," she said. "You look exactly like her."

"Good morning, Mrs. Steele," Lily said, pouring herself a glass. "What do you think?"

"You give me the shivers, Lily."

Lily finished her glass of juice, set it in the sink. "Tell Mrs. Hove I've gone into Santa Barbara to visit the morgue and impound yard. I should be back before lunch."

#

She drove the Mercedes into town, arrived at the morgue at 9 a.m. The man at the counter asked her name and other information. "Vergie Hove," she said, and answered everything as Vergie would have. It was a practical test, for Vergie had sent her to identify her cousin, being too lazy to do it herself. If the attendant saw through her disguise, Vergie would probably be more amused than shocked.

The attendant took a folder out of a file and opened it. "Hove, Daphne," he said, looking up. "It's good she had a handbag with a driver's license—Italian. Maybe it explains the accident, the reckless way they drive over there." He chuckled. "I'm sorry, Miss . . ."

"Mrs. Hove," Lily said. "Vergie Hove. I'm her cousin. Are you sure it's her?"

"Not until you ID her, ma'am. But we think so, based on the license and the car she was driving. Someone called you last week concerning the car, an Alfa Romeo. It's an old one, rare, and it's not likely someone impersonating Mrs. Hove was driving it."

"May I see her now?"

"Yes, ma'am. I'll walk you down there right now."

They walked side by side down a hallway through a pair of swinging doors into a large room with stainless steel drawers along the walls. At the far end, a man in whites sat at a desk watching a small TV.

The attendant located the drawer, reached for the handle, looked at her. "She was ejected from the car, no seatbelt, flew through the air, hit a hundred feet below. It was like she jumped off a tall building. Get what I'm saying?"

"I think so," Lily said.

"Barely recognizable. Please prepare yourself, Mrs. Hove." He slowly opened the drawer, pulled back the covering sheet.

A bloody, misshapen face, nose flattened, recognizable, but barely.

"That's Daphne Hove," Lily said. "She wore two wedding bands on her right hand."

"We removed her jewelry and placed it in temporary storage. You can collect it when you leave."

The attendant recovered the body, closed the steel drawer. They returned to the front counter. He retrieved a paper bag from a storage room and placed it on the counter. She peeked inside: bloodstained clothing, a handbag, plastic baggie with two gold rings and a gold wristwatch.

She told him where to send the remains, signed a paper, and left.

#

She pulled into a large fenced lot filled with vehicles, parked, and entered a shed. A man in blue coveralls came to the counter. She said she was Vergie Hove and described the Alfa. The man's eyebrows rose in a sign of pity—likely for the car more than its victim. He gave her a space number and pointed. "Do you want me to walk you out to it, ma'am?" he asked politely.

"No, but thank you for asking. I can find it myself."

"Please watch your step, ma'am. Don't slip or you'll ruin your pretty outfit."

She felt like telling him to shove it, smiled.

The sight of the Alfa made her teary. It had been such a beautiful car, those graceful, classic lines, voluptuous curves. What remained was the color red, bits of chrome, twisted and flattened like a crushed Coke can. The glove box was open, empty. She searched the cockpit floor—papers, empty cigarette pack, matches, ancient debris set loose on impact. Sunlight made it difficult to see, so she moved to the other side of the car, looked down, a glint of gold light caught her eye, down there, where Daphne's feet would have been. She leaned close, took out a handkerchief, reached down, felt it, the squared corners of an exquisite little gold lighter, picked it up, examined it: perfect, not a scratch. She was tempted to test it; no. She chuckled, wrapped it in the handkerchief, dropped it into a pocket.

About the Author:

Henry Simpson is the author of several novels, two short story collections, many book reviews, and occasional pieces in literary journals. His most recent novel is Golden Girl (Newgame, 2017).

THE MAN IN CUBICLE 2200

by Heide Arbitter

As a boy, he lived in a largely unfurnished thirty room mansion. His pious parents did not let him play with toys, nor make friends with children from the surrounding estates. They believed that the path to responsible adulthood was through religion. To that end, despite their billions, they led a cloistered life. Hidden away in the mansion's ornate incensed chapel, they prayed and meditated all day and night. They shunned technology, even though it had made them billions. They despised all manner of electronic devices and possessed none of their own. Their lonely son, at age three, demanded to know why they did not have a television. The parents said he was too young to ask. From then on, they lit their mansion with candles and refused to ever turn on the lights. They handed the boy a Bible and turned their backs.

Lack of electronics could not be said of the servants, however, who in the privacy of their comfortable quarters in the back of the mansion, gladly gave the boy access to smart phones and lap tops. One of the younger maids gave the boy a tablet for his fourth birthday. Within hours, the boy mastered skills to last a lifetime.

It was online, the boy read about dragons. He was curious why his distant parents never spoke of them, these magnificent creations of God. Sure, there were evil dragons, decimating with their fire breath, everything in sight, but there were also kind dragons with glittering wings and silken scales, who befriended a select few families, and they brought good fortune and happiness to these families who then went on to live with love, and wisdom, too. The boy decided to leave home and find as many good dragons as possible. He followed the path he had seen servant couples take on their days off and soon was beyond the mansion fences. He felt the wind in his face. The call of the unknown was scary. But, the boy was confident that dragons would lead him to his perfect family.

It is true, his pious parents did their best. They hired the most expensive servants to care for him, the most expensive tutors to teach him and the most expensive detectives to search for him. But after two weeks of looking, the detectives declared the boy dead and the parents changed their will to leave everything to a local monastery. And so, their lifestyle continued with but the smallest disruption.

It is strange that the detectives did not find him. As for those two weeks, the boy lived in the grasses only 500 feet from the mansion. At night, he gazed at his dark bedroom. He yearned for a warm bed, but he yearned more for the love of a family. And so, he picked himself up and walked the woods and streams, stars and lilac trees, looking and looking for miles and miles. Acorns and mushrooms were his initiation into lifelong vegetarianism. The boy loved being with the animals of the forest. He climbed hills, and slept in hollow logs. It felt like he spent many years searching, but in actual time, only four.

Eventually, this eight year old boy landed on the streets of the city, where the police picked him up on a rainy night. The boy made up a name and was assigned to foster care. There, he lived as an only child in a cracked basement apartment with a drunk foster mother and a drugged out foster father. But one night, after watching the fosters eat one too many veal chops, he decided the streets were a more appetizing home. When the fosters fell into a stupor on the kitchen floor, he opened the front door and left.

The fosters continued collecting their checks until one day, three years later, Children's Services knocked on the door demanding to know why the boy had gone truant. The police ransacked the apartment, peeled back the linoleum and dug through the dumpster in front of the building, searching for the boy's body. The fosters, blank faced and indifferent, sat at the kitchen table. The next week they received another boy to foster.

It true that the boy was truant, but he did not need school to help him learn anything. At the DMV, he searched garbage cans for cast off newspapers, rubbed newsprint on his cheeks to give the look of the unshaven, lied about his age, and got a driver's license and a job as a delivery person with weekly runs from the docks to Chen's Tea.

That was when the boy first saw the dragon cape. It simply fluttered out of the box he was delivering. It was the most beautiful thing in the world. Embroidered with golden dragons, the boy swore he saw them fly up and wink at him before settling back into the fabric, where they stared kindly at him. The boy could feel the dragons' magnolia breath empowering him. He stood in the alley and held the precious cape to his heart. That's when Mr. Chen, tall and virile, stomped over. The boy cringed. Mr. Chen always frightened him. This time, Mr.

Chen wiggled his grey whiskers and snorted. The boy handed him the cape. Mr. Chen invited the boy into the shop for a saucer of tea. And there, the boy remained for many years.

It would be nice to say that Mr. Chen taught the boy how to grow into a man, how to fly like a dragon, how to work a cash register, or even how to run a tea shop, but that was not true. On a good day, Mr. Chen ignored him. The tea shop was so immense, that no surge of customers, however big, could fill it. So, the boy spent his time walking the aisles, loading the aromatic shelves with Chinese Flower, Earl Grey, English Breakfast, Hibiscus, Chamomile, Peppermint, Raspberry Peppermint, Dark Chocolate Mate, Cucumber White, Vanilla, and Zen. Although he slept on the shop floor, it was ample payment for stacking the shelves with tea boxes and the sweeping and mopping of his job.

And, each year, when the holidays arrived, a girl, just about his age, would come to the shop. The boy, now a teen, glowed with delight. This was Ashley. The teen heard her name, when she asked Mr. Chen to stop calling her Miss Burnham. This beautiful girl, with her classic black curls and eyes the color of Matcha, did all of her holiday shopping at Chen's, filling cart after cart with teas like Lavender, Peach, Ginger, Apple, and the teen's favorite, Green. Ashley paid and Mr. Chen would carry her purchases out to her limousine where her chauffer opened the trunk for him. Mr. Chen would then return to the shop and be met with the scowls of his twelve sons who berated him, shouting that Mr. Chen acted like a servant to a skinny white heiress. Mr. Chen ignored them.

The sons could do nothing about their father, but they could about the teen. One time they caught him looking at Ashley. They dragged the teen into the storage room and kicked him black and blue. From that moment, the sons cursed at the teen daily, but the teen could not forget his beautiful Ashley and dreamt over and over again about the pink cashmere coats she wore, always with kittens, cats and mice embroidered on them. The teen concluded that Ashley was a veterinarian and perhaps he could find a position working for her in her pet clinic.

So, the next year, after Ashley finished shopping, the teen leapt onto his delivery bike and followed the limousine uptown, until it stopped in front of a sky scrapper. This was no veterinary clinic, for sure. It was the globally despised Burnham Enterprises. The teen saw the driver and Ashley went in, carrying the boxes of tea. He biked back to Chen's Tea, Googled Burnham Enterprises and gasped.

This was the company his parents founded, then sold, after they discovered that their good intentions in creating a place that would provide jobs, and sponsor peace initiatives had become a hot bed of evil, dark web activity with every monster, dictator and sadist logging on day and night. His shocked and penitent parents retreated to their mansion, took their name from the company, and after it was bought and renamed Burnham, were never seen in public again. With this understanding, the teen considered returning to the mansion, but after one night of thinking about it, he knew his destiny was elsewhere.

As it turned out, the teen made the right choice. A week later, while watching CNN, and sipping tea in the back room of the tea shop, the teen saw a horrible story. The mansion where he spent his early years had burned to the ground, and although the servants escaped, his parents had not. The teen gagged and abruptly stood up, spilling his tea. The twelve sons glanced in his direction, but none came over to inquire about his distress. And when the teen broke down sobbing, they simply left the room.

Although the teen loved Mr. Chen, to his knowledge his adoration was not reciprocated. He would miss Mr. Chen, the tea leaves, the clink of tea cups and the soothing quiet of the shop as he lay on the floor at night. But, he disappeared from Chen's Tea as he did from his parents' mansion. He rode his bike uptown and

applied for a job on the 22nd floor of Burnham Enterprises, the floor where Ashley had her office. He was still there 22 years later.

Now, no longer a teen, the man bought his own studio apartment in a downtown neighborhood. After work, he climbed five flights, usually without passing any neighbors. On the rare occasions he saw somebody on the stairs, he smiled, but his greetings were never returned. People moved out, but the man remained. And, as years passed, so did his hope for making any connection with those living around him.

Then, it happened. A new family moved in down the hall, and although the man never saw them, he thought perhaps, they would become buddies. He spent several weeks climbing over their boxes strewn along the hall, thinking of ways to befriend them. When they finally moved in, they did not knock on his door to introduce themselves or put their name on their mailbox. The man took this as a sign, but did not give up hope.

That night, the man came home from work, in a depressed state. He shut all the blinds and windows. The man took off his clothes, and put on the dragon cape. He pranced around his small home, spreading his arms as though he could fly, posing and grinning at every reflective surface he could find, the computer, the television, and the mirrors, which shot back a glimpse of this middle-aged costumed fool.

Yes, the man was not exactly attractive. His suits, although a bit behind the times, were clean. His full moon eyes were at times luminous, not quite green, but certainly not brown and always seemed to match the color of the suit he wore for the day. And, despite the insufficient diet of his youth in the woods, and stolen bits of pumpernickel from the fosters, his straight, white teeth boasted not one cavity. His nose, well, it was a nose to make a dragon proud, but a man less so. His ears were large and pointed. They appeared dragon like and when he wore the cape, the man felt most strong in his dragon fierceness.

The man danced back and forth until he heard screams from the apartment down the hall. Four gun shots pierced his reverie. The man heard footsteps of neighbors all around him running down the stairs, then, police sirens filled the air. The man cautiously opened his door and peered out, as cops and feds raced past, down the hall and into the apartment of his new neighbors.

The man considered entering the hall to provide what help he could. Instead, he closed the door, not seeing the little mouse escape from the apartment and dash into his, away from the only home he had known now decimated by a cartel hit. Trembling, the little mouse looked for shelter. Quickly, he hid in a corner.

"Okay, boys," yelled a cop from the hall. The man watched from the peep hole as the dead were carried down stairs. Sirens blasting, the bodies of this Witness Protected Family were transported to the medical examiner. Soon, someone pounded on his door. "FBI! Open up!" "Right Away, Sir." The man opened the door to three feds who pushed their way in. One laughed out loud. The others leered at him. The man tried to summon dragon courage from the cape, which he was still wrapped in, but he could barely raise his eyes from the floor as the feds interrogated him and pulled up the cape to see what he was hiding. All shrieked at the man's nakedness. Soon, they left, but not before muttering, "What a creep."

From his corner, the trembling mouse watched the man pace, then return to his trance like rhythms. As the sun rose, the man ended his dance and laid the cape on the couch. Suddenly, the cape looked shabby. Its golden threads seemed to be rusting, and its embroidery looked tattered. And, oh no, he could see holes in the beautifully sewn borders. The man refused to think about this or the massacre down the hall. Instead, he thought about how lovingly Mr. Chen treated the cape and how enraged Mr. Chen's twelve sons were, when by order of his will, they mailed the cape to this stranger. The man never did learn how the twelve found his address.

The acres of cubicles, on the twenty second floor, of Burnham Enterprises were a relaxing sight. So familiar in their one desk, one phone, one computer, one chair, that even after twenty two years, sitting in cubicle 2200, the man got lost and needed a guard to lead him to his destination. The man did not mind, for it gave him a few minutes to exchange workday words with the young guard, Pedro, who pretended to listen, but was actually thinking of his girlfriends.

Once located, the man turned on his computer. The phone rang. The man answered. The questions were always the same and the man would say, as politely as he could, "Try turning it off. Now, turn it on. It worked? Great. Don't forget to call with other problems. My name is..." But, by then, the caller had hung up.

Each morning, Ashley passed by on her way to her office. The man's heart beamed every time she drove by. Although others saw Ashley as a woman who was gawky and strange, to the man she was still beautiful. He shuddered as he recalled how she was beaten into submission by her marriage to Bixby, a spoiled trust fund snob. Since their wedding night, a motorized wheel chair was her means of travel. The man heard that the repugnant Bixby hung himself, but he was never sure if this was true or office gossip. That the man loved Ashley was true. That Ashley still adored Bixby was something he could never explain.

The man stood outside cubicle 2200 to see Ashley roll down the aisle with her kitten sweater and her mouse shaped barrettes. On this particular day, she looked even more beautiful. It was all the man needed to forget the challenges of the last few days. "Good morning," the man said. Usually, Ashley did not respond, but today, Ashley's glowed in a way he had not seen before. She looked happy. Encouraged, the man stepped towards her to declare his love, but stopped as Ashley looked as though she had simply never seen the man before. And that might very well be true, for the man carried the odor of the displaced, not tangible, but apparent in everything he did, and this often rendered him invisible. Ashley continued down the hall. Foolishly the man followed her to her office, where he tried to speak. But before he got the words out, Ashley slammed her office door.

The man ran back to cubicle 2200, and sat with his head in his hands, as his youth, tarnished with time, but painful, flooded him. He remembered how his heart burst with love the first time he saw Ashley. And he regretted, never getting in touch with his parents to tell them he was alive. Perhaps, that would have lightened their earthly burden. But then, a realization, one that had been lurking deep within him burst forth. He was with his parents. He had been these 22 years working in the very structure they built and then abandoned, just as they had him. Perhaps, this was the reason he felt so comfortable in cubicle 2200. He was enveloped in his roots so much so that the man broke down and sobbed.

Back at the apartment, the brave little mouse was still huddled in the corner. The man returned at midnight, and was standing in the middle of the room, thinking of Ashley, the cape wrapped tightly around him. Is that what tears are, the mouse wondered, but judging the man to be in a gloom, the mouse kept its distance.

At sunrise, the man sat on the couch. That's when he saw the mouse. The man's face softened, and the mouse ventured closer. "Hello!" The man yelled, more loudly then he intended. The little mouse hunched his back, and ran some distance from the man, twitching his small grey ears. "My name is Myka" the mouse bravely squeaked. The man did not hear. "Myka", the mouse shouted. The man smiled at the mouse, then got ready for work. Myka, dashed under the grandfather clock, until he heard the deafening footsteps of the man leaving the apartment and the ear splitting noise of the key outside locking the door.

Only then, did Myka tip toe out and approach the cape. It was beautiful, hanging on its hook.

Myka looked at it with gleaming eyes, gently climbed onto its hem, then onto the collar and down into a pocket. He stayed, curled in the warmth, until he heard the key again. Myka ran as fast as he could under the grandfather clock.

But, something about the man was different. The man carried in a paper bag, leftovers from his dinner down the street. The man kept little food in his spotless apartment, and not even a crumb or two left in the kitchen sink. And, Myka was so hungry. He sniffed the air. It reminded him of the place down the hall, and the witness protected family who fed their cat, Myriam, grilled cheese sandwiches. Best of all, Myriam would leave some crumbs in her bowl for Myka to snack on. Myka became almost fat after these satisfying morsels and for fun, best of all, he would stand on his hind legs and play the sleeping Myriam's whiskers like a harp, till she woke and playfully chased him back to his nest in the book case. And, that was only part of the fun they had. But, then, Myka had run out of the apartment and Myriam hadn't followed. Fortunately, there was an open door down the hall, the apartment of the man.

Myka watched as the man cut a corner of the grilled cheese sandwich into tiny, tiny bits, which he placed on a saucer. Then, the man put the saucer in front of the grandfather clock and waited on the old, brown couch. Soon, Myka crawled out, and seeing the man was sitting, slowly approached the meal. As the man watched Myka nibble, a feeling of family entered his heart.

But a noise outside of the apartment interrupted this. Cautiously, the man opened the door and went into the hall. Emerging through the opened door of the murdered tenants' apartment, he saw something wonderful. No, not the ghosts of the slaughtered family transported to heaven on the backs of benevolent dragons, but a snow white cat. She meowed and looked at the man pleadingly.

This was Myriam, the white furred cat that belonged to the family. Whatever their misdeeds this husband, wife and the wife's two brothers adored her. They discovered Myriam cowering at the back of a cage at their local animal shelter. She was merely three weeks old, too young for adoption really, but this family promised to bottle feed her till she grew, and so they took her home. Myriam adored her warm box next to the fire place, and the way the family threw balls to her, but when Myriam was two months old, the family noticed something. She did not answer to her name because she couldn't hear her name. Myriam was born deaf. And perhaps, it was because of this that the move to the tiny apartment was so hard for her. No, she did not act ungratefully, she was too polite for that, but she missed the warmth of the fireplace and the laughter of this now sad family. Until she met Myka, Myriam was lonely.

Nervously, the man walked down the hall to the cat. She did not appear to mind as he bent over to pick her up. She smelled so sweet and her fur was as soft as cotton. Her eyes were Matcha, like Ashley's. The man carried Myriam to his apartment and shut the door.

But now, the man faced a new challenge. Would the rodent be devoured? The man decided to take one of the biggest chances he had since running from the mansion. He would risk sharing his home with two new dwellers, no matter the consequences. The man placed the cat on the sofa.

At that, Myka looked out from behind the saucer. He could not believe his ears. Myriam was purring, a sound so soothing and very much loved. Myka breathed deeply. His whiskers vibrated with joy. His eyes locked with Myriam's and hers with his. Observing this, the man slept for the first time in days. When morning came, he was almost late for work.

That night, the man entered his apartment without looking around. He had read in the company email that the rumors of Bixby's demise had been just that, and Bixby had returned to Ashley. Now, the man knew his love for Ashley was lost, withered by time and circumstance. Without taking off his clothes

the man wrapped himself in the cape. He stood just outside the kitchen sobbing. Tears ran down his cheeks, no matter how hard he squeezed his eyes shut. After two hours, the man shook his head, annoyed he had given into emotion again. He opened his eyes and was met with delight.

His dragon guardians had found him at last, for sitting on the couch, paws around each other were the animals. "Thank you!" the man screamed to the still invisible dragons for helping him create a family of his own determination. He thought he saw the two animals grin in agreement. This was a good sign. As he glided over to pet them, he realized he had not given them names, let alone introduced himself.

Myka and Myriam sat together on the couch. As the man came near, his happiness was apparent. By way of greeting, the man flapped his arms and snorted welcoming dragon breath. Myka and Myriam looked at him, then at each other. "Hello," the man shouted. "We are family. My name is…" But, Myka ignored him and Myriam couldn't hear him. Both, knew they would tolerate the man, and even respect him, but they would never love him. And at that, Myka and Myriam snuggled closer, too overjoyed in their own love to pay the man any more attention.

About the Author:

Heide Arbitter's plays have been produced in New York City and regionally. Some of these productions include a one-act, HAND WASHED, LINE DRIED, which was produced at the Public Theatre; a full-length, FROGS FROM THE MOON at the American Theatre of Actors; and a one-act, TILL WE MEET, at Unboxed Voices. Smith & Kraus and Excalibur have published JILLY ROSE, SHARON and POPPY. Heide was recently interviewed on the radio, WFUV.

HIS HOME

by Effy Rose

It's the house I grew up in, but everything's different. Forty years ago, I left it to care for itself, and I suppose it has. It's still standing. Under a blanket of ever-creeping ivy, green as the springtime grass, which has all but taken over the roof, the familiar face, made of two eye-windows and a door-mouth, begs for a white-washing it will never get.

As a child, I counted it one of a few blessings to live in such a tall home. In a way, its height made up for my father's lows. Now, as I draw nearer, I wonder if I might be taller. If I stood back to siding, my head might peek over the rusted tin roof and come to rest in the clouds alongside my mother's.

I've outgrown this place, could never go back to change anything, even if magic potion made it possible. Could never sit quietly, still as a speckled fawn, listening, waiting for my mother's beating to end. She deserved it, I told myself, and when I couldn't muster it, she told me. I'll do better next time, she'd promise time and again. He's got a right to be angry.

I sit down on the rickety steps and look up under the overhang and find most of its beams are rotted through. If I listen hard, many a rainy nights' ping-ping-pinging still rings in my ears like it did on those nights when I rocked and rocked in our only rocking chair. Dreaming, thinking about better times I wasn't sure existed.

When my mother died, I was glad for her. I cried, but only for myself. On that afternoon,

I kissed her cold cheek, then ran. Tore off through the tall, sun-dried brush before they even laid her in the ground. Day after day, I ran, taking small bites of the stale bread I carried in my mother's only apron. When my stomach threatened to roar loud enough to give up my hiding spots, I'd slide my hand into the carefully tied mass of what was supposed to be red fabric, but looked baby pink from endless washes. When the bread was gone, I tied the apron around my waist for warmth. Not the kind of warmth your skin needs—that was provided by the high-summer nights' sticky, suffocating air. I was after the kind that starts at your insides and spreads into something mimicking happiness. It was her warmth I craved. More than bread. More than a new family, but that's what I got in Mr. and Mrs. Carlisle. They took me in—resisted my fighting, which rivaled that of any feral kitten—and turned me back into a person. And I'm forever grateful.

I find myself rocking on the step and it groans, begs me to stop, threatens to snap in two if I don't. I look behind me once more, and find the windows of this old house—his house—have been left uncovered. I could look inside, see what's left of the place since his passing, but I don't want to. Don't care to. Whatever is left isn't for me. I took what was mine long ago: my freedom. It's the only thing my mother ever wanted me to have.

About the Author:

Effy Rose holds an MFA from Lindenwood University. Her love of reading drives her love of writing. In an alternate reality where motion sickness doesn't exist, she might have studied to become an astronaut, but probably not. She lives in Florida with her husband, who is also a writer, and her dog, who is over it.

QUEEN'S GAMBIT

by Lazar Trubman

"I'm not particularly against telemarketers, but if they could only use a little more improvisation," says Bill Stubbs setting out the chessmen for our usual Friday game. "It makes me feel sorry for our language!"

I don't respond to that and help him with the setup.

Bill will be ninety-four next month, and if not for the arthritis, which makes his everyday existence torturous, he is a pretty healthy man. His mind is sharp, speech clear and his mouth is full of straight healthy teeth: what else could one wish for approaching the century mark? He gets a cold now and then and his blood pressure is a bit high, but it had been a bit high since he retired at the age of sixty, that is to say for the last thirty-four years. His 2005 Buick "Park Avenue", which he drives only occasionally, is in perfect condition, and he keeps its service records in a special folder under the letter "B". His neatness is staggering. Everything has its own box, folder, or shelf and cannot be moved or misplaced without his permission. He does his own shopping at the same "Safeway" and banks at the same branch of Bank of America for many years, where everyone greets him like a long-time acquaintance. At the supermarket, he always uses the help of a bag-boy and tips him two dollars only after his groceries are unloaded into the trunk in a certain order.

"I think this is management's fault," he conti-

nues to criticize the marketing business. "If they could only understand that there is a smart consumer on the other end of the line. Years ago it was different, but who remembers that, right?"

"I agree," I say, "they're just too annoying at times."

"Don't you think so?" he says wiping the rook with a light-green piece of cloth and placing it on the chessboard. "The last one especially: he was trying to sell me weightlifting equipment! Aren't they aware of how old I am?"

"No, sir, not necessarily," I must keep up the conversation.

Every Friday, before our game, he chooses a subject to reason about, and we sit on the wooden patio with scotches in our hands and a bowl of mixed nuts on the miniature table. It's after six o'clock, the sun is still up, but a couple of ceiling fans attached to the wooden cover makes the way of spending our time together more or less tolerable.

"Queen's Gambit: Queen E2 to E4!" he announces and slowly moves the Queen with his arthritis-deformed fingers: he always announces his moves and the chosen beginning. "Let's see what you've got for me this time."

"Queen E8 to E5," I say after a sip of scotch.

"Hmm," he says, also taking a sip, "you sure about that, aren't you?" even though this is my usual answer for the last three years. "Well, then you leave me no choice but Knight B1 to C3."

Every once in a while, a neighbor walks by and greets us with a nod:

"Another nice day in paradise, gentlemen, isn't it?"

We support neighbor's enthusiastic statement by slightly raising our glasses.

"I used to know all their names," says Bill after the neighbor disappears around the corner. "Not anymore: we don't see one another as often, I guess, and you know what they say about an old man's memory, don't you, Grigory?"

I think: do I want to live until his age? The thought is old, but the answer is always different.

"Your move," I remind him, "don't distract me with your smooth talk."

It takes at least a couple of Friday evenings to finish our game, but I got used to it over the years. As I figured long ago, Bill doesn't like to lose and usually shows his obvious dissatisfaction with himself only at our next meeting.

"I spent a great deal of time thinking about our last game and came to the conclusion that I really had a chance after your eighteenth move," he says tasting his scotch, "but it's easy to be smart afterwards, isn't it, Grigory?"

I mix myself a drink and keep quiet.

"And my twentieth move could've been much stronger, don't you think?"

I can't be silent any longer.

"That was my secret fear," I say, "but, thank God, somehow you missed it."

"Well, then," he says, and the previous game is forgotten.

At 6:30 p.m. comes Vergie, a Mexican woman who cooks for Bill since his wife died seven years ago. It took me a while to finally convince

him that he wouldn't survive without a hot daily meal. Vergie was recommended by one of the neighbors who himself used her sister's services since he became a widower. She is in her sixties, maybe older – you never know with Mexican women. Walking by us, she always asks me about my health and disappears into the kitchen before I answer her polite question. Every Saturday, as they agreed upon a long time ago, she puts together a menu for the following week and leaves it on the kitchen table for Bill's approval. Her meals always vary and she is a great cook.

"Pork chops this evening, Bill," she says coming out of the kitchen half an hour later with a tray. "I hope it won't be too heavy on your stomach."

"Pork chops are fine," says Bill.

"Call me when you're ready for the ice cream," reminds Vergie and retires back into the kitchen. She's as quiet as a church mouse and as poor. Every now and then Bill helps her with her medical bills, or car payments, or her grandson's insurance premiums, very unobtrusively, as if she were one of his daughters. "A day doesn't go by without me asking dear God to keep him alive," Vergie said once. "He is the main reason our family is still together."

The game is off while Bill is eating, so I stretch myself In the chair and enjoy the pleasant Northern breeze. Cutting his meat into small pieces, he says:

"Vergie's pork chops are by far the best I've eaten in many years. She told me that she marinates the meat for forty-eight hours before putting it on the grill. Forty-eight hours! Have you ever heard of such a thing, Grigory?"

"We do the same with lamb meat for a shishkebab in my country," I say, "but only twenty-four hours: it really depends on how old the animal is; an aged beef will most definitely require as much time, if not longer." Then I fall silent because he is busy again with his pork chop: he doesn't like to do two things at once, not that I know of.

My glass is empty.

"Get yourself another drink, Grigory," he suggests. "Don't wait for me."

"It won't help your situation," I say meaning our chess game and leave the patio.

Vergie overheard our conversation and is waiting for me with the bottle of scotch in one hand and the measuring glass in the other. While I'm getting the ice from the freezer, she asks: "The same dose, Mr. Grigory?"

"Make it a bit milder, please."

The sun had just fell off the horizon line and it's getting darker by the minute. Back on the patio, I turn on the light above the chessboard and occupy my chair.

"Care for some ice cream, Grigory?" asks Bill sending the last piece of the pork chop into his mouth. "I bought the kind that has less fat for you, keeping in mind your heart, of course."

"That is very thoughtful of you!" I say, really moved by his foresight.

"How's your heart anyway?" asks Bill taking a sip of scotch. "Hopefully, it doesn't bother you as often as before the surgery," he pauses while considering another sip. "An old friend of mine had a bypass surgery in the late seventies – lived almost thirty years after that."

"Some days are better than others," I say.

For a while we just sip our drinks.

"I really feel fortunate having almost all my relatives in town," says Bill suddenly, "even my children and grandchildren. At my age it's the most important thing. Even my sons in California call every week despite the fact that they both are very busy with their jobs. Even their wives!" now he falls silent – obviously tired after a long sentence.

I silently agree with him.

"Not a birthday goes by without them inviting me to their homes, not a holiday," he continues encouraged by my silent agreement. "And

what do you think of the Sunday dinners once a month, which I invented a couple of years ago, if my memory serves me well? They never missed one!"

"It was a brilliant idea," I support him, "keeps you in touch all the time."

"I hope it's not because I'm paying for the meal though."

"What an ungrateful thought!" I object sincerely. "As far as I know, they always have a great time, especially the grandkids – just look at their happy faces when they laugh. I think they really appreciate your company, and money has nothing to do with that."

Vergie comes out and takes away the tray.

"We'll have some ice cream," says Bill, "Grigory's kind has less fat."

She nods and leaves the patio.

"Your move," I remind him. "Let's concentrate on the game."

"Knight C3 to E5," he says after some time. "I need to develop my figures."

"Very good," I say, "very good."

"Last year my son Richard was trying to convince me to buy a Japanese car," he says while I am thinking on my next move. "And he almost succeeded, too...but it's not easy for my generation to forget Pearl Harbor, you know!"

"Pawn B7 to B6," I say and add indifferently, "Not my war, sorry."

I try to picture his son Richard, a sixty-year-old man in a wheelchair, who lives in California. I met him and his tonelessly speaking wife at last year's Thanksgiving dinner, and we exchanged a few sentences.

"What are you up to, Grigory?" asks Bill and falls to deep thinking. His eyes are half-shut, and I have this strange feeling that he is asleep, but a minute later he says leaning back in his chair, "G2 to G3 – I'm not going to make the same mistake twice!"

"Ice cream, gentlemen!" announces Vergie placing the tray on the table. "I used apricot preserve this time instead of raspberries and some sliced almonds."

"Apricot is fine," says Bill. "Isn't it, Grigory?"

This is usually our second break and after that we only have time for a few more moves. I like to watch Bill when he eats his ice cream, always half spoon at the time, without taking his eyes away from the bowl. It's quite dark already, and I say – meaning our chess game, "Your last move opened quite a few possibilities for next Friday, sir."

"You think so?" he asks filling up his spoon. "I think so, too."

"You're getting better and better every week."

"Instead of getting worse, you mean?"

"Your ability to see the disposition so clearly is staggering! One can only wish…"

"I've heard this before," he interrupts. "You're becoming a politician, Grigory."

He puts aside his spoon and rests. By this time he gets so tired that he might suddenly fall asleep for a few minutes. I don't bother him and enjoy the nice, quiet evening. Our game becomes less important – it's the company now that's priceless. Coming back from his short nap, he looks blindly around and apologizes:

"An age thing, I guess: my body cannot keep up with my mind anymore. Sorry."

"Well, then," I say. "Bishop C8 to B7 – and we can stop right here, unless…"

"Agreed," he says, and I move aside the small table with the chessboard on it.

Soon we're done with the ice cream, and Vergie takes away our bowls and glasses.

"Have you been writing lately, Grigory?" asks Bill adjusting his armchair to a more comfortable position. "Your last short story kept me in a state of tension for a while. Do you really think

that a young man can force himself to die just because his life seems suddenly senseless?"

"It was a relief for everybody that he did," I say. "I hope it was."

"It took me some time to get used to your style though," he says and falls silent again. I wait for him to continue. "The way you commit your thoughts to paper is different, the way your characters act…" He is silent again, and the pause is longer now. I hear the dishwasher working; then Vergie's soft singing. An idyllic evening, like all of them actually. I glance at my watch: 8:45 p.m.

A few moments later, Vergie is done with the dishes.

"Your pills are ready and I warmed a glass of water for you."

"Thank you, dear," says Bill, "you've been very helpful as always."

She wishes us good night and walks to her car. Why do I always think about her with a strange sense of regret, as if she is wasting her life preparing meals for a ninety-four-year-old man twice a day six days a week?

"I am not exactly a religious person," Bill interrupts my thoughts, "but the day Vergie stepped onto my porch was probably the most important one of my life as a widower. God, I guess, is not a bad fella after all."

"Not in my dictionary, no," I agree.

"I don't have any plans for the weekend," he says, "unless my kids will surprise me with another treat. Why don't you come again tomorrow or Sunday, Grigory, - we can watch a game or just chat about something."

"Sunday perhaps," I say, "but I can't promise."

He uses his cane to get off the chair, stands still for a moment, thin, round-shouldered, heavy breathing; then walks slowly towards the bathroom.

"My memory betrays me often nowadays," he says stopping at the open door. "I'm afraid I can't trust myself any longer and that creates a lot of confusion between me and my kids and grandkids..."

"Confusion?"

"Things I remember are not necessarily things they have told me," he explains avoiding my eyes. "That's why I could be wrong assuring you that nothing has been scheduled for this weekend. On the contrary..."

"I would've called anyway!"

"You better be ready next Friday – I'll kick your butt finally," he says and laughs. His laugh is weak and squeaky, as if somebody is tearing to pieces a thin sheet of paper inside his throat.

It is still hot inside my car; I turn on the air conditioner and drive off.

The way I spent my Sunday mornings has changed dramatically since the bypass surgery two years ago: I wake up around six o'clock, walk my usual two miles; then work for a few minutes with five-pound weights: an exercise which supposedly will make my heart muscle stronger. It's not any different this Sunday. The phone rings in the middle of my shaving.

"Good morning!" I say placing aside the razor.

"Good morning, Grigory, Bill Stubbs here. I completely forgot at what time you were supposed to be at my house; I'm sure it's not in the afternoon, because, as you probably are aware, I always spend my Sunday afternoon getting ready for the next week, and that could take a few hours: everything I do nowadays I do very slow..."

"I don't recall promising anything," I say drying my face with a towel, "but I guess I can spend a couple of hours in the company of an old drunk."

"You can fix yourself a "Bloody Mary" – it's still breakfast time."

Half an hour later I knock on his door and let myself in.

Bill is already in his armchair, with a glass of orange juice in one hand and a cell phone in the other; catching sight of me, he puts the glass on the portable table and says, "The world is running away from me at the speed of light, and there is not one damned thing I can do about that!"

"You're not alone, believe me," I admit.

"Fix yourself a "Bloody Mary", he says. "I bought some tomato juice last week."

While I am in the kitchen, he turns on the TV.

"I keep thinking about the character in your story, Grigory," he says as I occupy the chair next to the window, "the one who becomes so afraid of his confessions to the KGB Major, that he suddenly dies in the middle of the day," a short pause to stabilize his breathing, "He was a very young man, thirty or so..."

"It happens," I say. "His previous life had expired and he didn't know how to start a new one..."

"Dorothy usually calls me before noon on Sunday," he interrupts. "It's been like that since my Frances died, but not today. I wander if something happened to her." Dorothy is Bill's daughter, a retired schoolteacher who finally enjoys her life after thirty years of hard, ungrateful work.

"It's not even eleven," I calm him down. "She's got time."

"Before noon usually," repeats Bill, as if I missed this part of the sentence. "It always pleasantly surprises me. As you know, she's been a single woman for some time, and I am glad that my company could make her existence more bearable. Even though we disagree on a few things, we get along pretty darn good. She's had some bad luck with men, because she's too honest, too forgiving. Honesty and forgiveness are less and less desirable in today's world, don't you agree, Grigory? In my day that was the way of life...not anymore, I guess."

"She seems to be quite satisfied with her

retirement," I feel obligated to say something. "And – who knows – maybe this is how she wants to live her life: free and independent. After all, it's not easy to adjust yourself to someone else's habits when you're over sixty."

He doesn't respond to this, clicks through a few TV channels, surprised by the speed with which one picture replaces another. From the outside he looks like a five-year-old kid who is left alone in the house and for whom everything is as though for the first time: remote control, TV, strange figures, strange language – the whole world around him. Finally, he finds the right channel, and we watch a baseball game for a while. It's so quiet in Bill's house that even the familiar commentator's voice sounds alien.

"I understand," he says as soon as the commercial comes up, "it's her own life and she is probably visiting one of her colleagues or went to a movie theater... It's her own life, I understand," he keeps repeating the same sentence, which shows how unsure he is of his reasoning, "but it's almost midday," he turns the TV off and adds angrily, "Her forgetfulness is unforgivable! She is my daughter, for God's sake!"

His sudden anger is rather unusual.

"Listen to yourself," I say. "Just a minute ago she was a perfect daughter – and suddenly she is a betrayer, who deserves to be punished... And then again: why are you so sure that she enjoys your company? You're not the easiest man to be around..."

"Talking about yourself, Grigory?"

"Oh no, I usually have a reason: chess, for example, but mostly free booze."

He laughs weakly. "I was afraid you'd say that."

"You should get used to the thought that old age is pretty much a lonely existence."

"Not in my case, no sir!" he disagrees. "Call it luck, but all my kids and grandkids enjoy being around me. Take Terry, Dorothy's son: he drops by every time he is in the area, and not just for a minute; sometimes, he ends up

spending an hour with me, talking about his new business, asking for advice..."

"Well, that's good to know!"

"And money - yes! But I never charge him any interest and always give him as much time as he needs to pay back the principal!"

I let his remark go and finish my drink.

Our conversation took an undesirable path, and just to put an end to it, he dials Dorothy's number, gets a message and dials the number again. This time she answers the phone and they talk for a while. All I hear are short phrases, which make very little sense. Suddenly a grimace distorts Bill's wrinkled face.

"Whose birthday, Lisa's?"

Lisa is Terry's wife, also a schoolteacher. Unfortunately, I cannot hear Dorothy's answer; I leave the room to boil some water for coffee. What's obvious is the fact that today is Lisa's birthday and Bill wasn't invited. I hope I missed something, because this kind of news might easily destroy Bill's theory about luck forever. I come back with my coffee, ask: "So, how's Dorothy? I hope..."

"Strange," Bill interrupts impatiently, "they were in my house on Thursday, Terry and Lisa... they could've reminded me...very strange and very confusing, because I never intrude upon..."

"How about we finish yesterday's game, old timer?" I offer. "Your last few moves were somewhat unpredictable, and, to tell you the truth, pushed me off my comfortable path a bit..."

"If I am a burden to them," continues Bill ignoring my proposal, "they should've told me long time ago. I am a grown man, I would've understood... But they didn't!" he raises his voice and falls silent. His face is white; his frail chest is moving up and down with dangerous speed.

"You want to hear my opinion?" I ask casually, afraid that this sudden agitation could simply kill the old man. "Don't take it seriously! To reason soberly: what happened? They forgot to invite you to Lisa's birthday...alright, they didn't forget, the decision was well-considered. So what! Maybe they decided to give you some rest on Sunday. You are assuming the worst..."

"They were in my house on Thursday, Grigory, not a month ago!" he speaks much slower than usual. "Concerning Dorothy: I called her this morning and asked her to help me with my recycling: I missed last week's pick-up time. And she readily agreed... but not a word about the upcoming birthday!"

Now I am really worried, but prefer to keep quiet, sip my coffee, and look outside the window: almost midday, hot, birds twittering in the roadside orange trees. Truthfully, I don't feel that today's incident could be a real danger, real death.

"It's peaceful and sad in my soul, Grigory," says Bill and pauses as though demanding my attention. "Peaceful - because I lived a long and productive life, raised my kids hopefully the right way, loved my two wives. I was at war but I was an engineer so I didn't kill anybody, and the shadow of guilt doesn't wake me up in the middle of the night," he pauses again in order to accumulate enough strength for the next sentence. "I could've been a better husband and a better father I presume, but that, unfortunately, cannot be changed. Sad...sad – because I suddenly realize that this world can easily survive without my stupid neatness, crumpled thoughts and laughable confidence that I am needed by all my relatives..."

"That's a very frivolous assumption, sir!"

"My life has just expired, Grigory, and it's too late for me to even think of a new one," another pause, now to suppress his tears. "Why don't you fix me a scotch, my friend? I know, it's too early for that and probably not wise, but I'm willing to make an exception. Fix one for yourself, too – a milder one that is," his laugh is still weak, but I feel relieved nonetheless.

"Three pieces of ice as usual?" I ask standing up.

"Neat this time: you die only twice, right?"

"No argument here, old timer!"

"And get me a few slices of cheese: my stomach might not agree with an early drink without food."

In the kitchen I mix two drinks, slice the cheese and think: never before has he allowed himself a scotch in the middle of the day, not even when he was much younger, and never before without ice...

I run back into the living-room, but too late unfortunately: his hands lie peacefully on his knees, his body is straight, but his head is thrown back and it seems that he just fell asleep with his mouth open, in a manner of an idiot; he was probably trying to write me a note but didn't have enough time – his pencil is on the floor, same as his notebook.

"What a pity," I think and dial 9-1-1.

About the Author:

Lazarus J. Trubman came to America as a political refugee from a small town in the ancient land of Transylvania, which for years had been forcefully attached to the Soviet Empire, after experiencing firsthand the hospitality of the Committee of State Security, KGB in common parlance. After obtaining degree in philology and linguistics, he worked as a critic for a literary magazine and later taught literature and writing at a local college. In 1990, after three unsuccessful attempts, he finally boarded the shiny Boeing-747 bounded for New York. He settled in Tucson, Arizona, where for 25 years he taught languages and Russian literature. In 2016, after retiring from teaching, he moved to North Carolina to dedicate the rest of his time to writing.

Lazar J. Trubman has been writing professionally since 1983, publishing – when allowed by the censorship - two collections of short stories and a novel "It Won't Hurt". Another novel, "Adaptation to the Past", had been published in 2012.

Married, three grown children.

I COULD ONLY HEAR HER SILENCE

by Juanita Tovar Mutis

She failed me, failed our fate, failed the memories we could have built together. She stopped. Stopped replying, looking for me, meeting me. She paused the flow of emotions that ignited our connection.

#

I was laying down late at night, watching cars' lights come and go, filling the room with moving silhouettes. I texted you. I knew from the clues you left on social media and through one of your articles published online, that you were not well. I told you what I tell almost no-one. 'I really care about you.' I meant it. I was ready to be there for you, to hold you if you needed me. I was committed to give you my all, my time, my thoughts, my affection.

I pushed on the blue button, confidently, without anxiety. I did it as I remembered the last time we had been together. How your shoulders descended whenever I spoke. The way your eyes widened and your lips revealed a smile when you told me about your recent trip to Paris.

I recalled that after I told you I had recently lost someone, you put your hand over mine and opened your arms so I could meet your embrace.

Snapshots of the moments in which I enunciated my sins to you calmly, completely unafraid to reveal truths that could destroy my relationship, my stability, my life, came to mind. They reminded me how unburdening my secrets made me feel closer to you.

How it made me think that when you said, typed, rolled your tongue to the sound of the words 'I L-O-V-E Y-O-U,' you really meant them.

I saw myself falling, peacefully descending to the realm of dreams, feeling the warmth that our memories would elicit in my body, resting reassured of the connection that we shared.

#

She didn't answer. Hours, days, and weeks started to hit me, slap me on the face, hard.

I kept on looking at my phone. There was nothing. She had vanished. She kept on acting as if we had never happened. As if those quiet afternoons filled with uninhibited laughter needed to be erased. As if the dinners in which we sat raw and emotionally naked in front of each other needed to be wiped from my memory.

I could only hear her silence. It was loud, deafening. Pressing. It made my throat tighten, my teeth clench.

#

I went through the motions.

First there was *bewilderment*. My hands pressing on my phone, eyebrows rising when I would wake up to find no written trace of you.

Eyes not wanting to look, sight avoiding the Instagram page that narrated your everyday life. Feelings being puzzled by the big white smile you revealed on your pictures, the colorful places you visited, and the dark, grotesque humor you expressed on your captions. I did not want to look. I didn't want to listen to the inner thoughts that pierced and damaged me. They were approaching, pulsing through, slowly filling my mind.

Time kept on flowing, on hurting me with its passing of seconds, hours, and days.

Then *sadness* rushed through.

I first felt it while sitting on the subway. I was going to meet with your boyfriend. He had a professional opportunity I wanted to take, to seize. I kept on seeing the stops passing by. The car full of faces, began to close in on me. I looked down, trying to breath slowly, catching my breath. A pressure in my chest began to build. My nails now were tightly pressing, closing in on my thighs. That didn't work. Their voices became too loud, too quickly. The pressure of their shoulders against mine intensified, it felt aggressive. Now with my feet tapping on the floor, I closed my eyes, tightening my grip on the subway pole that grounded me. I kept on thinking: you just gotta endure three...two...one more stop.

The sun came down after the meeting. I could not hold it in any more. It needed to be released, to flood and overwhelm my mind. To rush in and empty me.

I called Karl and told him "I need to not be home, I need to take the night and take it all in, I have to get drunk. I must drown my mind with anything that comes my way. I have to figure out what I'm feeling."

And so we did. We sat in a dark room. His face lightly touched by the entrance's fluorescent light. Face to face we drank. Our eyes meeting only when the woman singing in the background stopped. Glances locking on each other in between her breaths and in those moments the saxophone filled in her silence.

I kept on talking. Couldn't seem to stop. Fast, quickly. So as not to catch too much breath. Talking to understand, to grieve, to flush the stream of feelings that had been confined within me.

Emotions fell down my cheekbones. Made my throat tighten, my face press up against the inner space of his shoulders: to hide my flushed cheeks, absorb my tears, and shield me from my own sadness.

Now there's *anger*. I feel it ebbing, rubbing up against me. It comes, it goes, in cycles, at night, in the morning. I could feel it flaming up my chest after your name lit up on my inbox.

I know it will be gone. Eventually, in time. I need to accept it. I have to gather the patience, the strength so I can bare to watch it disintegrate slowly, unfold right before my eyes.

About the Author:

Juanita Tovar is an emerging creative nonfiction writer with only a small scattering of published pieces. She currently writes for Spoiled NYC and acts as the creative director of their art department. Juanita is from Colombia and has lived in New York City since 2014.

MYSTERIES OF ENGLISH CLASS: GANESH

by Gregg Williard

Today's ESL class is a YouTube video of "How Ganesh Got an Elephant Head." There are dozens of versions of the story from the Ramayana, Mahabharata and other sources, many as cartoons or opera. We settle on a live-action one in Hindi with English subtitles. Most of the Bhutanese students say they understand the Hindi, but I'm not sure. Some of them know the story, but many seem mystified by it. This one looks like it is from the 1970's, in low-budget Bollywood style.

Queen Parvati, wife of Lord Krishna, is at home in their temple, a grungy fiberglass or papier Mache cave with fake snow on the ground. Everyone walks barefoot through it, and it clings to their feet in Styrofoam bits. Parvati is pining tearfully for her lost, or never was, son. She squeezes together the clay-like green turmeric skin paste she's been applying to her arms and molds a human form. Gradually it becomes a little boy. When she hesitates, a plaintive voice from within the lumpy figure urges her on, (translated as, "Please, innate me!"). In an animated Shazam flash, Parvati innates, and the statue, like Pinocchio, becomes a real boy. A pudgy, pouty boy who already looks spoiled rotten. She christens him Ganesh and caresses and kisses him with an ardor that looks more than a little weird. She commands him to guard the house and turn away everyone while she takes her bath. Lord

Krishna returns home and is barred from his own house by the boy Ganesh. Krishna is furious and cuts off the boy's head. Parvati is grief stricken, and commands Krishna to restore the head and bring her son back to life. Krishna says he cannot recover the head "because it is flying into space." Parvati's expression darkens and she's lit in a bright, menstrual-red light. She grows into a wind-and lightning swept giantess and glowers down at the cowering men, snarling that they will bring Ganesh back to life, or face her wrath. The terrified Krishna barks at his minions to bring the head of the first being they find on the road. The first creature they find is an elephant. They attach the elephant head on the boy's body and bring him back to life, endowed with special powers to overcome all obstacles.

What fascinates me is the Ganesh head "effect:" really just a small pink rubber mask with a little curling trunk that they deliver on a plate under a little towel. It recalls the rubber oxygen masks that bomber or jet pilots wore in the war movies and war comics of my boyhood. I was transfixed by these masks, with their ribbed oxygen hoses dangling, and the almost prosthetic hug from multiple straps. I owned several masks, purchased from army surplus stores with money I made mowing lawns. Over my face the masks smelled of mildew, mothballs, and, I imagined, heroic and terrified fighter-pilot sweat. Long lost child-hood memories opened up, vistas of strange, fugue-like playacting spells: I am a fighter pilot, flying a World War II prop plane or Korean War jet, sitting alone in my room in my cockpit, scanning the ceiling skies for enemy planes, eyes narrowed and darting over the menacing clouds around my bed. I see my face—eyes and forehead at least-- as depicted by two of my favorite comics artists, the penciler-inker team of Ross Andru and Mike Esposito in the pages of *Star Spangled War Stories*. They had a distinctive style for rendering the pilot's eyes that seemed oddly feminine. (The artists were also renowned for their work on the 1960's *Wonder Woman*, where the feminized men and masculinized women resonated with the role-reversal stories). In depictions of boy-men jet pilots in combat, they showed a wonderful attention to wiggling beads of sweat working across anxious foreheads, and a hint of grime (combat dirt? powder burns?) suggested by cross-hatching across the (always pink) skin. These details on my face, I remember, needed to be indicated to myself with sound-effects: cross-hatching sounded like a rapid *"cickachickachickachika"* and the sweat with a hectic *"buhbuhbuhbuhbuhbuhbuh."* These sounds mingled with the ambient drone or puffs of air blown into the mask to simulate subsonic or supersonic flight, with periodic and snappy exchanges with my wingman about bogeys, Zeros, Migs or escorts closing in, at seven o'clock, or twelve o'clock, or whenever/wherever, high, authentically muffled and guttural under the khaki-gray or black rubber embrace. As the story of Ganesh unfolded on the classroom computer screen I fell deeper into the newly awakened memories. In that play, time seemed to expand into a war game beyond dog fights, bullet-drilled Plexiglas, flame-outs, ejector seats, crash landings or much of anything, really. Only the whine of the engines, and the whistling air outside the canopy. And the kind giant sky. It must have been autohypnosis, some state of self-sedation or disassociation that was the real point of the whole game. Escape and safety behind a mask,

in an empty sky arcade, gazing out with expectant eyes. Girl's eyes.

The students begin talking together in feverish Nepali. I think that the story has aroused in them some powerful memories, different than mine but urgent. I call on one of the more fluent English speakers, Puspa, to help me understand. After a hard day of farming, I ask, did they tell each other this and other Hindu stories, gathered around a campfire, or hearth, or something? Was there singing and dancing, maybe even masks? (Prior to class, in a desperation of lesson planning—or the absence of it—I had entered a search on "Ganesh and boredom," and was rewarded with a link to Odissi: Ganesh Vandana: "...the oldest surviving dance form of India...a treatise not just for the eyes, but for the ears and heart as well! The various Bhangas, or stances, will pierce vials of energy in your soul and will leave you enthusiastic for the rest of your life!" I tremble inside to the promise of a "treatise" for my eyes and ears and heart, of my soul being pierced with vials of energy and enthusiasm for the rest of my life. It is what I keep searching for with anxious eyes over a mask. Innate me).

Puspa translates my questions, and their answers come after lengthy cross-exchanges and haggling. No, no, they never told these stories. Some of them had heard something about an elephant, but they never got together and told stories, or told anything. They were tired and wanted to be left alone. They ate dinner and listened to the radio. Some people had a tv. Then they went to bed. One of the students, Chandra, is shaking his head vehemently and laughing. Puspa explains that he says he is a Christian and doesn't pay attention to that Hindu stuff. Chandra goes on in Nepali with an intense-sounding story full of yanking and tugging motions, hands gripping the air as if wrestling snakes, and his own furrowed and anxious brow over bright searching eyes. At the end of his story the other students gasp, and some explode in laughter. I imagine some culture collision of Jesus and Vishnu, a battle royale of Vedic axes and astra tridents clanging and sparking against The Cross. Over more shouting and laughter Puspa says it is hard to translate, and he will try to explain later.

After class is over and the other students have left Puspa leans in close to me and blushes. In a low voice he says that Chandra's words were a little rude. "Don't worry about me, Puspa," I say. "I'm not Christian, or Hindu, or Buddhist or anything. Whatever he thinks about religion…"

"No, no teacher. It's about Ganesh. His nose."

"The trunk?"

"Trunk?"

I mime the trunk.

"Yes. The Ganesh trunk. Chandra says the nose trunk is like his thing."

"His thing."

Puspa mimes his penis.

"Penis."

"Yes. Chandra says his penis is like the trunk of Ganesh. Hanging down." Puspa mimes a flaccid penis, his mouth making a matching droop.

I nod solemnly, intrigued by the association. Puspa elaborates: "Chandra also told us about how his penis gets tangled up, like a shoelace, and he can't pee. Like a garden hose that has… doesn't let the water go."

"Yes. 'Kinked.'"

It is Puspa's turn to nod, closing his eyes and savoring the new word like a sip of the fresh chai he often brings me in a thermos emblazoned with Bucky Badger, the U.W. mascot he thought was a squirrel.

"Kinked. Yes."

Mysteries of English Class: Ganesh

About the Author:

Gregg Williard grew up in Columbus, Ohio. He attended the Columbus College of Art and Design, The New York Studio School and the State University of New York. His writing and visual art have been published, most recently, in Muse/A, Raleigh Review, 34th Parallel and Riddled With Arrows. His illustrated short stories appear as a monthly feature, "Williard World" in X-R-A-Y Journal, and he produces the radio show, "Fiction Jones" on WORT community radio (wortfm.org), reading unabridged 19th Century Russian novels live on the air. He teaches ESL to refugees in Madison, Wisconsin.

THE CHIPPED-TOOTHED HEART

by LaDonna Friesen

I pushed a button, and the rear van door beeped like a pulse. It felt hot enough inside it to be a heart. I loaded a couple cloth bags of organic groceries, one eye casually on the peripheral scene.

Behind me, a man with legs like a safari giraffe took one step for everyone else's three. His long neck slanted forward, stretching for a fallen leaf from a tree, a dollar bill riding on the wind toward a pocket of his frayed jean shorts. He had nothing in his hands but his own fingers, long-thin and bent, swinging his stride across the parking lot.

An Amish-Mennonite family rounded the corner of the van, and I tensed in my sleeveless top and black knit capris. I had stopped by the store after running two miles at the university gym. Compared to their handmade long sleeves and dresses, my upper arms were bare as the moon. At least my shirt was loose enough to let in some breeze. I slowly rolled my cart toward them with a gentle nod, and the wife pressed a quarter in my hand. We were at Aldi's, the only place where money passes benignly in a grocery lot.

A rusty maroon van was parked right next to mine with the window open. I reached up to pull down the hatch of my van when a woman leaned out. "Can I ask you a question?"

She was still in the driver seat, and I was in the back of the van. I didn't move. "What do you need?"

She shifted her body so that she could fully see me, and I saw an envelope with a list of tallied figures in one hand, a pencil in the other. Nothing to fear yet. In the window portrait, I could see the collar and rounded sleeves of a cotton dress with pastel flowers, the material soft-looking from too many washes. Her skin had sweated the folded collar a light brown.

"Well, I'm lookin' at this list and trying to decide what I can cross off. If I had three more dollars, I think I could get the vegetable shortnin' this man wants. Do you know if they sell only the big cans of vegetable shortning'? Do they sell the small cans? If they have the small cans, I think I'd have enough."

Never in my life had I bought that stuff. Depending on the brand, shortening uses fully hydrogenated oils, nothing like the organic extra virgin olive oil in my van.

I shook my head. Once when I was a child, my brother had given me a spoonful of white shortening and told me it was ice cream. It looked like a cloud on a spoon. Now, in the heat, I fumbled with the memory of spitting the stuff into the sink and using my tongue and saliva all night to un-coat my mouth. It was a rotten milky introduction to the other side of Eden.

The woman looked perplexed but not desperate. Her voice was an old melody, sweet and distantly familiar, almost motherly. "Well," she said, "I'm gettin' groceries for two shut-ins down Mt. Vernon way. One of 'em is 92. He tells stories of livin' on a can of beans for a week. He's full of weeks like that." She looked at her list again, some items with a line through them. "I just don't know what more to cross out."

I would rather people ask me for money than steal it, although she didn't look like the crook-fingered way we imagine the stealing type. Her gray-brown hair was in a frosted cinnamon bun, and she had a half gallon, chipped-tooth smile. Still, I kept to the back of my van.

"I don't think I have any cash, but I might have some change."

She looked away from her list at me again. "I think most people are like that anymore...just plastic."

I pulled my rectangular black wallet from my purse and unzipped it.

Her face jerked away. "I'm glad you didn't pull a gun on me."

My fingers stopped clinking coins, and I studied her, a little muddled. No one had said that to me before. Like averting shortening, I had never held a gun in my life. I can't even play a character with a gun on Super Smash Bros. But looking down at the black rectangle, I could see how fear might turn a black wallet into a death piece. I had read an article about an officer who shot because he thought the victim's phone was a shooter.

Maybe if the woman had seen my organic groceries in the back of a white decade-old mini-van, she wouldn't have suspected something. Or maybe I was just scaring everyone in my workout clothes.

My fingers scooped four quarters. "I have a dollar in change if it'll help."

She pressed the envelope into the steering wheel. "Well, it would sure be a blessing."

I took one step and held my arm out like I was reaching for a fist bump. She stretched hers

from the window, and here we met, two women with their arms lingering like Michelangelo's God and Adam, bodies separated in vulnerable space, fingers curved by the gravity of trust. My fist opened just above her palm and freed itself of four heads and tails, four bits of nothing but a partial can of shortening. Another innocent change of money—no weeds, just dough.

"Thank ya. God bless ya." Her eyes were like suns that found a few quarters to shine on. She smile-hummed her arm back into the van and turned to her ragged envelope of numbers.

I closed the hatch to her whisper, "I still gotta find two more dollars."

I don't know what she spent her dollar on, but I wish I'd had two more to give her. I only thought after that I could have gone with her in the store and paid for the shortening with a credit card, redeeming my brother's trick and helping the 92-year-old. But my fingers had curved inward again, slouching to my core.

When I got home, the back van door re-opened its beeping heart. Mine echoed when I saw my neighbor pulling the cord of a silent mower. She wasn't 92, but her lawn might be starting a new safari. Later, I leaned forward like a giraffe and pushed a mower until her grass shredded its life and stuck to my perspiring skin. I looked down at greened arms, more organic than olive oil.

About the Author:

I changed my major to English when a college professor helped me discover that writing and literature offer us layers of meaning about the human condition. Since then, I find stories and poems every day. I earned my M.A. in English and have served as a full-time English professor for 13 years, teaching literature and writing courses. Currently, I teach at Evangel University in Springfield, MO.

NACHES

by Jeffrey Loeb

West of the city the river road beckoned, all soft oak-leaves and ripening corn. It struck me as a place for reflection, so on impulse I cut north off the Interstate, over the state line. I'd cross back at the Leavenworth Bridge. Cracks in the worn asphalt boomed under my tires. The curvy highway, I knew, had started as hard-packed ruts worn 150 years before by the wa—gons of small farmers. It had also been used furtively, at night, by runaway slaves, because it afforded them access to the Missouri River sandbars.

I was teaching circuit-rider English that year at half-a-dozen colleges and universities, so the temporary job I was headed to was familiar. What wasn't familiar—and what I wanted to think about while I drove—was the students: federal prisoners taking courses on the inside. My actual paycheck came from St. Mary College of Leavenworth, but beyond the interview, with the first nun I'd knowingly talked to in twenty years, I'd been left pretty much on my own. While this arrangement let me evade supervision, I'd also had to invent my own curriculum.

The students—the inmates—were in the last semester or two before receiving their BA's. Given what I was to find out about the vagaries of prison life, especially at a maximum-security facility like Leavenworth, for a prisoner to reach this level was an enormous achievement. The average sentence was eighteen years, and the only way a man arrived there was to have screwed up somewhere else in the system. On top of that, in federal prisons, convicts served their entire sentences. No parole. Yet somehow, in this utterly demoralizing situation, these students, cramped by bunkmates and open toilets, had mustered the fortitude to amass over a hundred college hours.

I'd learned most of this while going through a standard orientation for anyone with business inside, from day workers to delivery people to teachers. The process had several steps, all evolved from keeping people at close rein: blood and urine tests, done at a windowless building near the prison; followed by an interview with a doctor whose thoughts were elsewhere (stirring only briefly at spotting traces of my back medication, but quickly sinking back into lethargy and signing the necessary forms); and a lecture from a uniformed, stone-faced guard who shared the following bit of wisdom: "Every one of these men has a con, and they're going to try it on you. Whatever you do, don't carry any messages for them, and don't accept any phone calls from them. They're smart, and they'll use you in a minute."

The final session had been with the prison librarian (a civilian like me, bearing no resemblance to the trustee rolling his cart from cell to cell in that year's big prison movie *Shawshank Redemption*), who took me through a subbasement housing books in order to design my curriculum. While we were descending into this morgue, he'd informed me that most prisoners had their tuition paid through Pell Grants since technically, however much some had profited from their crimes, they had only minimal income and had long since forfeited their locatable assets. He'd also told me there was only one rule about books: If there were enough copies of something on hand, I could teach it. I found stacks of them, loaded into dusty, deteriorating cardboard boxes, and began looking for what would consume me for the next three months. When I'd broken everything out, it was apparent I was pretty limited: an anthology for poetry and short stories, the play *A Streetcar Named Desire*, and a few novels. I decided on *Huckleberry Finn*, *Light in August*, and *Beloved*, largely because all three had been taught to me at some point. I had eighteen students, with three-hour classes meeting four evenings a week.

As I crafted my focus during May, two thoughts unsettled me: All three novels were about the debilitating effects of race in America; and, from what I knew of prisons, virtually all the inmates were going to be black or Hispanic, meaning each man was probably going to feel like he'd gotten a series of raw deals based on skin color. The closer the date grew, the more disturbing this thought became, and no matter how much preparation I did—re-reading all the books, studying critical opinions, making lengthy notes, and designing paper and test questions—visions of prison riots, with my poor, white body crumpled in a corner somewhere, wouldn't stop haunting me. These still played over the edges of my consciousness as I marked the turns of the river road that first night.

It took about an hour. As I drove by Leavenworth's dejected downtown and past the fort, my thoughts grew more unsettled. I'd sent word that the students should read a chunk of *Huckleberry Finn* for opening night. My anxieties seemed to come down to how to begin things. I'd convinced myself that the poisoned theme of race could somehow be handled if I just could put everything in context.

I pulled into the prison, its massive stone walls two stories high and turrets at each corner, automatic weapons clearly visible; in this case, it was exactly like the movies. The process for entering was lengthy, and I'd been warned to come an hour early. Most of this time was spent just waiting, waiting for enough visitors to show up so we could be searched together and processed through to another room, waiting there to be equipped with body alarms, and yet more waiting in a third room to be escorted by guards without weapons to take us through the final locked doors into the prison itself.

In the last cold antechamber, four of us sat silently with our own musings. It was impossible not to notice the reddish skin and long, braided hair of the other three. When they leaned together for a whispered confab, I heard the name "Peltier" and was reminded what "maximum security" meant. My brooding grew as the minutes multiplied, my mind returning to the class opening; everything would be fine if I could only solve that. No matter how much I massaged the words, I came up with nothing.

Eventually, my thoughts wandered to another situation I'd experienced with jails, one from twenty years before, back in the small Kansas town I came from. It must have entered my mind's eye with the bars and stone, or maybe because the night in Junction City I was thinking about, like my interview for this job, had involved a nun. It had been a humiliating incident, and, probably because of that, I hadn't thought of it in years. Suddenly though the whole memory came flooding in.

It was 1974. I'd been visiting from Boston, more like fleeing because things were a disaster back East. The sense of possibility I'd grown up with had long since disappeared. The country was mired in the long, dreary Nixon recession following the Arab oil embargo. With my lofty BA in English, I could command only sporadic jobs: waiting tables, carpentering, occasional substitute teaching. Also my marriage was rapidly coming unraveled; that was probably really what I was running from, and the drugs and drinking made it all worse. Thinking back during the flight to Kansas, in fact, I could only locate failed relationships and bad decisions, starting probably from when I'd dropped out of college and gone into the Marine Corps some seven years before.

There, in Junction City, I went with some friends to a club on the fringes of town, near the edge of Fort Riley, where one could easily find other essentially directionless people, mostly soldiers trapped in the crumbling post-Viet Nam army. When, somewhere around two in the morning, my driver decided to leave, I stayed. I have no idea why, but the coke I'd greedily snorted and the deluded promise of an alcohol-ridden night-without-end certainly figured in. Of course, this left me with no ride. As it happened, I'd known the club manager at St. Xavier High School from several years before; in my freshman year—his senior one—he'd gotten kicked out and promptly joined the navy, eventually earning himself a bad-conduct discharge. Now, he had grown into a thoroughly disreputable, 300-pound behemoth sporting ribald tattoos the length of his body. His name was Steve Rathbun, so naturally he was called Ratbone. He'd also previously been married to my cousin, Sheila—twice according to some accounts. So, on the basis of these multiple, if tenuous, connections, he agreed to give me a lift after he closed, somewhere around four in the morning.

We sped through deep night down a broad, lighted boulevard, the only car in sight, on into town past shoddy trailer courts—anyone above the rank of E-5 who lived off-base had fled to nearby Manhattan, with its college and veneer of class utterly lacking in Junction. Suddenly, Ratbone, a victim of his impulses even on good days, veered off the road and onto a gravel drive. He braked to a halt in front of one of the mobile homes, dust swirling in the green mercury-vapor lights. Moving lithely for all his weight, Ratbone leaped from the still-rocking

car, leaving the driver's door swinging open, raced over to the trailer, and kicked in the door. In my stupor, I sat gaping at the square of yellow light. Shortly, I heard shouting inside and jumped out myself. Stumbling up the rickety porch steps and on into the living room, I saw two small children sitting up on a dirty vinyl couch, wide-eyed and blinking, clearly just awakened, with only a thin blanket covering them. The shouting was louder—mostly threats and profanity—but mixed with sounds of a struggle. I turned back toward the noise, which seemed to come from the right, and as I rounded the first corner, I ran head-on into none other than Sheila herself. She leapt back and shrieked, "Jeff," as surprised as I was but with a firmer sense of purpose: "I'm calling the cops. You better get."

And with that she bolted past me toward the kids. I edged cautiously down the dark hall, toward the rear, the shouting growing more intense. In the back room, I nearly stumbled over a thrashing tangle of bodies. When my eyes adjusted, I made out a nude, heavily muscled man squatting on top of a squirming Ratbone pointing a military .45 at his head. Ratbone, supine body covering most of the open floor space, looked for all the world like a turtle on his back but—against all logic—was yelling: "Let me up, motherfucker. I'm gonna kill you."

Suddenly spotting me, the naked man swung the pistol so it was pointed directly between my eyes. Ratbone continued struggling, but I caught in a glance that he was firmly pinned, a hand to his throat. What I mostly saw, though, was the maw of the pistol's opening. It looked like a howitzer. I tried backing out of the room, but the man halted me with a shout. All three of us remained that way, Ratbone locked to the floor, wriggling and screaming profanities, until the police arrived and hauled the two of us off.

At the station, Ratbone was immediately thrown into the tank, but, thanks to Sheila's providing the police some hurried absolution for me, my status was a bit more uncertain. I was left moldering in a locked, dusty office. Finally, after about an hour, with daylight now beginning to stream through the smudged, filmy windows, a policeman entered. I knew him, a local named Haley. He was a few years older than me. I remembered he'd gone into the Navy just out of high school, at the very beginning of Viet Nam, but had only lasted a few months. I also recalled his bragging about wetting his pants to get out.

He carefully placed his clipboard facedown on the desk, then slowly dragged a gunmetal chair over. He plopped down in it backwards and stared at me for a long time. A cop's studied gesture, I thought, something they probably taught in their two-week training academy. Haley had always possessed an unusual combination of superiority and stupidity, something I remembered when he finally opened his mouth. Like Ratbone, he spoke unadulterated Junction City, equal parts black and Southern white, a verbal mix strewn from the leavings of impoverished enlistees stretching back to Custer: "What you doin' here, Jeff, round bad people like that? Thought you was in college or something."

"Just visiting, Don, just visiting."

"Breakin' in, though? Assault? Even a smart college boy could get his ass shot."

"Yeah, I know, Don. I was there, remember?"

I wasn't going to give him a thing. I had absolutely no respect for him. After all, I'd actually gone to Viet Nam. As he proceeded to lecture me about the direction of my life, basic how-did-a-nice-kid-like-you stuff, I paid scant attention to the words themselves. I knew though what he was getting at was completely true. Life had become a disaster; all my accomplishments—class president every year, Catholic Youth Organization president, co-captain of the football team, honor-roll—had come to nothing. And my sitting here watching the sun come up in a filthy holding room in Junction City, Kansas, listening to a dolt like Haley lecture me was an absolute symbol of that waste.

Of course, they had no reason to hold me, and Haley's sense of gratification, like his attention span, was fleeting. After a suitable time I was released into the rapidly warming 6:00 a.m. air to find my way home to my parents' house. Having no other choice, I took off walking, following approximately the same route that I'd taken to and from school years before. Fatigue was setting in, and a distinct pounding had begun in one of my temples.

Within a few blocks I passed the Catholic convent, where the nuns lived. I sat down on a small stone wall across the street and smoked the last cigarette in my crumpled pack, brooding over Haley's comments. Suddenly, I realized Sister Mary John was probably inside. I thought about her for a while, the cigarette growing shorter. She'd been the only teacher who'd really ever gotten through to me. I'd had several who'd caused fear, mostly by the routine slapping and hitting. And I'd had my fair share of martinets who conveyed what the book said and left no room for questions.

I finished my cigarette. The throbbing was now a full-fledged headache. Then—I still don't know why—I got up and walked across the street and knocked on the door. After a few moments, a nun answered, smallish, wizened, spectacled, just like I'd remembered nuns looking from first grade on. I asked if Sister Mary John were there. She stared at me for a moment and, apparently deciding from my disheveled appearance and the early hour that either resistance was futile or I really needed help, disappeared inside, leaving the door slightly ajar.

When she came back a few minutes later, it was with Sister Mary John. She hadn't changed, it seemed, and she didn't appear as surprised as I would have imagined. Politely, she asked me inside, almost like an invited, late-afternoon visit rather than at six on a Saturday morning. She ushered me into a small study and gestured toward a straight wooden chair, then pulled up one like it, facing me across a small ecumenical-seeming table. I realized in all my twelve years there I'd never been inside the convent and suddenly remembered the crude stories we used to make up about nuns. I felt embarrassed—too late now to do me any good. Sister Mary John fixed me with her blue eyes, and I couldn't help looking down. "What is it, Jeff?" she asked softly. "What's happened to you?"

I looked up at her—she was a large woman, at least as tall and heavy as I was, a size no doubt enhanced by her billowing black-and-white habit—and I remembered her classes from the three years I'd had her: freshman English, sophomore history, and junior English. She'd been direct and purposeful, demanding that we have the reading done on time and assignments finished. While we plodded through a stultifying history text whose Imprimatur ensured that it was essentially a de facto Ministry of Truth for the Catholic Church, Sister Mary John had softened its references to Martin Luther as a heretic and added much-needed context to its descriptions of the Spanish Inquisition as a heroic undertaking.

Sitting there years later on that morning, I couldn't recall her ever raising her voice when someone—I myself, often enough, it seemed—had fallen short. Somehow when she'd spoken in these situations, you'd felt like it was you who'd failed her, and you never wanted to again. I didn't know how she'd created this feel without ever saying the word failure, but I knew it was her capacity to arouse both guilt and introspection that was responsible for my sitting in the Catholic convent in Junction City, Kansas, a useless and thoroughly disheveled twenty-six-year old, at six in the morning. She'd taught me how to write, I realized, and how to read for all practical purposes, two of my only accomplishments; I barely would have touched books after high school if it weren't for her, or known what actual thinking was.

I wouldn't until many years later, well after this meeting, have the political consciousness to understand that there was a particular type of Catholic—Sister Mary John certainly being one

of them—motivated not so much by faith as by a sense of social conscience, and how the Church could help fulfill it. This instinct for justice was, of course, exemplified by JFK, whose shooting was announced in my English class by Sister Mary John herself, fighting tears as she spoke. When 5,000 Marines landed in Da Nang a bit over a year later, an initial wave that was to grow by 100 times, my football coach, an ex-Marine himself, led the cheerleading in our school, and her voice somehow receded. She would have had to experience significant distress watching Kennedy's idealism eroded by Viet Nam, and, I suddenly realized, I knew exactly how she felt about the whole disastrous enterprise.

"I don't know, Sister. It got away from me. I guess I want it back, and I don't know how to get it." I told her some specifics; I can't remember what exactly. We talked for probably an hour; it was summer, so there was no school, but still, nuns had some things to do, I'm sure. To her credit, she didn't offer me religion. I probably wouldn't have been there if she'd been that type. I don't know what, in fact, she offered me; it's been too long ago, but what I do recall—and what I remembered suddenly sitting there in that prison holding room waiting to be led in to the prisoners I was going to teach—is what Sister Mary John told me when I left. Standing in the front doorway of the convent, full sunlight light now bearing down, looking at me straight on, she'd said this: "I always expected more from you than you did from yourself."

Stunned, by those words, and by my own sense of failure, I'd carried them off that front porch and into the ruined day, and then the next one just like it, down all the days, until twenty years later, married, with a child, a college teacher, I found myself sitting there in that prison a few minutes away from beginning an American literature course. The other people were culled from the group, and soon a guard led me in: weighted down by the unfamiliar body alarm, brief case in hand; past the enormous-seeming prisoners walking round and round a huge in-door center turret, like pilgrims at the fountain at Mecca; all glancing momentarily at this puny alien in their territory before choosing with massive dignity to ignore me; and on into the classroom, where my students awaited me.

They were who I thought and feared they'd be: only one was white, all of them clearly worked out daily, and they looked at me as if I were some kind of functionary, barely tolerable but somehow temporarily necessary. Also, though I wouldn't start finding this out for awhile, they had their little cliques and ways of establishing rank, and each of them was a type of con man, though, of course, not one of them was guilty. And I was nervous; I would have been foolish not to be—the guard left the room after depos-iting me, an opaque-glass wall providing scant comfort. I hurriedly wrote my name on the board. Small talk didn't seem to be the kind of thing they'd particularly respect, and the thought of introductions was absurd; we didn't have that much in common.

I turned to face them. They were seated at lunch tables in a long, narrow room, four men to a row all the way back. I took a breath, pro-nounced my name, and started mumbling something about the structure of the course and the requirements—just the kind of thing that you'd tell a college class on the first day, but which I recognized with a sinking feeling carried absolutely no credence with this one. After I'd limped through most of my introduc tion, the realization creeping up on me that exactly what I'd feared about first impressions was happening, Sister Mary John's words sud-denly from somewhere leapt to mind. I located a bit of courage and stopped my frenzied chattering, paused for a second or two looking from man to man, and then repeated an ap-proximation of those same words: "I expect more from you than you do from yourselves."

Shocked at the sudden realization of my utter arrogance, I must have cringed visibly. They didn't know me. And I had absolutely no idea how they regarded themselves. I could instant-ly tell some were taken aback, looking at me differently. But the thing was I'd meant it, and I guess they intuited this because within minutes we'd launched into the novel, and when, with-in a short time, I began reading aloud from the raft scene where Huck apologizes to Jim, I paused momentarily at the word "nigger," one of them sensed my discomfiture and rescued me, the most impressive-looking one of all—huge arms, sculptured body in a tight blue t-shirt, wearing a stocking cap that rimmed a perpetual scowl, and apparently having only one eye left. His name was Galyn Harris, and I later found later he could write like an angel; I still have his papers. He said, "Don't worry, Doc, we know that word." General laughter followed, and with it a sudden sense of drained tension.

It was a contentious class; they argued and disputed, night after night, all the way through *Huckleberry Finn*, and they suffered alongside Faulkner's half-white Joe Christmas in *Light in August*, and eventually beheld Toni Morrison's profound and transcendent reveries in *Be-loved*, together perhaps the most damning trilogy possible of the racial inadequacies this country suffers from. And, despite the heated-ness of their arguments and the depth of their feelings, never once did I feel threatened—and never once did I get a late paper, nor one of them fail a reading quiz.

I detected in many the beginnings of some in-sight that evaluation, rather than reaction, was a valid means of addressing problems. The most perceptive of them, I saw through their papers, actually looked within and discovered how the inevitable anger they had often felt (and most certainly acted on) turned into unre-mitting self-destruction.

Several years later, I got a postcard from one of them, Robert Harris. It read only, "You are missed." Overcome with flattery, I googled his name and found he'd written his own appeal brief to the Supreme Court, where it was denied for exceeding the statute of limitations.

Harris's crime had been rape, classified as federal because he'd taken his victim across state lines. So much for romanticizing convicts; I guessed the guards, after their fashion, had been right.

Still, curiosity, or something, moved me to call St. Mary College, which, I noted, was now a university, whatever that meant. After a couple of barren conversations, I got passed by chance to the guy who'd been in charge of books all those years before. He actually remembered me, he said, but the program was caput: Congress had taken Pell Grants from prisoners. No telling where my students were, probably all still inside somewhere. He himself wasn't at the prison anymore; the college had transferred him to records. So much for that, I thought, hanging up. I didn't actually know why I was even looking for them.

A couple weeks later, I got a letter on St. Mary stationery—one line, no signature: Every single prisoner had graduated.

Even though they knew they'd never see the outside again.

Transferred to records. It rang in my soul like a mantra.

About the Author:

Jeff Loeb is a writer who lives in New York City. In prior lives, he enjoyed long careers as, in roughly this order: US Marine, bartender, construction worker, waiter, truck driver, furniture mover, college teacher, radio reporter (WBAI - D.C. Bureau), assistant city manager, cable television company manager, photography studio owner, farmer/rancher, academic writer, and high-school teacher. He has a PhD in English from the University of Kansas.

GOING HUNTING

by Cynthia Close

We were driving from Boston to my parent's home in New Jersey. Pete had the rifle in the back of the van. It was Thanksgiving and deer season in Jersey. My folks lived on the side of a gravel road in Mine Hill, not the kind of industrial landscape usually associated when anyone mentions New Jersey. There was a densely wooded area behind the house.

My dad, having served as a B17 bomber pilot in WWII, left any interest in weapons of war behind him and never went hunting, but when he met Pete his testosterone level rose. He became interested in hunting equipment. He bought professional hunting bows and a target on a tripod that he set up where the yard met the woods. The bows were huge. It took incredible strength to pull the string back far enough to send the arrow to the target. My younger brother and I humored dad and gave it a try. My brother was no athlete. I can't remember if he managed to hit the target. I certainly couldn't. Mom didn't venture out of the house. She was safely ensconced in the kitchen with the turkey.

Pete, the ex-Marine, served the country late enough to miss Korea and early enough to avoid Vietnam. His natural athleticism was recognized by his superiors who selected him to represent the Marines in the 1600-meter event in the 1960 Olympics in Rome. He effortlessly excelled at anything he tried and this Thanksgiving he wowed the family with his ability to get a bull's-eye every time. Even while downing a few beers, his aim stayed true. After dinner there was still enough light to go hunting. It was doe season. Pete had a special license that permitted hunting doe outside his home state for a limited time. He retrieved the rifle from our van and suggested I join him. Everyone else opted to stay home.

The woods behind the house emerged abruptly at the edge were Dad stopped mowing the grass. Pete gave me a fast track lesson in hunting. He showed me how to walk without making noise; a seemingly impossible task on the crunchy brown oak leaves that blanketed the ground. Then there was the gun. He wanted me to shoot it. I'd never held a gun before. I resisted. Annoyed, he said, "Learn how to use a weapon and you won't be afraid." So heavy, I struggled raising it to my shoulder. He demonstrated how to aim and warned about recoil. His hand supported the barrel while I aimed at a tree. "Pull the trigger slowly!" he commanded. POW! My ears were ringing, and the shock to my shoulder almost knocked me down, but I didn't fall.

"O.K., that's it! I did it once and don't want to shoot again."

It was a beautiful late fall afternoon, and the woods seemed so benign. Pete urged me to stay. Reluctantly I trudged on. We'd been walking cautiously over an hour, pausing occasionally to look and listen. Pete held the gun comfortably across his body. I'd almost forgotten why we were here. The low setting sun sent deep shadows across the leaf-strewn ground. Pete stopped. Not moving. Not speaking. I glanced to my left without turning my head and saw a deer, motionless, about 75 feet away. The delicate creature appeared as a statue, dappled light serving to camouflage its light brown body. It was a doe. At this distance, it was a sure shot for Pete. I was standing to his right. He raised the rifle to his shoulder and took aim. Mindlessly my heart pounded, bursting, without a thought, my arm flew up, propelled by an innate, barely acknowledged sympathy for all living things and pushed the gun straight into the air. BLAM! The deer turned and disappeared. Pete stumbled slightly and turned to me in shocked disbelief. I had yet to absorb my radical act. We walked back to the house in silence. He never took me hunting again.

Fast-forward 45 years. I am now a well-worn woman of 70, no longer married. Irrational confidence has propelled me through decades of living a vibrant life in cities in the U.S. and Europe, pursing careers in the arts and film. I'm comfortably retired in Vermont's largest city which is hardly a city at all. When I told my Boston and Manhattan friends that I would be moving to Vermont to be closer to my grandchildren in Montreal they thought I would shrivel up and die. "You don't drive!" they said in mock horror. And--"you don't ski, or hunt, or know anything about tapping maple trees for syrup." While all that was true, the storied Vermont environmental consciousness and liberal politics (I live two blocks from Bernie Sanders) had a decidedly au courant vibe not unlike the Harvard Square hip in Cambridge where I most recently lived.

Nature remained an abstract concept best admired from afar. I preferred firm concrete under my feet rather than a leaf covered forest floor. I hated camping and the quite dark of a rural road terrified me. I wanted to hear my neighbors night and day to know I was not alone. Now, for the first time in my life, I lived alone. Not only alone, but in a place where nature cannot be denied. The fact this dramatic change was by choice feels both strange and yet inevitable. Perhaps there is something hard wired in our human DNA drawing us back to our primal source as we age – the ashes to ashes, dust to dust scenario. Finding another man to share what's left of my life would be a buffer to aging and I figured this effort would take time.

As things worked out, after a few false alarms, forays into relationships that left me tired and bored, I encountered a man whose life ran parallel to mine on opposite tracks. My new male friend was born into a large, disadvantaged family living in Vermont on the shore of Lake Champlain. I was born in Queens, New York City's most diverse borough. College educated in Boston, I spent most of the 1960's on the streets of that fair city, protesting the Vietnam War. He was the middle child of five kids often left to his own devices, and was drawn to the wildness of his surroundings where he became an expert fisherman in all seasons and learned to hunt, getting his first 6 point buck before he hit puberty. School was less a priority for him so by the time he hit high school the military seemed like a good option. Vietnam undercurrents were roiling the surface of things yet had not broken out in the full-fledged protests that found me in a student takeover of the president's office at Boston University and later found him as a tank commander in the Marine Corps in the jungles of Vietnam. Bearing a Bronze Star for valor after enduring 6 years of intense warfare left my new friend battling PTSD that would not be recognized as an issue until decades after he returned home to bucolic Vermont. Smoking marijuana helped, a habit he picked up in the military. He avoided the more deadly heroin, which he said was rampant throughout the armed forces and most heavily used by those who served on the ground. Ultimately, it was a return to the woods, lakes, and streams of his childhood home where the sounds of the loons over the water on a foggy spring morning helped to drown out the constant ringing of tinnitus that invaded his head along with the nightmares he kept at bay with the comfort knowing his 22 caliber hunting rifle was in reach.

On the day we met, he was driving a white, 350 Super Duty Ford pick-up truck. We had agreed to meet for a getting-to-know-you drink on a cold January afternoon in a Burlington café. That drink stretched into dinner and later, after discovering I did not drive, he offered me a ride home, apologizing that the only vehicle available was a truck, suggesting that Cinderella's coach was more apropos. That afternoon ended hours later in my driveway sitting silently in the dark, side by side high off the ground in the cab of that white truck. He was a charming storyteller, who knew how to use silence. Buoyed by his broad shouldered, cliché handsome Marlboro Man looks, I felt myself tumbling into something that felt suspiciously like love.

Our mutual physical attraction grounded the relationship. His tales of fishing salmon from the rivers of Alaska to the depths of Lake Champlain ignited idyllic memories of fishing with my grandfather in a tiny rowboat off the shore of Long Island Sound where I spent my childhood summers. My new man caught buckets of perch, northern pike, and bass that he cleaned, filleted, and cooked to perfection. He delicately fed me my first perch and I thought I had died and gone to heaven. He had a freezer full of venison. In preparation for the first party he took me to, he engaged me in making a huge pot of venison stew, along with BBQ veni-

son back strap, a frequently requested dish from his circle of friends, most of whom were also hunters and fishermen. It was obvious he was held in high esteem.

We met in winter and by early spring he had cleaned up his favorite rod and reel for me and lured me with enthusiasm on to his boat, where I found myself breathless in the middle of Lake Champlain surrounded by the beauty of the still snow capped Adirondacks on one side and the rolling Green Mountains of Vermont on the other. I nearly fell overboard from excitement when I reeled in my first salmon, a keeper. He documented my catch with his cell phone camera as he now has done with each new achievement while he gradually acquaints me with a world of living and dying creatures beyond the human kind.

During the fall hunting season he took me scouting for deer. He treads lightly on the earth and has always been able to sneak-up and surprise me, even in my own house. I never hear him coming. This skill may have saved his life on the killing fields of Vietnam. He has a bow permit. I'd never seen a professional hunting bow before. Its lethal medieval look reminded me of the movie *Hunger Games*. Just the sight of it lifted the hair on the back of my neck. My nose twitched catching the whiff of fear as it rose from deep within my body. He hit the bulls-eye every time at the range where he had the bow restrung for the upcoming season. I stood watching in awe, my ruffled white blouse in sharp contrast to the camouflage wearing men and their women who at twice my size were better equipped to pull back on that bow and let it rip, as many of them did that afternoon.

After bow season comes rifle and after that black powder. He hunts them all. He has reached his quota every year he has hunted. The evidence hung on the wall above his TV and filled his freezer, feeding him long after the season was over.

His most prized gun is a 22-caliber rifle. A Remington Model 60 originally made by Marlin Firearms Company in New Haven, Connecticut, in continuous production since 1960, reflecting its popularity among hunters since the year it was introduced. He tells me it's the most accurate gun he has ever used. It has a beautifully polished wood grain stock and he demonstrated how to site the target using the barrel-mounted scope. He very carefully showed me the proper way to handle this firearm indicating his respect for an instrument with the capacity to take a life, a power he had relied upon to save his own.

The more I thought about it, the more I was challenged to overcome a life-long fear of guns. I felt protected by this mans love. That love would insulate me from the inevitable political fallout if I revealed my newfound desire to shoot a gun to my liberal friends both here and back in the asphalt encrusted confines of my former life. Risk taking is not unfamiliar to me. As an artist and writer risk is an ingrained part of daily life. Those risks are largely existential, invisible, and rarely include the actual possibility of physical harm or even death. His experience of risk was at a whole other level. I confess my desire to shoot to my lover. His soft, quizzical smile, followed by quiet contemplation tells me he's thinking over my request. Listening is another rare trait that has endeared him to me.

Over the next few days he educates me further on proper gun etiquette. We go to gun shops. I want to buy my own bullets. I feel like a stranger in a strange land in these places where weapons abound. Consciously sucking in my breath, I draw my shoulders back, trying to look like I belong, worried these rugged people dressed in camo will spot me as a fake, an interloper, a threat. Driven by curiosity and now

challenged by my own nerve to move beyond the borders of my fear, I walk out carrying the box of ammunition for the 22.

A dairy farmer on a dirt road far south of the city of Burlington opened a section of his property to informal target shooting. On the appointed day of my baptism into gun culture, we drive out to the edge of a field, blocked off by a rusted old iron gate, beyond which stands the target range, just out of sight. There is a weathered box attached to the gatepost next to a crudely written sign that suggests a donation be left as thanks for using the range. My man instructs me to hop out and open the gate so he can drive the truck through and on down the grass-covered hill, passing a small cud-chewing herd of cows bringing us closer to where we want to be. My excitement rises as lingering summer heat from the early fall sun gradually leaves my body. I'm dressed in tight fitting jeans and an equally body skimming T-shirt, so that nothing gets in the way of my handling the gun.

The "range" is nothing more than a large, relatively flat, grassy, open field, with 4 tightly packed hay bales set on tripods at distances from 25 to 100 yards. When we arrive three rough hewn benches behind table height wooden boxes set at the fields opposite end backed by a line of trees are occupied by a man and his two teenaged sons. They each had taken a position, we'd heard the gunfire on the way to the site, but they politely move over, giving us one of the spots.

I glance toward my man, my trainer, my mentor for reassurance and he nods for me to take a seat while he gets the ammo and readies the gun. The sun is now low in the west, not quite blocking my line of vision toward the hay bales. He shows me the paper target he brought before running to attach it to the bale at the 50-yard marker, making sure the other shooters hold their fire while he affixes the target. They decide to gather their equipment and pack up, leaving the range to the two of us.

The 22 is laying across the table in front of me, tame, its beautiful polished wood and metal gleaming like an art object, daring me to hold it in my hands. My attention is riveted on the gun. All I can see is the bullet being loaded for me, and I hear the oft- repeated instructions again, sounding as though they are coming from far away. He hands me the gun. It feels heavy with importance as though the weight of it is a cautionary reminder I now hold the power to kill in my hands. Elbows on the table, stock resting gently against my shoulder for support, finger poised near the trigger as I squint through the scope adjusting the cross-hairs where I think they should be to hit the target. I'm totally focused. Squeezing the trigger, a sudden blast, I blink, the recoil feels orgasmic against my body. I have no idea where the bullet landed. He runs to the target, bringing it back for me to see. I'm shocked. A near bulls-eye. Suspicious I wonder if somehow he had poked a hole through the target ahead of time, as a reward. He insists, "no, no, it was you, all you, you did well. Try again." Now I'm high. I'm eager to prove that the first time is not a fluke. I pick up the gun that now feels somewhat familiar. The bullet slides into the chamber. The crosshairs are right on target. I don't flinch. Pulling the trigger, again the sudden blast echoes through my body with a warm rush. I'm hooked. I want to immediately replicate my actions. This scenario repeats itself 10 times. The last three my attention shifts to a dangling coffee can on a string that hangs in front of the target. He set it there to test my abilities. Blam, blam, blam. Now I'm ready to see how I have done. I carefully, respectfully, lay the gun down while he retrieves the target and the coffee can. Smiling, with a touch of pride he shows his earnest student the concentrated circle of bullet holes near the bulls-eye and the can peppered by black ringed punctures from all three bullets.

Satisfied, I help pack up our gear and hop in the truck. A man who has confronted death on the battlefield, and faced the ghosts that still haunt him at home has helped me to leave decades of unfounded fear rattling around safely inside a coffee can.

About the Author:

Armed with an MFA from Boston University **Cynthia Close** plowed her way through several productive careers in the arts including instructor in drawing and painting, Dean of Admissions at The Art Institute of Boston, founder of ARTWORKS Consulting, and president of Documentary Educational Resources - a film company. She now claims to be a writer.

In addition...

To support this claim, she is a contributing editor for Documentary Magazine and writes regularly for Vermont Woman magazine, Art New England, Professional Artist magazine, and Art & Object. Her creative non-fiction appeared in the 2014, 2016, and 2017 anthology, The Best of the Burlington Writers Workshop, and her essays have been published in various literary journals including 34th Parallel, Woven Tales Press, The Black and White Anthology, The Seasons of Our Lives, Across the Margin, Montana Mouthful, and Agni among others. She has read publicly at many venues including the Cornelia Street Café in NYC. She was the inaugural art editor for the literary and art journal Mud Season Review launched in 2014.

A PISS ON THE CHEEK
by Walker Thomas

My escape took me as far as Tucson, where I ditched the car and volunteered for the draft. I bussed to El Paso for basic training at Fort Bliss. A grandfatherly major gave us forms and a pep talk.

"Boys, you're men now. Time to realize that Mom and Dad won't always be there to decide what you should do. From this moment on, you'll make all the important decisions in your lives. It starts when you fill these out."

Maybe the rest were boys. I knew the major's mind and I was with him all the way.

I filled out tax forms, insurance forms —all the forms, except a prepared letter like I'd seen on the back of cereal boxes at the boys' camp where I'd been a counselor. It announced my pleasure at having been called to duty, along with my promise to write home every week and an invitation for parents to attend my graduation from basic training. We were to add Moms' and Dads' addresses for a clerk to put on an envelope, and our Fort Bliss barracks addresses for parents to write back. I pushed that form aside. I'd driven across the country to be done with Mom and Dad, and the Army would be the last step in sloughing them off like old skin.

And then, an officer called my name out of all the others in a roomful of newly acknowledged men. I snapped to attention and gave my best salute.

"Yes, Sir!" I said.

"At ease!"

He resumed his grandfatherly tone. "Son, we can see you're excited to be in the Army and we appreciate that. Oversights are usually frowned upon, but we'll make an exception in this case. You've forgotten to fill out one of the forms."

"Sir, was that the DD-XXX?"

"Why, yes it was."

"That wasn't an oversight, Sir. I chose not to fill that one out. Thank you, Sir."

I sat down, pleased with the rapport so soon established with a ranking man.

"Who is this man's commanding officer?" the major bellowed.

Capt. Thomas called out from the back of the room. "I am, Sir."

"Capt. Thomas, take this man out of here. Do whatever you think appropriate. If you decide on courts martial, I'll sign off on it."

I walked sheepishly to the back of the room past other nervous eyes and out to the hall.

Capt. Thomas was a low-keyed ROTC officer serving his required time after college. He offered a sympathetic look, but I could only glare back. Recovered from the initial shock, I seethed. I'd been making adult decisions for a long time. The Army had asked me for one more, their major fucked it up.

"I can see you're pretty wrought," Capt. Thomas said.

He gave his winningest smile.

"Why don't you go back to the barracks, get a good night's sleep and drop by my office after breakfast?"

Before my hand was halfway up to salute the next morning, Captain Thomas reached across his desk to shake it.

"So, what's bothering you?" he asked as if of a college roommate.

"I shouldn't have to tell you this," I said, though with a lessening of my initial surliness.

I told him about life under the thumb of an abusive father and of our final, violent confrontation.

"I can stop it here," Capt. Thomas said, "but you'll need to tell every commanding officer you get or your location will be released."

I got a letter from my mother a few days later. I went to Capt. Thomas in a rage.

"That son of a bitch! I told the major you had good reasons and that I stood behind them."

We both stared at the floor around our feet, and then he raised his eyes.

"That's okay. I'm the only one who can release your next duty station. But you'll need to go straight to that commanding officer or he'll give it out. That's the way it's going to be as long as you're in the Army."

I was sent to take an electric generator course at the Army engineer school in Ft. Belvoir, Virginia. I didn't repeat my tale to my new CO. It was nobody's business but mine.

I'd been there a couple of weeks when the kid in the bunk above pretended to masturbate with wild pelvic gyrations. The whole structure shook while I tried to read. I put my foot into where his buttocks bulged down through the military-grade mattress. I lifted him, bed and all, toward the ceiling. I lifted the steel frame

out of its supports when I did. The bed teetered a moment as the jerk sat up. When he flopped back hard onto the bed, it broke loose from its supports and crashed down on my head.

A friendly junior officer visited me in the hospital the next day and asked me to drop in on the CO when I got out.

"Some SNAFU with your paperwork. Anyway, the captain wants to meet you."

A Pennsylvania senator had demanded my location on behalf of my bereaved parents. My CO at Belvoir read between the lines. He wanted to talk before he acted on the government's request. He made a quick study of my situation and promised to keep my current location and next posting a secret.

Someone up the line released the information without his permission. In a letter, my mother bubbled with news that a psychiatrist had assured her that my father had no treatable psychoses. I didn't write back. I'd already been told he was a sociopath.

Half my class flunked out early and went to Nam: easy targets sent to sit beside loud, gasoline-powered generators at jungle outposts. Because I made the little effort required for good grades, I stayed on to learn how to generate the precise power needed for Nike guidance systems. After my rude introduction to the reality of a GI's impotence, I'd become the kind of knucklehead who'd study late into the night, so I could score a perfect zero on a test. I was careful to miss every question, but instructors' reputations were on the line, and I never scored lower than I had on the first test I'd taken before a bed on the head convinced me that military life was a sham. I'd be sent to a peaceful place when the second level of the course was done.

We used Nikes in Germany and Korea. I'd be sent to Korea. I would go straight to my CO when I arrived, but the brass in Washington, tired of headaches from commanding officers who didn't fall into line, would release my forwarding address on their own. Someone even posted my APO in a Philadelphia newspaper. Sympathetic letters would come from high school girls who thought the address was for a jungle outpost in Nam. And I'd get happy domestic scenes from my mother. I would have to wait until I was out of the Army to shake off family ties.

In the few weeks while I waited at Belvoir for the Korean assignment, I met self-proclaimed genius and American Nazi, Private Freudlich. With his name, maybe the Nazi part was a dark joke, but it went past me back then.

I asked how he always got out of the Tuesday work details.

"Tuesdays I chat with a psychiatrist," Freudlich said. "You should try it."

"How?"

"I told the CO I felt depressed, a little weird, like I didn't fit in. He sent me to Psychology. Easy as that. Now I meet with the psychiatrist every Tuesday. Next to me, he's the smartest guy here, always stops me when I begin to *intellectualize*."

I'd awakened to a spray on my face a few nights earlier. I tried to bat it away a couple of times before I opened my eyes and saw a drunken soldier in boxers, one hand holding onto my wall locker, the other holding his part that was pissing on me. I jumped up.

"Martin!" I yelled.

He just kept pissing. I grabbed soap and towel and ran to the showers.

I returned from the showers to a barracks still filled with snores. Martin snored in his top bunk. A few beds down, my old, impermeable Army mattress held the puddle of his piss.

I stood at his bedside, eyes at the level of his snoring face.

"Martin, Martin."

He slept soundly.

I brought a cup of water back from the latrines and tossed it on his face. It splashed onto Johnson in the next bunk, priming him to fight.

"The hell!"

"I've got to wake him up. He pissed all over my bed and now I can't find my glasses."

"So why the fuck you pouring water on me?"

"It splashed."

"What's going on?"

Martin was waking up.

"You pissed on me. Where're my glasses?"

Martin, now the picture of forced sobriety, climbed down from his bunk and walked over to mine.

"What're you talking about, man? Somebody played a trick on you: poured water on your bed."

"No. You pissed."

"It's just water, man."

Martin scooped some from the still unabsorbed puddle and brought it up to his face.

"It's water. Smell it."

"Don't! It's piss."

"You threw water on me!" Johnson couldn't let go of his own hurt.

"Just go back to bed," Martin said, our calm center.

"He's all fucked up," he said of me to Johnson.

They returned to their beds, the recipient of errant drops still grumbling.

With urine puddled in a waxy, body-oil-slick depression in my vintage Army mattress, I sat up all night in the latrines.

Where was my rage when Martin pissed on me? My father would have come up off that bed and torn his head off his shoulders. I would have, too, but a violent streak had taken a brief respite. It would return soon. In barroom brawls, I'd tap into the rage I felt in the moment my father attacked and I hit him in a panic of self-defense. I'd learn to use that moment when fear and rage combined to make me all-powerful. He was a still-strong and youthful thirty-nine when he attacked, and had a fifty-pound advantage over me, but I left him unconscious in my mother's arms. My year-younger sister, raped by him since she was a little girl, thought he was dead on her way past and out into the snow. She'd seen our abuser dead. When she ran, she ran from me. Violence had worked when I needed it, and would again, but it made me the monster.

The day after my late-night soaking, Martin said, "I remember it now. I did get up to piss. Shit, man, don't tell anybody. I'll look like a damn fool."

I took that story to my already sympathetic CO and added that a Pennsylvania psychiatrist had advised me to follow up on my abuse. The CO sent me to Psychology.

The admitting psychologist was an easygoing black man drafted after he'd completed a master's degree. He refused an officer's commission and had just learned he was soon to be reassigned as a rifle-bearing grunt in Nam. Wednesdays became my days to complain about the inequities of Army life to a man who'd faced bigotry all his life and then the threat of death in war.

On my third visit, I blurted out, "Why don't you send me to the psychiatrist. Freudlich gets to see the psychiatrist."

"But Freudlich's crazy," the psychologist said, "There's nothing wrong with you."

Freudlich crazy. I'd never thought of that.

Something *was* wrong with me, though. Guys were developing post-traumatic stress disorders in Viet Nam while I came to the Army with a case already established. Diagnosed years later, mine reflected none of the experience of war and its terrors that rose beyond any I could imagine, but the symptoms of sudden-surfacing residual anger and uncertainty were the same.

I hate to imagine where I'd have ended up if the Army hadn't come along to refocus my life. I look back now at two valuable years' experience. At the time, though, all I saw was a lack of the personal freedom I'd struggled to obtain.

About the Author:

Walker Thomas wandered into a desert-mountain wilderness and stayed eight years. A Piss on the Cheek is drawn from a just-completed book manuscript that describes the experiences of those years and the life that compelled a man to live alone in a cave.

KILLINGS AND ABDUCTION
by Tamas Dobozy

The summer of 1981 was the summer of murdered children.

The bodies had been turning up for a year in the Lower Mainland of British Columbia, mainly the Vancouver area. Places like Surrey, Langley, Coquitlam, Richmond. But the killings intensified in May, June, and July of 1981. The victims were between the ages of nine and eighteen—drugged, raped, tortured, bludgeoned—some of their skulls so shattered the bones were loose behind the faces, like broken glass in a bag.

It was the summer Tamas learned to read the news. He was twelve. He went through the reports as if as if the name of the next victim was in there, somewhere in that jumble of letters, and if only he could decipher it another child might be saved—a child who might be him. But no matter how many times he scanned the paper, the letters remained lost, dead things. They didn't show the future, they marked only where the past had ended, forever. Decades later, after what happened to Pete Boules, Tamas would regard the questions he'd brought to those articles the way you'd think of totems left before a black wall, like offerings to no god.

The boys spoke of the killer on late July nights in Port Alberni. Tamas was visiting Pete for the week. They didn't know it then, or maybe they did, if fear can be considered knowledge, that the killer would be caught on the outskirts of town just over two weeks later, in early August,

while trying to kidnap two hitchhikers. Had everyone in Port Alberni had the same premonition? It's said you know when you're in the presence of a psychopath, and Tamas would have that feeling in the years afterwards—in the classroom once, in a parking lot with a teenage boy, beside a redneck at a bank machine—but only one more time with that intensity. It came through loud and clear in the July dark like a transmission playing on their nerve endings.

There was another boy there, Sebastian, also visiting. He said the killer had pounded nails into the heads of the children. He probably wanted to know what it felt like, Sebastian said. He probably asked them, nail by nail, what are you feeling now? The children were screaming and thrashing, torsos buckling up and down on whatever plank he'd tied them to. Sssshhhhh. It's okay. Tell me how it feels? Here, let's try another one.

Tamas was tangled in his sleeping bag. He could barely make out the others in the dark, as if they were on a lake, but not a lake of water, black liquid of some kind, and they were drifting apart. All he could see were their outlines.

He laughs when they cry, muttered Sebastian. He reads them things their parents say in newspapers. How scared they are. How much they miss them. Your parents' eyes look dead, he whispers. Like they already know you're never coming home again.

Shut up, Sebastian, Pete said, you're scaring Tamas. Sebastian paused a minute, gauging Pete's threat, then continued. The killer is all there is. All that's left is what he wants to do to you. That's what you've become, what you are—whatever pain he wants to bring into this world. If he could, he'd prefer to keep you alive forever so he could keep hurting you.

There was no second warning. Pete leapt onto Sebastian. Clambering onto his chest. He grabbed the edge of the sleeping bag in both hands and held it over Sebastian's face, elbows locked, jerking it down again and again, bearing down with all his weight, Sebastian's feet thrashing under the covers. Shut up! Shut up! Shut up! It wasn't until Tamas tackled him that he stopped, sobbing. Sebastian tore himself free and scrambled backwards like a crab, hand out against another attack.

After that, Mrs. Boules put the boys into separate rooms, where no doubt each of them sat awake, curled into the tight space where the mattress met a corner of the wall, or sitting on the edge of the bed in the glare of a light kept on to burn away the images—the nail in the head, the raised hammer, the crooked grin. The image of a child begging to be saved.

The next day they ate breakfast in silence, the newspaper headline writhing across the page. The questions around the killer, his acts, the narrowing investigation, seemed to Tamas written in Pete's home that morning, and in Pete's sleepless face, absent its lopsided smile, its joy and its bravery—filled with a fear that had not yet found its object.

But there were better parts to that July. Pete gave Tamas comic books. The old Frank Miller *Daredevils*, with their grainy elegance. They were already valuable by then, collector's items. But you can have them, I'm giving them to you, because you're my best friend, Pete said. That summer they fought wars with marbles of burgundy fruit picked from trees whose leaves flashed red when they turned in the breeze. Pete called them Japanese cherries,

and they stained the sidewalk in front of his house, their clothes. Pete was always on Tamas's side, between him the other kids. It was the summer of afternoons in Sprout Lake, Pete warning Tamas against getting water in his mouth. Beaver fever, he said. It'll turn your guts inside out. A summer of last childhood maps, tracing paths through old-growth cedar on the edge of town, private kingdoms soon to be replaced by official charts that had none of that season's familiarity. The summer of Pete taking Tamas to the canal and telling him about the 1964 tsunami—how it swept away the cars, trees, houses. He bought them ice cream with his paper route money, they looked at Deni Eagland's photos of houses dropped on top of trucks, streets cracked down the middle and fallen to either side, a car tilted up on its front bumper underneath the edge of a mobile home like a ballerina in mid-pirouette. The summer they were stopped by three teenagers in a Camaro who knew Pete and wanted them to get into the backseat. They wore jeans and jean jackets, torn along the seams, tight in the ass and crotch. They had hair past their shoulders. Smoking cigarettes. We got some weed, the one who'd gotten out of the car said, four inches taller than Pete, staring down at him. No, said Pete. The driver and the guy in the back seat exchanged glances. What about your friend? Maybe he wants some. Pete dropped his backpack. What, you're going to fight? Us? Pete stayed where he was. Not all at once, he said. The teenager laughed, but there's no fun in it. What about your friend? Is he going to fight too? He won't need to, Bela replied. The guy sneered, but he was slouching already, eyes drifting to one side. Tamas saw what he saw: the expression on Pete's face, like looking through a sheet of ice at someone trapped inside but still furiously alive. Just a matter of time, the teenager said, getting back into the car. One at a time, Pete said, but afterwards he was shaking so bad he had to sit on the curb. It was the summer they ambled home in the heat, arms around each other's shoulders, home from their victories.

Years passed. They kept in touch over the phone, once every few months. When Tamas was sixteen he returned for another summer visit, finding Pete fascinated with reruns of *MASH*, repeat screenings of *Apocalypse Now*, *Full Metal Jacket*, *Paths of Glory*—the old romance of war blossoming on the screen in the oranges of firebombs, the cinematic reds of spilled blood, the creeping black of fade outs. Tamas would remember Brando as Kurtz, the ritual sacrifice, the ox bellowing under the knife. Otherwise, Pete was lifting weights in the basement, so muscular he looked overinflated, body parts mismatched. His father and he had been arguing. Pete wanted to join the military. Wanted to be a marine, a ranger, special forces, recon. They'd nearly come to blows over it. Mr. Boules was five-foot seven, white haired, his only weapon a laugh so unerring, so on target, it singled out faults you never knew you had. His spit crackled when he laughed. He wants to go to war, Mr. Boules said, walking in on Pete and Tamas watching *Das Boot*. He wants to get blown up. But he can't even get a summer job. Fuck, Pete growled, rising from the chair. Leave us alone. But Mr. Boules didn't show the slightest fear down there, six inches under Pete, his shoulders no wider than a wire coat hanger. He turned to Tamas. See, he's ready to fight. Brave soldier. But he can't even apply for university. Pete shouldered past the old man, knocking over a side table covered in plastic flowers. Mr. Boules watched him go, shaking his head.

The next night, Tamas got sick on Southern Comfort in the back of Pete's car. Pete drove home, put him to bed, then sopped up the mess on the floorboards, hosed down the mats, sprinkled baking soda all over—not a word of resentment. He greeted Tamas's hangover with a laugh. They'd been up on a cliff overlooking a lake, outside of town—Tamas remembered the night, stars over a distant shore, a narrow road through a tunnel of leaves. Pete said he'd kept him well back of the cliff edge. He said it was not so far from here, just over the rise, where the two girls had been

picked up by the killer. Charmed, they'd said, by his intense manner, his jokes, a spirit of adventure.

Six months later, Pete was at the University of British Columbia. His parents had filled out the application forms for him. Mechanical engineering. But he'd already drifted from the courses he should have been taking, first into kinesiology, then sports history, then a course on Greco-Roman art, and finally literature, much to the alarm of Mr. Boules, who saw Arts courses as the trash heap of intellectual effort. There was verbal violence over the phone. Finally, Pete stopped calling. When he returned for summer break, he refused to move back into his room, preferring to stay in a trailer in the backyard—an Airstream Bubble, clad in high-gloss aluminum, so shiny it could barely be looked at in the sunlight—that his family had used, years ago, for summer vacations. He came in to eat, use the shower, pick up laundry. Meanwhile, the trailer filled up with books he bought by the pound from second-hand stores—Virgil, Goethe, Eliot, Yeats, Heidegger, and Pete's favorite, Joseph Conrad, whose *Nostromo*, he told Tamas, he preferred to read backwards, drawn along the protagonist's terrible journey into innocence, each layer of experience coming off like a strip of skin, back to that state where, once again, the world could do its worst. It's corruption that dies, Pete said. Innocence kills it. Every time.

Tamas stared at him in the trailer. It was the summer of 1990. There were books everywhere—heaped on the camper table, the bench seat around it, the shiny covers shifting and slippery underfoot. If you fell, they'd close over you like dirt. Not a stone to mark your spot.

Pete was working on a book called *David*. He'd produced a page and a half that he read aloud that night—a rush of emotion lingering in its own poetry. Beyond that, there wasn't much to it: a seated figure, a man, then scant light, either the first or last of the day, it was impossible to tell from the writing, only that the light was parceled out like coins. There was a tin bowl on the trailer's stove filled with the ash of other pages, hundreds of them, the ones that had come next, failed for having departed into plot, character, specifics of time and place.

Afterwards, Pete asked Tamas to read his poetry. He read only one, recalling the visit long ago, lying on the floor, their voices whispering cruelties into the dark. Pete watched the words fly past like a dog gazing at cars on a freeway. He was complimentary, but it didn't matter, not to the poem, which Tamas knew was bad, not least for naming the killer, but also for wondering whether the dead can still read, peering into our world for the thrill of seeing their names in print. Tamas shrugged, looked around. He had already learned the most best lesson of writing: there are things in life more important than poetry.

Pete and Tamas didn't see each other again for many years. Pete went back to university, studying no one knew what. Once in a while a box would arrive to Tamas's house filled with books—Yeats, Rimbaud, Eliot, Baudelaire, and a beautiful copy of Villon, French on one side, English on the other, the margins illuminated with roses and swifts. Tamas would lose that book across the years, gone to travel through other hands, but not before he'd memorized two lines someone had underlined in pencil: "My boon companions, this for you / Who make so free in every place." He knew it was Pete. He was the only one desperate enough to deface such a beautiful book. It was as if Pete, fearing his own words, had used Villon instead, while he still could.

Tamas went through the other books not as he would later—passage by passage, refusing to go on until the page yielded itself, margins filled with a tangled handwriting he'd later strain to read—but simply by letting them drift past his eyes, taking easy pleasure or none at all, lingering on what was beautiful, then letting the music run on. The most honest reading he'd ever done.

As for Pete's letters, they were a mess. Filled with excerpts of what he was reading, in no particular order or attribution. But Tamas recognized some of it—Lautreamont, De Sade, Nechaev, Lovecraft. Research on terror, Pete wrote, for the novel. He described days of writing—ten, eleven, twelve hours at a time. No food. Breaking only to go to the bathroom. He gathered material, he said, by walking Wreck Beach alone at night; riding the number 14 bus through the Lower East Side's dirty carnival of junkies and prostitutes and the homeless; visiting campgrounds along the north shore in the deserted autumn, spying on the few RVs and tent-trailers still courting that cold loneliness. The novel was still stuck on page one and a half.

Then the letters stopped. Tamas would never be able to say why, exactly, he'd broken off his own correspondence, only that he'd started looking elsewhere for more rigorous information. The letters with Pete that were too high-octane, too flashy, to lead to any real literature. It was a writing that burned itself out in the correspondence, as if that's all there was to the writing they were talking about, literary or otherwise.

Pete lingered in university another year. Tamas got reports from Mrs. Boules filtered through his mother. There'd been trouble in residence. Conflicts with other students. Pete locked himself inside his room for days, once or twice with another terrified student. Or else he was absent from campus, sometimes long as a week, nobody knew where. Security found him staggering around the western shore one February evening, wild-eyed, lost in the beach's endless variations of gray. He was taken to a clinic, checked by medical staff, released into his own care.

There was a fear in Mrs. Boules' reports that went beyond misadventure. Tamas imagined her wringing her hands in bed, beating back the dark with the glow of a lampshade, just as his own mother had done when he was living at home and out at night and she was worried. Always up, lights on, these mothers greeting their sons with a frown as they came in, their concern slowly squeezing them to death, or threatening to, until finally it chased them from home. Thinking this way made Tamas feel better about Pete. He was only going through what they'd all gone through.

But Pete left university that year. He was done with it. What remained was rage—at his mother for smothering him in concern, at his father for misunderstanding his ambitions, for failing to see that none of this, what was happening, was an inevitability, that the whole path had been carefully picked out by Pete himself. He hated them for letting him come home.

He was in the trailer again. The trailer had been moved to a ten-acre lot the family owned on the outskirts of Port Alberni, far from other people, anyone he could hurt. Then he was gone. Disappeared. Nobody knew where, only that he'd hitch-hiked to the ferry terminal in Nanaimo, where he was caught on security footage disembarking in Vancouver. After that, nothing.

A half year later his parents started receiving phone calls, from places always a little further south. Portland. Sacramento. Los Angeles. The calls came in late at night. They were brief. The rasp in Pete's voice made them think he'd been sleeping in the cold. He would open with one long sentence, five minutes in length, after which he had nothing more to say, nothing to ask. His silence stretched as long as the distance between them. But it hummed with bewilderment, exhaustion, rage. He spoke of migrations south. Streetlights in Blaine Washington glowing like no other. That he could see better by night than by day. The length of the Oregon coastline measured in footsteps. Different shoes—Adidas, Nike, Reebok—their relative thickness of sole, tread design, longevity. Ten pairs, so far, he said. What I need are boots.

When his parents asked how he was getting money, they heard crickets chirping, the crash of waves, cars zooming in the distance.

He spoke of rats in the fringes of palm trees, watching them skitter down at dusk to feed on vineyards in northern California. Buskers with home-made instruments—old radiators, wire-frame lampshades, untuneable radios—humming snatches of melody. He described a shade of neon so vivid it was as if he'd picked it up and carried it on his back.

None of the conversations lasted. Pete never said hello or goodbye, he just drifted off, like the sound of the passing cars.

Later on, it was police on the other end, asking questions. Did they know a Peter Boulez? They knew a Pierre Boulez, Mr. Boules replied. French composer. The police were evasive with further information. Wrong number, I guess, they said. Later, they'd be more probing. They asked for a physical description of their son. But it didn't match at all with the person they were looking for. When Mr. Boules asked why they were looking for him the officer said it was a police matter. They couldn't comment on an ongoing investigation. God knows what Peter looks like now, his parents must have thought. He could have lost a hundred pounds, or have grown a beard down to his knees. Or the reverse. Fat as a god from scavenging junk food out of garbage cans. He could have shaved his head, or dyed his hair blond. He could have dressed as a woman. Lost a leg.

None of the police officers called back twice, until the end. That was when Pete was finally caught and identified, in San Ysidro, near the border with Tijuana. He'd tossed a cinderblock through a shop window. He'd done it, he said, because a gang—and he was too frightened to provide names—had taken him prisoner and forced him into criminal activities—couriering drugs, hiding weapons, acting as a lookout during robberies—and beat him up and threatened to kill him when he didn't comply. Getting arrested had been the only way to escape.

His father drove five long days to California to get him. Pete was so thin, ribs like the rungs of a ladder. He had a beard you could twist into a scarf around his head.

He was silent in the car, not responding to questions, not to his name. When they came to a rest stop or restaurant he'd turn and gaze through the back window and begin to speak, in a rush so total, so incoherent, it was like a stampede of gibberish, making his body vibrate. All the way north the rearview mirror taunted him, until outside of Tacoma he tore it from the ceiling.

They put him back into that trailer on the outskirts. He wandered the woods, traced the track of streams, an elusive presence even to his parents when they came to visit. Sometimes he simply didn't appear. Sometimes the trailer door was ajar, leaves and twigs on the floor, as if it had been left open for days. Mr. and Mrs. Boules searched the woods. They had a feeling he was out there, shifting from tree to tree, spying on them. If they did by chance run into him, if he didn't know they were coming, if they snuck onto the property and up to the trailer, it wasn't five minutes before he was shouting that he'd kill them. Then he'd destroy the nearest breakable thing: a window, a headlight on their car, a glass he was holding in his hand.

He was still bench pressing three hundred pounds, still writing the thousands of pages stuffed into closest and cupboards and drawers of the trailer. The rest littered the floor, covered in muddy footprints, or were folded into the dirt around the entrance, or even, a few of them, impaled on the branches above the trailer, shedding sentences into the passing breeze. Pete's narrative had become endless, like a series of trap doors opening one onto another, with a thousand protagonists—the unquiet sleep of war photographers in Vietnam, political scientists tending trash fires in Central America, a woman repairing brooms used in the corridors of Suceava Prison.

Pete seemed to care about words only in the act of writing them down. He didn't even bother to burn the pages anymore. There were no books anywhere.

Tamas and Pete met for the last time in 1992. Mrs. Boules called to say Pete had moved home again. The trailer was unlivable now. Would Tamas be interested in coming for a visit? That summer, he was working as a broke hustler in the pulp and paper mill in Powell River. It was the bottom job—shoving slabs of paper back into the pulper, feeding sheets into rollers spinning fast enough to rip off your fingers. He worked in steam rising off machines, on his feet right across the twelve-hour shifts. Sure, he'd come. He was happy for a day off.

Pete picked him up at the ferry terminal in Comox. He still had the beard, but it was closely trimmed. He still walked bow-legged like an athlete. The eyes had deadened in his head, but they weren't completely dead yet, only hard, refusing the light. They softened at the sight of his friend.

He wondered if Pete should be driving. Once in a while he'd accelerate in response to nothing. A passing leaf. The sight of oncoming traffic. A stretch of empty road. Tamas kept bracing for the fatal twist of the steering wheel into the other lane.

Pete's first words were a warning: Terror is not being able to find someone who you can tell what you think. The statements in your head, he continued, lifting his hands from the steering wheel and twitching them by either ear. It's the condition of adulthood, the withholding of information. Tamas reached one hand for the steering wheel, but Pete grabbed it as they began to veer across the line.

From there, Pete recalled the last few years. He spoke of weeks spent walking south along the Amalfi coast. It sounded as if he'd transposed his misadventures in the US to some other country. He'd spent a whole night trapped on a cliff edge, the Tyrrhenian Sea frothing beneath him. He held onto the rocks until he couldn't feel his arms. When his knees began to buckle he rammed sticks down each pant leg into the heels of his shoes. In the morning he inched his way down into the village, where they treated him like a cripple.

It reminded him, Pete said, of the time his father sent him to a boarding school in Montreal. Tamas asked when this had happened, but Pete just kept talking. He and some of the other boys had gotten into a fight with a gang from another school. He lay in a meadow afterwards in the dark, feeling the blood drip from cuts in his head. There had been a clarity to it, like a kid confronted with something sweet. Pete couldn't remember what happened next. How he'd stood up, or if he'd been helped. The memory stopped dead.

He had no plans for the future, and recommended Tamas do the same. The future, he said, is as gone as the past. When asked if he still wrote, Pete replied, Often. When asked what he was listening to, he said there was so much he could no longer tolerate—the Doors, Rolling Stones, David Bowie—and left the answer there, in a ruin of silence. When asked if he still remembered that night, years ago, when they'd lain in the dark, speaking of the killer, Pete shook his head and said he didn't. He had a vague memory of the smile of someone who'd gotten away with it. No, Tamas said. The killer was caught. He's still alive. Once in a while he writes letters to the families describing what he did to their kids. He collects a pension. He uses the outrage to get himself into the news. Pete looked at Tamas and smiled, lopsided, in all his terrible freedom. He got away with it. Tamas looked at Pete as if not remembering the killer might be the worst of that killer's work. You don't remember Sebastian? The things he said? Hitting him? Who's Sebastian? Pete asked, smiling out of some dark interior.

In Qualicum, they pulled into a rest stop so Tamas could pee, though what he really wanted was to climb out the back window of the men's room and run away. When he got back to the car, he found Pete staring at the steering wheel as if he was a child again, twelve years old, not sure how to turn over the ignition. Do you have a girlfriend? he finally asked. Tamas nodded. Yes, I do. At the answer, Pete's face assumed a cartoon expression, as it

had long ago—Bugs Bunny seeing Elmer Fudd disguised as a lady rabbit. Then his face settled back to flat. There's a woman, Pete said quietly. Works for the city. Comes by every week. Rides one of those power mowers. Cuts the grass along the sidewalk, and on the traffic island. She's a real fox. Tamas watched his face. You should talk to her. Pete looked away. What would I say?

The road flashed ahead of them in rain, foliage spilling from ditches to either side, leaves plastered to the asphalt like an orange and gold foil.

They arrived in Port Alberni at lunch time, Pete still calm, talkative, Tamas calmer to have him out from behind the wheel. Mrs. Boules met them in the driveway, smiling at nothing, filled with nervous energy. I'm so glad to see you. Pete could really use someone to talk to him.

She fed them ravioli. But she didn't eat, nor did she sit. She hovered at the end of the table, hands clasped, staring. Tamas and Pete looked from their forks to her and then each other.

As the meal ended she reached on top of the fridge and pulled down a document, six or seven pages, and held it to her breast. Pete pretended not to notice. He talked about a necessary disorder in libraries, especially personal libraries, one that couldn't be brought about with shelves. Tamas nodded, but he was watching Mrs. Boules, who seemed to be waiting for a break in the monologue. Pete's eyes flicked in her direction every other second, and then he'd speed up, the words coming faster and faster the longer she stood there clutching the papers. A floor—that's what you need for books. Preferably one with an area rug. Uneven surfaces. Chairs, coffee tables, sofa, pillows here and there. A kind of terrain. Landscape. Hills, valleys, plains. So, you'll know where to find the books. You'll know the *geography*. Rivers, for instance, are the best places to store poetry. The dialogue had become frantic, each word another plank in a trestle he was extending, further and further, away from where his mother waited.

So many problems, she finally said. The words were tiny explosions crackling under Pete's sentences, collapsing his diatribe into a cloud of dust. He looked at his mother. She placed the papers in front of Tamas, where his plate had been. It was an article: "The Onset of Schizophrenia in Late Adolescence: Leading Signs and Symptoms."

I have been asking him to read this, she said. For years. Just read it. Pete glared at her. You're interrupting, he said. You can't just . . . His face twitched sideways, fighting off a sudden ferocity, then twitched back. Look at this, said Mrs. Boules to Tamas, ignoring Pete. She pointed to an underlined passage: In most cases the afflicted will not likely be willing to admit that what he or she is experiencing is . . . But Tamas never got a chance to finish reading it. She was already on to the next page, a paragraph marked in red that spoke of linguistic dissociation, an inability to report from the other side of schizophrenia, to articulate experience in any language other than the one supplied by the illness. She moved quickly to the next bit of underlining.

Apart from getting to his feet Pete didn't know what to do. Tamas could smell him now, sharp as an ampoule broken under his nose. His hands were in the air, as if pushing something away. It was a silenced question, as bewildered and honest as a child denied dinner for no reason.

The old lady continued on, her tone neutral as a clinician's. She pointed to a passage. Voices in the head. Wild paranoia. Unable to distinguish enemies from friends. A refusal to accept treatment, to swallow the pills, to reconcile with anything said. Violence, she finished, but here there was a crack in the smooth flow of her delivery. Violence, she said again, with a force so powerful Tamas felt it like gravity. They were accomplices now—Mrs. Boules and him.

Let's go! Pete shouted. Let's leave this place. But he was walking toward his mother. Tamas stood, caught his friend's arm, led him to the porch off the kitchen, and turned back to Mrs.

Boules. Please stop, he said. Whatever you're doing. Please stop. Her hands fell helplessly to her sides, still holding the article. He needs to go to the hospital, she said. He needs to take his medication. I thought that if I showed you what he did, in front of him . . . Her voice faded.

Tamas stepped into the warm afternoon. Pete prowling the edges of the porch. Now we're gone, he said. Now we're out. The way she talks, he continued. All day every day. The eight hundred articles. Flights of fancy. The peace betwixt.

Mrs. Boules pulled back the lace curtain over the window. She was holding a plate of baking. Tamas asked Pete if there was another way inside, downstairs to his room, where they'd be left alone. But Mrs. Boules opened the door. This is the way to his room, she said. His room is this way. You can be alone there.

Tamas wanted to stay outside, but she was gripping his hand, pulling him in, her desperation equal to Pete's. It had been ten years in the making. Watching her child being dismembered, piece by piece. Tamas wondered what that was like—trying to distinguish between the normal course of teenage rebellion and your son's disappearance. She only wanted to hold her boy in place. In the living room she removed an awkwardly placed picture frame. There was a hole behind it, right through the gyprock. Do you see? she asked. Would a normal person do this? Tell me. Tamas shrugged, muttering about house parties he'd gone to, young men punching holes in the wall for no reason other than the doing of it. Mrs. Boules waved a hand in his face. Come. He felt oddly passive, dazed, as if he'd been drugged, letting her guide him down the stairs. There were more holes here, none of them covered. Behind them Pete stopped on the landing, facing away. Don't do this, he whispered. Don't do this. Don't do this. The fist-sized holes looked strategic, like a message of dots and spaces. Mrs. Boules pointed at a door leaning against a wall, splintered and cracked where there'd once been hinges. From the landing, Pete's rage came at them like microwaves. He was pacing, hands clenched, uttering what sounded less like recollections than warnings, fragments of time flashing up in him, scenes, incidents, occasions they'd need to avoid in order to prevent such violence, as if muttering them was enough to divert the future. But Mrs. Boules didn't care. She kept going. Look at this. She reached into a box and pulled out the halves of a picture frame that looked as if it had been broken over a knee. Tamas looked at the box, the holes in the gyprock, the broken door, and wondered if she'd set it out this morning, like a kill room. Look at this, she continued, opening a bag filled with shards of porcelain. Herendi, she said. Inherited from my mother. With tears in her eyes, she mimed the action of stomping her feet to show how it had been broken.

Shut up! howled Pete. In an instant he was down the stairs and pinning her to the wall, shaking his mother so hard it seemed all of her would rattle loose, arms and legs and ears and eyeballs falling to the floor. His eyes were bulging in their sockets, the skin of his neck sunken beneath the cabling of muscles. Please stop doing this! he howled. He's the only friend I have left. It was the only time, that whole day, that Pete seemed to have found the right words.

Tamas raised his hand, but didn't know where to place it. The rage was so powerful it seemed to exclude Pete, to have absented him from himself. He was nothing more than a space where he'd once been, a vanishing so absolute there was no way to engage with it. Still Mrs. Boules spoke to her son, firing words into the emptiness. No, she shook her head. The marks you leave on us. The nights we have to call the police. The time they took your father to the hospital. The words came out stuttered with Pete shaking her. Mrs. Boules' head flopped back and forth as if severed from her spine. I am trying to help you. But first you have to admit you need it. Tamas could hear the screech of love in what she was saying, that terrible malfunctioning engine, bludgeoning

her son in a final attempt at saving him. It was an assault as brutal as anything Tamas had seen. He raised his hand, but Pete had already stopped shaking her. He was the only one who remembered me, Pete whispered. Now I'm all gone.

Tamas dropped his hand then, and Pete looked back as if his friend had been lifting a hammer. But in an instant his eyes changed, something blew through and settled in, and he let Mrs. Boules collapse onto the floor. Then Pete walked through a door off the basement hallway into his bedroom. It closed behind him like a wall.

About the Author:

Tamas Dobozy is a professor in the Department of English and Film Studies at Wilfrid Laurier University. He lives in Kitchener, Ontario, Canada. He has published three books of short fiction, When X Equals Marylou, Last Notes and Other Stories, and, most recently, Siege 13: Stories, which won the 2012 Rogers Writers Trust of Canada Fiction Prize, and was shortlisted for both the Governor General's Award: Fiction, and the 2013 Frank O'Connor International Short Story Award. He has published over seventy short stories in journals such as One Story, Fiction, Agni, and Granta, and won an O Henry Prize in 2011, and the Gold Medal for Fiction at the National Magazine Awards in 2014.

MEDIOCRE EXISTENCIALIST

by Rebecca Kirschbaum

You slurred about how you loved yourself while you hung from a balcony, two stories in the air, staring at the frozen ground beneath you.

It was a night drenched in booze, somewhere in Kentucky, sometime after midnight. You smelled of tequila shots, cigarettes and marijuana. You wore a dress with flowers that dotted your many curves and a beanie that gave you a bohemian vibe. Your hair was loose and matted from flipping it around at the Irish pub, when we were hanging out with those people we used to know, before they chose heroin over life. Your brown locks—a million highlighted and salon-enhanced hangman's nooses—curled around your throat, twisting into a knot.

 "I love myself too much."

That's what you said. You said you didn't want to kill yourself.

The stars were loud above that residential street, lined in tall trees older than us by three lifetimes. The winter trees mourned their leaves and called for them to return. The people were sleeping. The road was filled with historical homes worth way more than the mobile home I grew up in—and the property it was tossed on—the flimsy structure eventually abandoned and forgotten.

To you, you with the death wish, I said, "Stop being stupid. You're not going to jump."

You only repeated, "I love me."

For me, this was Kentucky. My hometown. The new mid-south. A heritage I both wanted to understand and to escape. A place filled with opioid abuse, the remnants of poverty and coal mining culture and somehow also, the filthy rich. I grew up half-joking about the barns the thoroughbreds lived in.

The racehorses lived like royalty. How I lived in my formative years is still undefined In my mind—it's an understanding I still reach to have—you could maybe call it white trash. In the summers, our trailer was infested so profoundly with fleas, my feet were red and blistered with their bites—one foot, one white sock, blackened in a matter of seconds with those biting bugs.

Underprivileged me, I'm not the one who hung above the cement, teasing death. Though life had told me I was less than, though I struggled to find meaning and context, though I too hated myself because the world had told me that standing in line for free milk and government-issued EBT cards for groceries rendered me useless—I'd never played death like a fool.

Death is savvy, a heartless asshole that makes decisions willy nilly and hands down verdicts without rhyme or reason.

At the time? You, my friend, treated suicide like an easy impulse buy and I likened death's persona to God, really. *Death and Jesus, both of you fuckers ... you stay over there. I'll be over here. I don't want either one of y'all's help, thank you very much.*

You, however, my dear wealthy friend, who treated the balcony railing of that old beautiful building like the playground we grew up swinging on—you probably still think that you matter. You do, of course. To me, to the people who know you. I mean more in the universal sense. You believed this moment registered in the grand scheme of things. That though we are invisible from outer space—hell, even from a damn airplane—you were important enough that if you did happen to die because you were morbidly goofing off, the world would care.

You seriously believed that.

There are more people in the world who don't know your name than who do. They won't ever know your name, let alone have an opinion on or a reaction to your death.

You don't get it, though. Because you've always mattered to the world you interacted with. Nobody discounted your medical emergencies because your insurance was provided by charity. Nobody stared at you because your sweet, kind mother didn't appear presentable, because her large boobs protruded from her low cut top. Nobody judged you and your food as it slid down the conveyer belt because the card you slid in the reader was from the government.

You've never measured your life in the remaining balance on that food stamp EBT card. You weren't tucked in under ten blankets and still cold in the winter because your heater broke and your family didn't have the money to repair it. Your memories are filled with dolls and tea parties. If your kid fantasies were real life, I

would have been the one bringing you and your friends food. Serving you.

Old money. A heritage of pharmaceuticals. Trust funds. Money was everywhere, tucked away in bank accounts by white people who generally cared enough about the places their sperm landed, about the uteruses that flourished with their babies, they planned. For you. They planned with dollars and decimals. The world was and is your oyster.

If you slipped and fell on your head, and nobody put you together again, yes—your family would have cared. Your small corner of this big big world would have mourned you, the newspaper might have even written about you.

In that boozy moment, you were a mediocre existentialist. You questioned your life and your purpose because of the sorts of things I wish I was privileged enough to be concerned about. I think you did love yourself too much, to be honest. Because if you realized you didn't matter, that with death, eventually you'd fade away, you would have been with me, on the correct side of the rail.

I rarely had the impulse to stand like that, to take a risk, because if something went wrong but also right, if I fell but lived, I'd only have expensive medical bills I couldn't pay.

You made me hate myself more by hating yourself. The night you did that to me, it was cold. I wasn't wearing a coat, but the coat of our old friend, Tucker, an once star football player who let himself go. That friend had a beard, and he didn't shower as much as he used to, he drank a lot and did a bunch of other drugs, too, and every time he got drunk, you know how he brought up his brother.

His big brother was named after a character in the Bible, and I don't remember which one. You might know. His brother was wild and he kicked Tucker's ass all the time when they were kids.

When we were around sixteen, remember how Tucker's brother wrapped his motorcycle around a tree out in front of our high school? The EMT told the kids who pulled the brother out of the bushes he would have lived if they'd only left him alone—that statement I've always objected to. He had no way of knowing that for sure. Let sleeping dogs lie.

Because the kids that pulled that guy from a tree? They live with guilt over that and will forever. Honestly, that's probably why that guy who graduated a few classes above us drank himself to death, died with his fingers down his throat. What was his name, again? Do you remember?

The night you, my childhood best friend, flirted with suicide, we were all staring up at stars that shivered against the blustery night. Frost was collecting on the grass below us, and it caught the light of headlights when a few cars drove by.

Just before you stumbled over the rail to hang yourself, Tucker and I were sharing a cigarette. You, the girl who loved herself too much? Were sipping from a bottle of old, sour beer and sitting in a rocking chair. You were mad because you thought you were fat, and because the guy you'd wanted to go home with was inside, pounding another girl, forty-something pounds lighter than you.

Bet you don't care about that anymore, do you? Bet.

You were and are profoundly, deeply, soulfully beautiful and wild. Smart. Articulate. Savvy. Creative. Sexy. You didn't and don't see that about yourself anymore. Life, mistakes, one too many penises at one too many college parties, privilege gone wrong—it all rendered you a shell of who you once were. Or so you thought and felt.

I'd given up trying to make you feel awesome. The truth was, those days, we all felt like shit.

"He would tell me to stop being such a pussy," Tucker said, talking about his dead brother. He took my beer out of my hand, took a long swig of it, and numbly blinked at me. "He would tell

me to get a job. Stop being such a pussy. Get a job. Live my life."

I nodded. "If he were here, he would definitely tell you that." I peered into the air next to him, staring at the empty space where his brother's head would have been, had his ghost been standing there. We're superstitious in the Kentucky foothills, a side effect of Appalachia. "I'm sure of it."

"Do you think I live my life?" he asked. He passed me the beer and took the cigarette from my hand. I watched him suck at the end of it, as the hot fire at the end of the stick lit up, a glowing light at the end of a bright white tunnel we'd never reach the end of.

I shook my head. "I think you do the best you can."

Comparatively, given the depth of Tucker's musings about death and loss versus the purported reasons you were moping and smoking, I'm still not sure why you crawled over the balcony railing. Maybe it went deeper than the things you bothered to complain about.

"Oh shit," Tucker hissed.

"I love myself too much to kill myself," you said, simply.

For a minute, no one spoke. The neighborhood dogs barked, a siren wailed, the television inside muttered about the woes of fame and fortune.

You did not distinguish whether you felt Freudian or chemical or familial self-love.

"You're about to be gravity's bitch," I said, the world slipping around on the bubbles of too much beer. "Knock it off."

You swayed and the fence groaned.

Alcoholism. It had once directed your car into a tree on a country road, but the cop who found you let you go. I never asked why and you never elaborated. Drunk driving was dangerous, but also a privilege I didn't have. No mistakes. No room for a misstep. This one time, I slipped into your car, knowing you were toasted, and I waited to see if we made it home because at the time, frankly, I didn't care what happened to us. I remember squealing tires, but no broken glass and never any blood.

We lived that time and all the times that have led up to now.

"You don't think I love myself?"

"No."

"Do you think I'm pretty?"

"Yes."

Tucker flicked the cigarette into the street. It fell for what seemed like forever and sparked. He offered his hand to you and it was that simple. Tucker helped you over the fence, and you fell coming back over, fell onto the safe side of the fence, falling to the floor of the patio with a *thud* and a prolonged whine—*owwwwfuck*—and then came the tears that might have reeked of vodka, tequila and nicotine, had you sniffed them. Snorted them like drugs.

You said, "That hurt."

For real, though. It did, it does, it always will, but we move and we are moving and we will always be moving forward because, as my grandpa always said, the alternative ain't that great, or he said something like it. We are all mediocre and that's the point and maybe someday, we'll be cool with it. In the meantime, we're just you're basic, boring white people. Me, I'm your basic white trash, grown-up.

Mediocrity. Mid-south style. I'll take it with a shot of Bourbon. Never top shelf. Maybe I'll sleep with the horses tonight. That'd be living in the lap of goddamn luxury.

About the Author:

Rebecca Kirschbaum is an writer with a heart for Appalachia and the poor. Her work has been called modern Southern gothic, boundary-bending and compared to that of Flannery O'Connor. Her stories have been published by Still Point Arts Quarterly and The Furious Gazelle, as well as seen on stage in San Antonio and San Diego. She is the recipient of a Write Well Award. She often writes to represent the underprivileged and a culture of poverty that is frequently left out of media. Those human beings are her people. She writes so they, too, have a voice.

MEDIEVAL SURGERY AND ITS CONTRIBUTION TO THE THIRD MILLENNIUM

by Dr. Raymond Fenech

Who isn't overawed by the progress that medicine has made in this third millennium? Yet few people know that basically all that we have today is all thanks to the profound effects of the Renaissance on the progress of medicine, as scholars emerged to point out the mistakes and the stagnation of the previous centuries, replacing these by much of the knowledge upon which medicine is based today.

In fact, many operations attempted in the middle ages have been undertaken in the 21st century. Among others are the removal of bladder stones, births by method of caesarean, dentistry operations and even cataract interventions.

Cataract removal was a painful surgical procedure, which basically involved the use of a sharp pointed instrument, such as a needle or knife. Such an operation hardly ever saved the patients' sight, but once medical influence from the Middle East reached Europe, cataract surgery was radically improved. The sharp pointed instrument was substituted by a syringe so that cataracts were extracted by suction.

Surgery then was only reserved for life/death situations because most operations resulted in the inevitable demise of the patients. If by some shear miracle the patient survived, he would succumb as the result of an infection, or some other complications.

Real anaesthetic as we know it today was not available and Dwale was the only alternative. The following are the ingredients and method to make this medieval anaesthetic:

•*Gall of one cow (if child), one boar (if man), or one sow (if woman)*

•*Briony, three spoonfuls*

•*Opium, three spoonfuls*

•*Hemlock juice, three spoonfuls*

•*Henbane, three spoonfuls*

•*Vinegar, three spoonfuls*

Mix together in a glass vessel and bring to a boil. Take three spoonfuls of elixir and mix into a potel* of good wine, and mix well.

When it is needed, let patient sit against a good fire and make him drink thereof until he falls asleep. Then you may safely cut him, and when you have done your cure, take vinegar and salt and wash well his temples and his cheekbones and he shall awake immediately.

A potel is equivalent to approximately 3 bottles of wine."

Ether as we know it now was first used by medieval Swiss physician, Auroleus Phillipus Theostratus Bombastus von Hohenheim, known as, Paracelsus. However, Ether didn't really earn the deserved acclaim and didn't come into use until it was re-introduced in the United States 300 years later. Alternatively, Paracelsus turned to laudanum and opium as the method to numb pain.

Surgical history was marked in 1543 when the Belgian anatomist, Andreas Versalius published his book, *On the Fabric of the Human Body*. In this book, he described the discoveries he had made while dissecting human corpses, thus removing many of the anatomical misconceptions, which had been widely accepted ever since the time of Galen.

Probably one of the more important surgical discoveries in the Middle-Ages was made by Abdul Qasim Al-Zahravi (936-1013 AD) known as Albucasis, another Middle East surgeon who contributed immensely to this science by the numerous illustrations of surgical instruments, some of which were invented by himself.

The Arab surgeon designed an arrow spoon, which could remove arrow heads from the bodies of wounded soldiers. The spoon had the capability of attaching itself around the arrowhead so the barbs could be pulled out without causing further damage to the wound.

In his designs found in the *Compendium,* Albucasis gives detailed descriptions and technical data of the surgical tools and their use. This extraordinary work not only provides a well-illustrated text designed to assist the surgeon with details of each treatment, but also includes different types of dressings for the various wounds.

In the same book, he also describes novel procedures such as the use of catgut for internal stitching. Catgut is a tough thin cord made from the treated and stretched intestines of certain animals, especially sheep, used as surgical ligatures. Albucasis also describes surgical interventions for the removal of gall stones by entry through the urinary passage, thyroidectomy and cataract removal.

Today when one goes to the hair dresser or as this profession was referred to in earlier days, the Barber, one goes to have his hair cut, trimmed, washed or to get a different hairstyle but not in the Middle-Ages. Besides getting one's hair trimmed or beard shaved, surgery was also on offer as part of the services offered by barber surgeons, who also practiced bloodletting, a very common procedure very much in fashion in those days and thought to be an essential healthy exercise. Barber surgeons mostly dealt with dagger, sword and arrow wounds. In most operations, patients were given a piece of leather or wood to bite on, or were made to drink large quantities of wine to numb their senses. .

One particular operation, Trepanning (Trepanation) goes even further back than the Middle- Ages. In fact, archaeological discoveries have unearthed fossilized skulls indicating that this surgical procedure goes back as far as the Neolithic Age.

The surgical intervention consisted of cutting the cranial bones with a small cylindrical saw, a trepan, which was equipped with a centre pin that extended just beyond the blade of the saw. The pin was inserted first to ensure the saw did not slip whilst cutting the bone.

The first metallic catheters were used in the mid-1300s. Such interventions were necessary when patients experienced urinary blockage mostly caused by various venereal diseases. Because there were no antibiotics, this intervention was very common. The operation consisted of the insertion of a urinary catheter through the urethra into the bladder, thus relieving the blockage. When the obstruction was such that the metal tube could not surpass it, other procedures were used. All the methods were as painful as dangerous.

Any modern pregnant woman today would surely think that having a child is a very normal and safe procedure. But this was not so in the Middle-Ages, when pregnant women were advised by the Church to go to confession and prepare for their funeral. All midwives assisting women during labour then were regulated by Roman Catholic law and licensed by a Bishop.

Dead babies that failed to be delivered were removed with a squeezer after being dismembered in the womb with sharp instruments, whilst retained placentas were pulled out by counterweights. Midwives who detected the baby to be in an abnormal position thus slowing its delivery would try to turn the infant *inutero*, or reposition the foetus by shaking the bed.

Haemorrhoids was always a condition that plagued thousands of people and in the Middle-Ages this condition was also as common and painful. Actually, it was the Irish monk, St. Fiacre, patron saint of haemorrhoids sufferers who is said to have had this condition himself, until one day he sat on a miraculous stone that finally gave him relief. The stone survives to this day and is said to have his haemorrhoids still imprinted upon it. Many used to refer to this condition as 'St. Fiacre's curse.'

In the 12th century, a new cure was suggested by Moses Maimonides, a Jew physician who disagreed with any of the previous cures and recommended the *Sitz* Bath, a common treatment used to this very day. The *Sitz* Bath is a simple procedure of sitting down in warm water to help relieve pain.

Amputation in the Middle-Ages was a very common surgical intervention mostly performed on numerous soldiers who took part in the various wars. Here is a descriptive account of such an operation from Henri de Mondeville's, Cyrurgia (Surgery) 1312. Monteville was the private surgeon to the two kings of France, Philip IV and Louis X:

When a surgeon encounters gangrene that has resisted all other treatments, he must ampu-

tate the limb to save the patient's life as well as to arrest the advance of the gangrene. Thus, if the end of a digit is gangrenous, amputate through the next joint; that is the rule to follow elsewhere. For example, if the gangrene reaches the palm, amputate at the wrist. If it involves the forearm amputate at the elbow. But if it extends into the upper arm the patient cannot survive.

By no means does this article cover all the surgical procedures, or discoveries which made a name in surgery during the Middle Ages. However, it does give readers a glimpse of how this art came about and all the pain that patients had to suffer before the more recent advances of scientific knowledge brought about the rapid progress from which we are now all benefitting.

References

Medicine in the Crusades: Warfare, Wounds and the Medieval Surgeon (Piers D. Mirchell), Cambridge University Press, 2007

Biomedical Ephemera

Cyrurgia (Surgery) (Henri de Mondeville), 1312

Medieval Masters of Medicine, Watch Tower Bible and Tract Society of Pennsylvania, 2015

Surgery in the Middle Ages: Trepanning (Michael Foster) 2014

About the Author:

Raymond Fenech embarked on his writing career as a freelance journalist at 18 and worked for the leading newspapers, The Times and Sunday Times of Malta. He edited two nationwide distributed magazines and his poems, articles, essays and short stories have been featured in several publications in 12 countries. His research on ghosts has appeared in The International Directory of the Most Haunted Places, published by Penguin Books, USA.

THE PERFECT POEM

by JR Solonche

SONNET X

X is the first letter of the fewest words, one

reason why X is my favorite letter.

X is a person, a thing, an agency, a factor,

etc. of unknown identity. X is the Roman

numeral for 10. X is Jesus Christ, God's son.

X is the designation used by the motion-

picture industry for films no one under

17 years of age may attend. X is the sign

that kisses you at the end of a letter.

X is the power of magnification.

X is the signature of an illiterate.

X is used on a test to indicate an error.

X is the last letter I write on most of what

I write. X marks the empty spot.

WALLET

I open my wallet which contains who I am.

It is right to be made of skin.

There is one one-dollar bill, more than enough for a phone

call if I can make the change.

There is a picture of my wife as an infant.

There is a picture of my wife as a teenager.

 There is a picture of my wife as my wife.

There are three plastic cards which give me credit for being me.

There are two library cards which, alas, I use seldom.

There are two health insurance cards which, alas, I use often.

There is a stub with which I will redeem a watch that needs a new crystal.

It is the watch of my wife's father who is dead and who,

therefore, has no wallet.

I carry it in my hip pocket.

I have never lost it.

It has never been pick-pocketed, although for years I lived in a big city

and traveled the subway, wary of a large population of strangers.

THE PERFECT POEM

The perfect poem is not square,
although I used to think the perfect poem

would have to be square.
I probably thought that the perfect would have

to be square because I read a lot of sonnets when I was young,
which, you know, sort of look like squares.

Now I know the perfect poem is not square.
Now I know the perfect poem is a sphere.

Now I know the perfect poem is the shape of the earth
or of any other body in space whose core is molten iron.

About the Author:

Professor Emeritus of English at SUNY Orange,
J.R. Solonche has been publishing poems in
magazines and anthologies (more than 400) since
the early 70s. He is author of Beautiful Day
(Deerbrook Editions), Won't Be Long (Deerbrook
Editions), Heart's Content (chapbook from Five
Oaks Press), Invisible (nominated for the Pulitzer
Prize by Five Oaks Press), The Black Birch (Kelsay
Books), I, Emily Dickinson & Other Found Poems
(Deerbrook Editions), In Short Order (Kelsay
Books), Tomorrow, Today & Yesterday (Deerbrook
Editions), If You Should See Me Walking on the
Road (forthcoming from Kelsay Books), and coau-
thor of Peach Girl: Poems for a Chinese Daughter
(Grayson Books). He lives in the Hudson Valley.

THE LOVE OF LATIN

by Howard Sage

Amidst the cost of all

that encompasses the

blankiverse these days,

tolls to pass this way or that,

lights to save pedestrians from

stalled vehicles en route

to dump their loads of food,

oil, chairs, desks, even

lumber here and there, betwixt

shuttered edifices that once

thrust bagels, foods, and band aids

at lined down customers,

in the midst of all the

paraphernalia that humps

upon the locus termed earth,

why do I recall only the note

you wrote on the back

of my business card to help me

read Catallus in the original?

Why?

En Route to Arequipa

I

At six I woke, ate,

bought our tickets for our

journey northwest to

Arequipa; we would stay two days,

move on to Puno by the Lake,

turn back to Arequipa and on,

further north, to Lima, to

complete our circuit begun

by air a week before. But

here we were, tickets

in hand, walking slowly

to the gate of Tacna's dead.

II

Before we approached closely,

a boy, smudged face, of many boys and girls

mumbled he would carry water,

if we would pay; no

one bargained. Flowers bought

at the door; we entered through a portal,

a tiled hall open to the

air, and slowly

through the dust walked

to the graves.

III
Aisles, left and right,
lay open to
our look; title, name
and dates, some clean
and neat, some obscure.
The boy's hands, all yellow
and blue with swishing
pails, taking their own route
arrived to find with us the shelves
we sought. You bore your flowers
and your bag.
I carried flowers in one hand.
    IV
High on a shelf your father lay.
Near him a cracked glass showed
Weathered wood, vintage 1911
dead. "Bring the stool,"
and the boy carried a ladder
twice his size
bent from many steps for you to
climb the awful climb, the
steep ascent bringing with
brave legs and
hands water first and
then, arranged and placed,
dipped in Tacna's wine, the flowers.
In shadow and sun the boy un-awed and I, taut,
saw.
    V
Down,
down you climbed, began
your descent, flesh
having returned to
flesh, to honor its
life, conception,
our life. Down,
down. Water and flowers for your
father's
father,
my tears for my mother's father;

past the grave
of Tacna's poet, home
from Paris; past
Italian clans;
in front of
Anglo busts; through
portals;
facing other water carriers; past the
flower stands without
a word from us or
them; home;
at night, North
west to
Arequipa.

About the Author

Howard Sage has lived at HMC Street, Houston, Texas; 182 First Street, Perth Amboy, N.J., 6 Belsize Crescent, London, N.W., 3, and Tatung Lu, Tainan, Taiwan. He edited and published award-winning Pulp magazine for ten years, including in one issue his interview with Ralph Ellison

BABY POEM

by C.H. Coleman

Naughty

Feel delicious? Okay!
"Decadent," say it,
think: herding happiness
isn't always enjoyable.

One button too far on
a billowy blouse reveals
enough already – two, now
an interstate billboard,

augments valley viewing.
Obvious, but not obnoxious.
Enough already! Walking
a third time through creates

an emblazoned image, finally
dots his eyes on crossing t's.
Confidence? Wobbly legs, his
welcomed mouth opens,

"Hi. I'm..."

Casting

Down the hill
at tree-canopied road's end,
there's a boat launch,
where many tire tracks show
where many journeys have begun,
and a rickety dock beside it.

At the end of the dock
a lure could be cast a mile
or farther or closer
or wherever in this world
any angler wills it to go.

Out early on my second day,
I feel the old codger's boots
stamp stamp stamp, coming
forth to where my feet dangle
above the still water.

His white mane captured
beneath his billed ball cap,
lips part between a face
full of white facial hair.
He whistles all the way
tweeting Amazing Grace,
a songbird's song, early spring -

like winter's finally over,
like the seasons, I am reborn.
The old codger's on his way
to teach me how to cast my line:
how far, how when, how where
to begin being in my new life.

A Better Education

You're going to school,
my father said, as he pulled
warm sheets and blankets
from my single bed.

You're going to school,
said my mother, as she pulled
a pillow from beneath a dream
playing in my sleepy head.

Stiff as an iron statue
lacking liberty, I figured
no use arguing my case,
I alighted in fast stead.

That musical's famous song,
it's a hard luck life for kids,
who can't get adults to follow,
always the ones being led.

My imagination of adulthood
resembles a Christmas poem,
delicious, sugary sugar plum
dancers dressed purply red.

Mom 'n Dad forgot that school
sucks joy from kids' lives,
only the geekazoids benefit
from great books not read.

Shoved outside in winter,
gloves, scarf, slice of bread.
Meander to the bus stop,
other kids too seem dead.

You're not going to school,
for sure I'll tell my own kids,
pulling covers around them
as I tuck them in their beds.

You're not going to school,
I'll promise to those kids.
Daddy thinks better you stay
home and play hooky instead.

Baby Poem [otherwise untitled]

You're pregnant.
Ignorance earned us
a six-week head start.
And now we must decide
on whether or not we'll opt
to proceed. You tried when you
were married and nothing ever took.
I prayed for extermination and the other
she agreed with me and we parted almost
parents. But never really were a couple ever
again. But here you and I are, together we
are pregnant with a six-week head start
and we had always thought you could
not and we knew that I could and
now we're on the verge of break
up, but now we're in this, a team
and you start thinking of names
and I think you're right and we
agree we're gonna have a baby.

HIS HAND

by Amelia Abdullah

Dear mama,

Mama

The first word of love to ever leave my lips

The strongest name to call a woman

The hardest job to take on

The mightiest soldier to ever walk the planet

The most beautiful grace to ever touch our hearts

Each day you rise with the only intent of providing for yours

The children you encased with love in your tummy

And the ones you birthed through pain and agony

And patience

Taking time to slowly learn our every desire

And love all our flaws into our strengths

You pursue your dreams through building ours

You give yourself up to make us bigger, stronger, and smarter

For all the times you stood by me

For all the love you gave to me

You lifted me up

Higher than the stars just so you could have something to look up to

Something that reflects your beauty and love in return

Three similar faces that resound in your heart

Three faces that belong to your skin

A mother's love could break any barriers

Formed between her child and any enemies

A mother's love is the strongest bond

Specifically crafted by God himself

To share time and space with a creation and their creator

A mother's love resides in me

Through you

My creator

Sea Life

The lack of gravity swiftly grabs my interest
As I float on top of a new world.
Colorful life one hundred feet beneath me
Magnetically attracts my focus
Of serene magnificence.
Fishes of vibrant colors put the rainbow to shame
As they feed off the coral reefs
Which house fishes by the hundreds
In curvy cubbies protecting them from enemies.
Random flamboyant sea fans waving hello
With their thin mesh frame
Acting as a shade for some

Scattered star fishes who lie on the sea floor
Lethargic and stationary
Next to their slimy twin
The sea cucumber.
Slithering snakes moving fluidly
Towards their prey.
Bubble-like jelly fishes pump towards the sky
With their sensational long legs.
Admiring the hidden treasures of the sea
In a breathtaking moment.
Fascination of underwater life
Relaxing my every cell.
Thoughts of reality disappear
As I slowly become one with the sea

His Hand

My light skinned skinny little fingers intertwined with his dark long fingers.

Our hands rested on his long dark jeans. His hand was warm and soft. Sort of comforting.

We were on the school bus with other high school kids who were rambling on about their day but

I focused on our hands. The contrast was outstanding and made me worry a little.

I couldn't help thinking about what people would think about an African American and an Asian dating.

People love to talk and spread unnecessary lies. My family wasn't too welcoming of other races but

I was always taught to never judge people so maybe they would be ok with it.

We were friends just the day before but today we were holding hands the way couples do.

I never had a boyfriend before so I wasn't sure if these butterflies should be in my stomach.

He sat slouching a little in a navy blue polo collared top. He had his black book bag in his lap.

He had a low haircut that was shaped up nicely, full lips, deep brown eyes, slightly long eyelashes, and a flat nose.

He had no pimples or facial hair. I had seen him every single school day but today he stood out.

He had a mature sex appeal that I couldn't help but be attracted to. He voice seemed gentler. His gaze seemed like a God's Angel looking at you awaiting for your demands.

He whispered something in my ear but I couldn't really focus on anything but him. I finally had a boyfriend. For the first time, I was going to feel what love was like. Or at least get to feel a guy holding me.

He leaned over and asked if I would be his girlfriend. I looked him in the eyes and gave him a nervous cheesy grin and said, "Yes."

We were at my stop, so I let his hand go. As I got up and started to walk off, I looked at him. His eyes and soft smile told me not worry.

Everything was going to be ok.

Father

His ugly unshaved chubby face disgusts me. I only see the wrinkled forehead

The evil eyes, and all the hurtful names on his lips.

His thinning hair does nothing to compliment "Devil" written on his forehead.

He stands 5'10" with a bulging stomach and stick legs. His big hands

Only remind me of the past.

I remember the beatings as a child…and the beating for my boyfriend.

I never forget the look he gave me every time he yelled.

Fire red face and nostrils flared as if breathing all the oxygen for the world.

The heavy breathing that made his chest move faster than a baby's.

His eyes would always be red…red as the blood that was in my eye from being hit with a gold ring.

I couldn't go to school because he didn't want anyone questioning my face.

My so called beautiful face…his face…I hate my reflection.

I only see him and all the scars he left on it.

My eyes swollen and puffy from the tears. I still see the ring in the corner of my left eye.

We have the same nose with the slight bump at the top.

I hear "bitch, slut, stupid, dumbass, wasted sperm, mistake."

All this pain hidden behind my perfectly straight pearly whites.

It's funny how a little smile can hide so much.

Here We Go Again...

Slowly our laughter faded into silence.

We were eves dropping on the dispute between them occurring in the bathroom.

It was hard to hear but we felt the hostility shooting us down.

I thought to myself, "Here we go again."

He came out giving us that evil look...the one that could kill.

As he made his way to the stairs, the same anger in his eyes showed in our eyes.

We returned to watching the VMAs then, she came out yelling about something irrelevant.

She made no sense and neither did their argument.

Why are we fighting over the small things these?

What ever happened to being a family?

Why is it so easy to point and blame?

Confused we scrambled at her request trying to figure out how to turn this mishap into laughter.

We could not fulfill her wish so she yelled more aggressively.

As we headed to bed, our heads hung low in disappointment.

Questions and actions replay in my head at attempts to understand the situation.

I guess I was not supposed to understand so I remained angry and puzzled.

I fell asleep thinking about how we got to this point and if there was any hope to bring back the joy.

I hope the future looks brighter because my brothers and I are simply lost.

Mommy is hurting and Ahmad refuses to leave.

About the Author:

My name is **Amelia.** I am a free-thinking writer who uses poetry as an outlet for depression and anxiety. I have been through a lot of ups and downs trying to find my passion and purpose in life. Writing has been a judgement-free zone for all of the negativity in my world and the world we live in. My hope is to share my thoughts for others to know that they are not alone in going through life's challenges. Always remember to smile. Enjoy.

PROLONGING

by William Snyder

PROLONGING

She told me to
wait a little while.
I said okay,
I'll wait outside.
Ry Cooder, Joni
Mitchell, somebody
in Chains—
they play and play.
I slept last night
in the hollow comfort
of the downstairs couch.
Alone.
I asked her
to come too,
but she decided
against it.

Rain falls.
The tip tip
   on a jutting eave
   puddles around me.

COMPANY

The café door open to the street, the seven
tables occupied tonight, one by troopers

in uniform. A bony cat slinks through chair legs
and rungs. We listen to the calms and quicks of
conversations until the owners, two brothers,
bring our food—fresh prawn, onion, butter,
bread. Suddenly, the cat leaps to our table. I
brush it off and the owners chase it, apologize,
pat our shoulders, bring fresh wine. The troopers laugh, pound backs. One pings his glass
with a fork.

The cat creeps back. A trooper tempts it in with
coos and a knife, its blade spearing shells. The
cat leaps toward the dangle. The trooper raises
the knife. The cat eyes the shells, springs
again—four, five, six times—claws spread, ears
erect, but the knife jerked up just far enough.
Someone behind us makes a hiss. The owners
polish trays at the kitchen door. Another leap.
The trooper darts his hand, throws the cat and
it tumbles. Another hiss. A whistle. The cat
leaps, fur-lines taut. The trooper slashes downward, but the cat twists, the blade flashing
past.

The cat licks its flank. The trooper drops the
knife—blade first—but the cat springs aside.
We hoot for the cat, clap. The trooper smiles,
leans back, thrusts his legs—accepts our applause. A woman glowers, reaches toward the
cat. Tail quivering, it licks the bread, the juice
and prawn she's offered.

About the Author:

I have published poems in <u>The Southern Re-
view</u>, <u>Atlanta Review</u>, <u>Poet Lore</u>, <u>Folio</u>, and
<u>Southern Humanities Review</u> among others.
I was the co-winner of the 2001 Grolier Poetry
Prize, winner of the 2002 Kinloch Rivers
Chapbook competition; The *CONSEQUENCE*
Prize in Poetry, 2013; the 2015 Claire Keyes
Poetry Prize. I teach writing and literature at
Concordia College, Moorhead, MN.

REFLECTIONS ON TIES THAT BIND

by Jan Little

If marriage offered a narrow tether like Denmark's attachment to Europe,
I could have conformed that much to a husband's wants
And gladly given all that connected me to him along that shared side,
Yet still have space to feel whole within myself
With time alone to welcome sunrises.

But in an era of coupledom,
Children, churches, friends appear as too tight enclosures
Like that of landlocked Poland vulnerable in its total connection to others.
The need for time to self-define would have pulled at those seams
I chose to sew myself into

—So, torn between need to soar with dragonflies
Or serve those who had depended on me, would leave me
Only ever be a halfling to them and to me.
And I would self-bind myself to a tree of love and know that
That to break even one branch to see the sunset
Directly and with no filter would break a dear heart.

Always my need to meander and to become
A nomadic jig-sawed raft, like Ireland, separated just enough
Would cause wars over custodial privileges—But after a while,
Loneliness would lead me to dock ports of serial monogamies
Until the yen to roam again arrived to leave
Those voices waking me from seaside talks with mermaids.

Yet love's allure—to matter most to another—
To have another matter most to me--
Still calls to me as Penelope's steadfastness
Did to Odysseus—
Like him, I could happily winter in love's arms
With freedom to sail in spring's seas.

About the Author:

A member of the Florida Writers' Association, I am a retired college instructor and AP English teacher. I am revising a murder mystery, writing a fantasy, and have written short stories and poetry. I live in Orlando, Florida.

LITTLE BLACK BOY

by Daniel Jackson

LITTLE BLACK BOY

after William Blake

As a stubborn child my father hit me,
his hand glistening black as Afro
Sheen came down like coal-tar
and dyed me blue as a Nelly Queen,
because I sparkled, I gleamed, found my light
in the shade and danced in the dark.

My father spank me on his knee
with an open fist before the Motown,
he shook me down and slapped the music out.
His finger like a switch on my cheek,
he said,

No son of mine will dance limp wristed
Take my hand come let me show you
put them on my waist boy
Don't be scared!
Lead real slow
Don't let the woman lead you
Dammit boy!
Move your feet and hips together
no not like that that's too much hip
        Never mind.

He blames my mother because he can't
believe a son of his would birth such radiance,
he said, little black boys with too much pride
in their hips leapfrog through life
lacking some part.

BOP: QUEER GOSPEL

Life, Death, Resurrection

If he had another voice
it'd be that of a singer
(Could he be twice blessed?)
and sing himself a better-made man,
for being born black & queer.

> *Look now, there is in this body*
> *a voice, the voice of a Man.*

When he was but a pickaninny,
swaddled, he saw the world
on his mother's cast-iron back.
When he grew up, the world saw through him
and then the suffering began.
A black, queer body hurls itself
over the very difficult task
of surviving a reliquary of screams.

> *Look now, there is in this body*
> *a voice, the voice of a Man.*

In his mother's high-heels he stands
on pillars, praiseworthy, in a looking glass.
Startled awake, his tiny voice
rouses his mother, and her helping hands
steer him down, untying
that ribbon dancing in his voice.

> *Look now, there is in this body*
> *a voice, I am a Man.*

BARBER SHOP

The barber's stony fingers
inched up my neck—
the tips of them I wanted
to fasten an ache within.

Sprayed off tongues, insults
unfastened to the smoke of Phillies.
I shrunk and overheard the word "faggot,"
as though I were deaf; their words guffawed.

With gestures, grunts, slaps across the lap,
two fathers spat, shaming their kids. Mine,
sat atop his rocky mountain, hard as stone,
watching me roll down in that chair, sinking.

How it must've felt to have another man's hands
at his own son's neck for the first time?
He sat indifferent, as I shrank
in that leather, unmoved to anchor
in me some rope, a touch

of reassurance, that what I felt
at the length of the chair's arm,
that bulge behind the barber's smock,
was nothing to fear.

LULLABY FOR THE WEARY

II.

Now the doctor tells me I got the gout
in my feet too, spent standing spent waiting
on a platform to go home from my night job,
for the train in the cold and rain the shit
I wipe from the asses of strangers.

Just so I can see my children go
a day without begging or stealing.
What work a woman ain't done harder
than any man? a mother's feet is as callous strong,
and it hurts just the same wearing new shoes.

Each time this body cries for a little more rest.
I lay down and get up with it. Each day it cries.
For the night's wide-eyed with live sonata,
Crickets surround this chair and I listen.

THE WEAK REVEAL THEMSELVES

You should play with boys.
If I had of been 'round
you wouldn't be this way:
you'd be running
after 'em girls,
instead of running
way from 'em.

She's to blame.
I tried to find my way inside,
so that when you grow up you
ain't never have to ask yourself
what part of you was missin'.
I tried to leave a piece of me inside.

Football, now that's a man's game.
Wouldn't you rather play with boys
and toss around the pigskin?
A man shouldn't be 'fraid
to get hit,
and you could be a runnin' back
since *you* like to run
from 'em girls.

Come sit down, boy.
You hear that? Listen.
This music is the reason you's here—
this here's baby-makin' music:

Take my hand,
Come with me, baby, to Love Land
Let me show you how sweet it could be …

Don't go blamin' me 'cause I wasn't 'round.
It's your mama's fault,
she kept me from you.
No son of mine…well you know what I mean.

About the Author:

Daniel Jackson, a poet from New York, has received his degrees from Hunter College, New York and Emerson College, Boston where He studied creative writing. His work has appeared on the Lambda Literary poetry spotlight, *Calliope Magazine, The Santa Anna River Review,* Black Napkin Press, Faultline Journal of Arts and Letters, and other small journals. He was an assistant poetry editor at Redivider: A Journal of New Literature and Art, and a prospective 2018 Lambda Literary Retreat for Emerging LGBTQ Voices Fiction Fellow.

MIND OF A BOY

by Jhier Wells

Mind of a Boy

When I was a boy
summers were waves waiting
to carry me to the ocean's center.
When I was a boy
summers were trees stretching out
its limbs for me to lie on.
When I was a boy
summers were sun rays kissing my skin.

I was a boy,
who longed to run the fields where
weeds shrunk themselves just so
I may know the sun's light.
Yes, I was a boy,
who jumped over the cracks of the
sidewalks just so that I wouldn't
disturb the roses that existed there.

I was a boy
who fell in love with
my idea of youth.
An idea that deepened
the moment my soul sat quietly
and admired the beauty of the star
rather than chase it.

Answered

"Fool in love," said my soul to my heart,
"Indeed, you are easily led down a path
of vanity, towards a darkness that will
swallow you whole, with no light left;"
And my heart cried unconsolably.

As I sat in front of Lisa, I watched the sun
kiss her brown sugar, honey skin,
while her lips reached to taste mines,
my heart buried a piece of the light it knew:
"I'll find my way out, I have to!"

Soul of Fire

Her soul was pure fire.
People gathered around to
bring warmth when life had
become cold and dark. She
alone was their comfort.

When Hate Wins

the night's been having a party
drinking the blood of the fallen
that has soaked the streets
while the stars cry

too scared to come out
the sun hides its face
and watch in terror as souls wander
the city in search of prey

as love pleads with hate to
stop getting high for just one second
so that the streets may be cleared
and the city can mourn

About the Author:

I am a poet, who is finally releasing my poetry
for the world to read. I am devoted to changing
lives through my writing by sharing my journey.
My hope is to inspire young men, like my son,
to do better for themselves. Past publishing
credits include: Ink & Voices.

AFTER HIS TOUCH
by Leanne Talavera

After His Touch

That's how they'll get you, through
your eyes. It's your eyes
that will cradle flickering irises. That
will swim in white paranoia.
It will ignore the faces in fear
they'll meet another, and not like
what they see. They will glaze with
the guilt of weakness, and
shake with the shiver of awareness.
It's the eyes that will fall with
the sense of recognition. The alarms
that will go off when the wind
moves with an arm, always
mistaken for a weapon to violate. And
traumatize. In the eyes is where
you'll weigh your routes. When to
avoid. And when to risk. It's where
victims will be branded, like pigs
ready for slaughter.

        To be eaten.

Marriage

A single grey thread
        that stretches through time
clings to the trenches
        of your cheeks. Right below
the floppy disc
        that hangs from your
right eye. Yet
        even as it slowly
peels away, like
        the flakes that bloom
fully off the skin
        on your toes. Or
the letters of my name
        from the white
of your tongue. I
        will still love you
with the days honey
        poured from your fingertips,
soft with the ravings
        of a fleeting youth.

How Ironic

There's this thing called
relationships
I've never been in. But
if that were the case
I shouldn't be telling you how to
keep one. And there's this thing called
dates
that I've never been on. But
if that were the case
I shouldn't be telling you how to
do them. But there is this thing called
love
that I kind of know because
it comes and goes
just like my fear of the dark. But
if that were the case
I shouldn't be telling you how to
do it. Because
as if anyone knows how to do that,
anyway.

About the Author:

Leanne Talavera is from the Philippines, and is currently an undergraduate at New York University Abu Dhabi. She intends to major in Literature and Creative Writing and (possibly) History. Her life would be meaningless without tea and coffee.

FIREHOUSE BABY

by Austen Roye

1. hang in there

my springboard is a type of
social solitude
publicly isolated with head down
in plain sight.
managed two maybe three
hours of sleep and here now
far from home
foaming over ideas of
empty typewriter rooms
a desk by an open window that
makes me think of cigarettes.
I am trying to quit smoking
I am trying to tell you something
I am trying to remind myself
what it is to be
idealistic.

I am right there on the cusp
of not knowing what the hell
the kids are talking about
not out of touch maybe
out of steam out of drive
just out of it.

people who have cosmic visions
have too much time on their hands
life is too short to party
with palm readers.

my angel of death
only reads books if they're

first editions and says
he has my all figured out
because I'm a Gemini.
he hands me an ironic pamphlet
with Gandhi on the cover
doing a pull-up captioned,
"Hang in There."

he asks me
what seems to be the problem
your disposition is negative
your vibes are anxious
your aura is shit-brown.

one day he'll take me
as yours will take you
the game is rigged
which should be enough
to unify us all but somehow
doesn't.

I can't have visions of grandeur
doctor's orders
something about a low blood
cell count I don't know
I wasn't listening.

at any rate
out of any conflict I'll
take the one I know
I can win
which is the human heart
at war with itself.

besides I'm too
emotionally invested
but then again
that's probably just
the Gemini
in me.

2. curtains

I'll pay one day
for everything.

one day I'll pay for
looking so cool
smoking all these
cigarettes.

whether steaming in my
skin in Texas or a hotel
balcony in Budapest
tomorrow next fall or
craned over shoving a
broom over lifeless floor
tiles bleach and piss a
wheelchair by a window
a balloon on a string
in my hand wondering
if administrative assistants
ever win Nobel prizes.

here I am
a fish in a bowl
exploring a plastic
shipwreck.

3. firehouse baby

I said to myself,
I'll write a comprehensive study
of average everyday activities
stricken with the weight of
crippling anxiety and paranoia

a life overcome by fear
which makes that life
anything but average.

regard fear as a living breathing thing
but never give it a name
because if you give it a name
it becomes all too real.

the way they don't name pigs
destined to be slaughtered.

a name makes it all too relative
much too real
and therefore makes it all the more
difficult to abandon
to bury to cast out.
with a name your fear becomes
a beloved house pet you can
no longer afford to feed.

your fear becomes a
firehouse baby.

these are the notes I scribbled down
after eight or nine beers in sweatpants
pine needles pile of smoldering ash.
notes on a novel
and less than a page written of said novel
after a solid year of
someday
someday
someday.

I was spinning on wine one night
in bed beside her in the dark and
she said

tell me a scary story.

so I coughed one up as best I could
in such a state as I was in
did my best to raise and lower my voice
pause for dramatic effect
whisper when necessary.
something about ghosts
I don't remember.

the next morning I woke heavy-headed
and she told me she'd had nightmares.
it was the story she said
it had left her a bit shook
to which I was both apologetic and
selfish as it is
somehow proud
believing nightmares to be a sign
of half-decent storytelling.
she suggested I try writing horror
and maybe I will who knows.

I used to think genre fiction
was dog shit on my shoe
for which I sincerely
apologize.

but writing about not writing
is hardly writing at all isn't it?
how many publishers' desks have
cracked and caved under a million or so
half-ass drab faux farces of ghost stories
1700's period clothing
bonnets beards top hats carriages
ancient burial ground bones in basements
and don't you ever go in the basement
footsteps in attics doors bursting open
and slamming shut anonymously
ominous faces in windows
always the creak of disheveled houses
and always the woods always the woods
running into it running out of it
the young couple the car breaks down
and in they go
you know the story.

how could the woods be anything
other than a catalyst for
death darkness evil
and not just a shit-load
of trees?

writing about not writing
a comprehensive study
average everyday activities
stricken by the weight of
crippling anxiety and paranoia.

notes on the novel
I read them back to myself out loud
then sat down and wrote
this poem instead
if that's what this is.

that being said
consider this a horror story
and if it gives you nightmares
please know that I am both
apologetic and selfish as it is
somehow

proud.

About the Author:

Austen Roye has contributed to numerous independent presses and literary magazines. Most recently, he published his first poetry collection, God Save Your Mad Parade, through Crisis Chronicle Press. He resides in Denton, TX.

HERE FOR THE FOOD
by Tim Wenzell

Shoes (Global Warming Version)

A true woman evacuates with her shoes
and makes certain that all of them,
wrapped in garbage bags,
fill the trunk so that
he will take the back seat with his things
(whatever they might be).

The Artimus River
broke two dams and the St. Sebastian walls
with their ivy, their moss, and their history,
and dropped them to the sludgy bottom.
The mud rose in clumps and fell along the banks
like vanished turtles,
dotting the shorelines when the rain let up
and producing some kind of landscape:
 torn chunks of houses, diminished chimneys,
and brown wet sofas
falling back into earth

They will never build here again--
and in a thousand years, or maybe five hundred,
(or maybe tomorrow)
when the oceans converge into a thick salt sludge
filling like a hardening glue
 into the spaces that are left
a true woman will open her trunk
and pick out the right shoes
for the occasion.

Further Notes on the Spiders of New Guinea

Do invertebrates dream?
For example,
does the Brain Coral dream
it is a human brain
inside a skull, looking out
through land-rooted eyes at
a world beyond
the bottom of its sea?

What about the Bay Ghost Shrimp
dreaming of being real?
or the Aggregating Anemone
wishing in sleep to finally be calm?

What about the Cave Cricket
chirping in its sleep for daylight?
or the Missouri Millipede
walking upright in a dream
 on just two legs?

Does a House Spider drift off
after the lights have been turned down?
Where to? The deep forest where lights
 never click on, where webs are
never swept away by brooms?

In the deep sleep of an earth
alive with everything,
I would like to think that house spiders
can weave webs that rise
 into the upper canopies of rain forests,

fabulous filaments so graceful and long
that they disappear into Whitmanesque infinity:
no tears, no slamming of doors, no shouting,
no brooms, no lights to go down.

Instead, it is a party of the living,
day and night, with the company of other
dreamers:
The ant colonies marching in, the beetles
crawling home,
the crescendo of the crickets, loud and long,
and the dark, iridescent and beautiful spiders,
massed together with webs open and
lying in wait for everything to awaken.

Here For the Food

My grandfather left my father's family
In the middle of a cold night in 1933.
He said he was going out for coal.
That was two years ago
and on the day I turned twelve:

Now, I am the man of the house and we must
eat,
so I am here for the food.
I understand your mother died, and I feel for
that.
She must have been a wonderful woman, raising such mourners.
I see her there up at the altar in her fancy box
So I will file in line and cry for her with you.

But I really need your reception
More than anything.
You will have a spread, after all.
I brought my pants with the large pockets
To fill with finger foods
while I fill your world with lies
about how I knew her:
Yes, I will say between bites, she was like a
mother to me.
And if you knew the truth instead of the lie I
have provided,
You would understand why I am taking your
little sandwiches.

I saw my father again yesterday.
Gaunt and out of a car,
He walked across the baseball field
And handed me a dollar bill
While I stood on second base.

But I did not know that I had seen him
Until I went home and described a shadow-
stranger to my mother.
She handled the dollar in her hands, unsure of
where to pass it.
But I am a man and I can rise above her trembling
and her stare into space, and I will use that
dollar if she doesn't.

I check the obits, and another rich one has died,
this time an old man down on Devoe.
So here I will be again, working up a good cry,
getting ready again to tell someone in a line
and in the back pew of the church
about their beautiful grandfather who helped me
fund and find my way.

Someone Seven

I am crying:
my cat Speckles has been hit by a truck,
thrown into underbrush by rolling tires,
and I am standing in the roadside dust
watching the truck disappear into a wall of
thick air.
And where are my mother and father?

I am six and angry. They have just told me
that I can't watch the Flintstones
because I will stay awake and stare at my ceiling
and have bad dreams about a barefooted Fred
locked outside by the cat all night.

I am seven now, not six,
no longer worried about Fred knocking
for Wilma, not after the non-cartoon cat I hold
in my hands
looks into space and knows
that someone seven and crying, or six and angry,
won't be able to save it.
And where are my mother and father?

This is the windiest day I remember:
The dirt arrives in little tornadoes at my feet
and
a cold invisible wall pushes against me
and my suddenly still Speckles
locked inside my arms
on the side of the road.

The light disappears.
Fred won't wait out there forever--
Wilma will open the prehistoric door,
stop his shouting, allow him to finally lay down
on his stone bed and sleep, and in the morning
I can bury Speckles on the opposite side of the
pool.
But where are my mother and father with the
shovel?

Ellen

She ran into herself
like a parakeet into a hall mirror
and couldn't fly for a while,
she of the missing make-up,
absent of pointed shoes mounted on racks
hanging from her closet door--
no fabrics hanging on wooden poles in veils of
plastic,
confronted instead with a tape of her own
voice

screaming at some hour, scream
that seeped through walls
and under doors, woke neighbors
and deluded her from beauty.

About the Author:

I am widely published, including a novel,
twenty short stories, and many poems in literary journals, as well as scholarship in the area
of Irish ecocriticism, including a book (and
another forthcoming), and many articles in
peer-reviewed journals. I am an Associate Professor in the Department of Languages and
Literature at Virginia Union University in Richmond, VA.

RUBY THROAT

by Jessica Sabo

ruby throat

sit down she says
make yourself comfortable
put the napkin in your lap / keep your hands folded / sit up straight she says
cross your ankles
lift your chin
act like you are interested
I don't like sitting / I have too much energy I say
my foot shakes under the table
a hummingbird beats its wings inside my chest
and I feel like I can't breathe
my lungs are concrete
I am swallowing dust / my tongue is caught in
quicksand
pick up that fork she says
sit up straight
wipe your mouth
don't move too quickly, you'll seem anxious she
says
don't you dare take seconds
remember these things
my lips are sewn shut and my toes curl
I am staring at the fork
my brow is sweating
it is askew and a tick betrays my body
I am counting the minutes of the clock
my eyelids twitch / the bird is inside my brain
now
she is manic, stinging me with her beak like a spi-
nal tap to my meninges

I grip my thighs under the table
I won't tell you again she says
she points to the fork
there are people in this word who are starving she says
stop wasting my time
look at me when I am talking to you / lift
your chin / stop shaking your boot
what is your excuse
I am sorry I say
look at all of them she says
look at their bones
they are an army / battle ready / aiming fire
rings of soot around their eyes as they hurl
their meat through murder holes
and claim the bodies left behind
who the fuck are you?
my shoulders are uneven
I say I am one of those bodies that needs
looking after
I taught you better she says

Cradlesong

I remember the crack of your tongue against
the floor.
The whiplash reminding me of how you'd shut
me up so hard
that my body would turn inside out.
Monsters crawling inside your closet, through
the walls, inside the bathtub drain,
and they were coming for you *again.*
I told you to rise,
run faster.
I was never any good at saving you.
Even now, my knuckles are embedded in your
wet marrow-
fish-hooks into wired bone that cling to your
muted voice.
The last night we spoke,
I heard your demon whisper to me across the
static-
how to hunt you in the dark, how to find you
by scent.

When you finally freed your bones,
I was there to remind you
of how they still belong to me.

About the Author:

Jessica Sabo is a freelance writer and artist currently living in Orlando with her wife and two rescue pups. She is an LGBTQ+ advocate, an ardent supporter of the performing arts, and aspires to publish poems on topics related to eating disorders and other mental illnesses in order to promote awareness within the community. Her work can be found in the annual literary magazine, ChannelMarker.

RETICENCE

by Rick Adams

reticence

a heart shattered
like a broken
mirror; the shards
of glass slit
the wrists of
a man's desire

plagued with loneliness
and fear and
hatred and distrust;
happiness lost a
trial and was
sentenced to death

a soul abducted
and held captive
by emotional scarring
that may never
fade and may
never be forgotten

an occasional facade
of compassion and
geniality mask a
natural and sincere
cruelty and resentment
and blatant disregard

withdrawn from a
world of love
and warmth and
empathy; distant from
wide open arms
and welcoming hearts

these that are
not known may
never be known
about the beautiful
woman and her
barricade of reticence

my five friends

last night was spent with my five friends;
my five best friends in the whole wide world.
their names are Cabernet,
Pinot,
Merlot,
Bordeaux
and Shiraz.

they are always there when I need them;
they relax me
and soothe me.
they help me through my problems,
dull my pain,
and help me sleep at night.

they will never ignore me,
avoid me,
desert me,
deceive me,
lie to me
or steal from me.

we were all together late last night,
my five friends and I.
when we started the night,
they were full of body
and color.
before I knew it,
four of my five friends
were gone.
the only one left
was Merlot.

it was late
and I was tired.
they're good at that,
my five friends.
they're good at
making me feel tired
and sleepy.
they're good at playing tricks on me too.

"how do you feel?" asked Merlot.
"I feel good," I replied.

"well," said Merlot,

"just wait until morning…"

About the Author:

RICK ADAMS is an aspiring poet and short story writer. His work is influenced by life occurrences and human behavior with recurring themes that include isolation, alcoholism, depression, and longing. He currently resides in Texas and holds a Bachelor of Arts degree in Radio, Television, and Film, as well as a Masters degree in Information Systems Management.

RESILIENCE

by Andrew Hubbard

My first name is Marybeth
My last name changes about once a decade.

I bought this little log cabin
With a stone-fenced vegetable patch
For a backyard, and started
Reading gardening books,
Started getting my hands dirty
With some honest work.

The rock garden walls
Are home to little lizards
Beautiful, and quick as thought,
With graceful, brilliant blue tails.

Yesterday the cat was playing
With a blue tail on the porch
And I said to him,
"Hey mighty hunter, did you eat the lizard?"

My neighbor was visiting, and he laughed.
"It's a blue-tailed skink," he said.
"If something catches their tail
It comes off and they grow a new one."

I marvel:
"Now that's what I call resilience!"

I feel admiration
And a sense of kinship:

I can't regenerate body-parts
But life-parts I'm good at.

Fire me?
I'll get a better job.
Garnish me?
I'll make more money.
Divorce me?
I'll find a better-looking man.

I've bounced back from disaster
So many times I feel almost immune
On my good days…

On my darker days
I amend the old saying,
"What doesn't kill me makes me stronger."
I say instead, "What doesn't kill me—
Wears me down bit by bit
Like a file on soft metal."

That's all right—
We all have some dark days
And when I do
The garden helps a lot
And so do the skinks
With their endless scurry
And their unselfconscious passion
For being so utterly and intensely themselves.

JULY 2017

Taking Care of Mother

Beside the sink in the old farm kitchen
We have a red-enameled water pump
With the long handle flung into the air
In a salute it has held for over seventy-five
years.

We got it when mother was a little girl.
She says her mom was the proudest woman
In town: and for good reason—
No more walks uphill from the well
With a bucket of water in each hand,
No more shoveling snow to the well in winter
And breaking the ice on the wellcover with a
hammer
While the screaming wind made her eyes tear
And the tears froze before they could reach her
chin.

Now the pump's an antique, a monstrosity,
But mother dotes on it as much as ever;
Won't even discuss getting running water.
She even resents the electric lights
And whenever we lose power she gloats
How kerosene lamps don't go out in an ice
storm.

We're alone. Dad died long ago.
I was an only child
And mother won't talk about that.

I never married, never came close
The story of my love life would fit
On the back of a postage stamp with room left
over.

Mother cared for me, now I care for her.
That's a kind of rough justice I suppose.
I used to dream of getting free
But now it feels too late
And this life with mother
I truly believe it's a visitation for my sins.

She has three gingham dresses, blue, brown,
and pink.
She rotates between them, but favors the blue.
When we go into town I try to buy her new
clothes
But she won't. Says they're too dear.
(How long since you heard that phrase?)

She remembers about twenty five stories
About her family and her early years.
She tells a couple every day
Until she gets through them, then she starts
over.
She doesn't know she's doing it of course
But it's been going on twenty years
I could tell the stories myself by now.
She starts every story by saying,
"Did I ever tell you…"
And that's what most makes me want to
scream.

I can't let her cook.
She burns things till they catch fire
And she doesn't turn the stove off.
That leaves me, I cook. We eat together
And she farts through every meal.
Of course she can't hear it, so she doesn't
know.

Last month I was so far past fed up
I took her to a senior home in town,
Checked her in, and paid her first month's
keep.
She was docile enough during the process
But after lights out she opened a window
And somehow got to the ground in one piece.

She walked five miles toward home
Before the police picked her up at sunrise
And brought her back here.
They were amazed.

"That's one tough old bird," they said.
She is that.

She was mad as a wet hen
And so were the people from the home when
they called.
They wouldn't even give me my money back.

She caught a really bad cold in that escapade
And it won't go away so now I sleep with her.
I'd rather sleep with a squid, but sometimes in
the night
She coughs so bad I'm afraid she'd die
If I weren't there to help.

I don't get much sleep
And I've picked up a cough of my own now,
Along with blood in the morning phlegm.
Not a very good sign.
If I go first, I want my stone to say,
"Whatever she did, she paid for it."

About the Author:

Andrew Hubbard was born and raised in a coastal Maine fishing village. He earned degrees in English and Creative Writing from Dartmouth College and Columbia University, respectively.

For most of his career he has worked as Director of Training for major financial institutions, creating and delivering Sales, Management, and Technical training for user groups of up to 4,000.

He has had four prose books published, and his most recent books, collections of poetry, were published in 2014, 2016, and 2018.

He is a casual student of cooking and wine, a former martial arts instructor and competitive weight lifter, a collector of edged weapons, and a licensed handgun instructor. He lives in rural Indiana with his son, his wife, a giant, black German Shepard, and a gaggle of semi-tame deer.

SIMULTANEOUS WORLDS

by Mark Hurtubise

Momentary Tree Visit

Oak -

holder of leaf nations,
passageway for squirrels,
jay and crow scribe.

From its kiln, the sun exhales
afterlife upon you.

*

Stepping into your silhouette -
a breathing . . . irreversible memories
or prophecies from parallel sides?

*

Suddenly, your shadow lifts
then scatters . . . like a flock of birds
to chase air-light.

*

We are
someone's idea.

Simultaneous Worlds

Present

We grieve, we laugh spontaneously
like a key turning in a lock. Yet,
it takes so long to love forever –
except for the infant.

Future

Taken by doves without shadows,
we gaze beyond the earth's curve
to hear the single chord,
while the sun still follows moons
to study the singularity of smiles.

About the Author:

Mark Hurtubise. During the 1970s, numerous poems were accepted for publication. Then family, teaching, two college presidencies and for twelve years president of an Inland Northwest community foundation. Recapturing poetry's euphoria and appreciation for the authors he read four decades ago, he is attempting to compose again by balancing on a twig like a pregnant bird. Recently, his work has appeared in Bones, Ink In Thirds, Atlas Poetica, The Spokesman-Review, Stanford Social Innovation Review and Alliance (London).

LOVED LETTER

by Thea Tomaini

Loved Letter

A letter sent from a long-lost lover
Opened with much hesitation trepidation
Unfolding it in thirds and turning it over
Reveals the paper to be blank.

It mirrors the look on my face in confusion
Mouth hanging open, brain upend pendant
Searching the paper for some mark or sign
Some character in palimpsest to give it mean-
ing.

But it is silent, no voice on its surface
Blank like a tombstone, the name eaten by
lichens,
Like a sold-out hotel with every room empty
Like the face of an actress in mink eyelashes.

Like the wearied look on the ocean's broad
face
As it bumps the sand on Malibu beach
Like a student's essay in big looped letters
Asleep on the page and safe from meaning.

Like an old revenant with nothing to say
Resigned to his fate and unwilling to frighten
His haunted house quiet and undisturbed
The Ouija board still, no names yes or num-
bers.

The letter sits on my desk all night
While I lie awake with my face to the wall.
Listening concentrate close by the paint
I put my cheek to the cool white plaster.

I fold up the letter and put it away
Deep in the socks where no one will look.
The sign on the restaurant says, "Steak and
Magic,"
I sit at the bar to wash out my mind.

Is this your card? No, my card was blank.
Lady, there aren't any blanks in the deck.
Well, that's the magic, now, isn't it?
I am waiting to see the one that I picked.

Laurel Canyon Boulevard

Hollywood calls it magic hour
When purply tufts crawl toward the horizon
Across a sky still specked with blue,
They chase the sun in desperation,
Reach for their beloved as she pulls away.

The firmament lights itself from within
Below are shadows of hulking foothills
And flickering blips that mimic the stars,
Futile attempts trapped in bulbs of glass,
They cannot offer themselves to the twilight.

Phantom shapes and wisps of limbs
Parts of people walking pieces of dogs
Noises felt and sensations heard
Faint light in dim-light barely can see
Nothing until it's in front of you.

And she saw nothing as she stepped off the
curb,
Followed the faded orange arcs
Once bright, now sunk into layers of pitch
Her fingers crinkling a stiff green bill,
Granted from her mother's reluctant wallet.

Screeching wheels and a long honk horn
Sent her flying, then hard slam down
But in the mid-dusk, in the half-light unseen,
She rose incandescent above the dark figures
That gathered in sadness and shock on the
street.

The wind whipped up and wound right through
her
Spun her over the hills and dandled her high
Her arms raised up to embrace the gusts,
Her feet kicked out with pointed toes,
And she lit the broad flat stretch of the Valley:

A brand new restaurant with the door locked
tight,
A pack of stray Chihuahuas living next to the
freeway,
A newlywed couple with chickens in the yard,
A mansion abandoned in a hurricane fence,
A flapper's bob dyed the color of acid.

900 calories a day,
100 degrees above zero,
60 hours in non-union rehearsal,
30 dollars for sea urchin sushi,
10 o'clock and time for bed.

Squeal pink lip gloss laughter
Soft finger curls to stroke her face
Ballet flats batting the air
Dandled in the cooling night
She tumbled up.

Unenchanted

I know that house. I knew that house. Used to
be

A woman would come in an old Dodge Dart
She'd check on it, look in the cracks and the
crannies,
Where children's voices were stacked in a corner
And the sounds of breakfast were piled in the
sink.

Where the heavy feet of a father's work boots
Made a shallow dip in the threshold,
And tiny hands searched over their heads
To jam their fingers in the keyholes.

Where the clicks of a mother's knitting needles
Tapped between the plastered walls,
And homemade curtains slapped the breezes
That stirred around the hallways.

The woman would step through the weeds on
the walk
And yank on the padlock hanging on the door.
She'd send some guy a few days later
To patch the screens where the rats got in.

A tiny LA cottage with its breath blown out
The summertime streams through the rotting
eaves.
It warms the face of the linoleum floor
And lights the air with jasmine.

The rooms stand bare and drowsy-still
The echoes in the hallways call out goodbye.
Muffled by stucco and strangled by vines
Its specters gone Back East on the wind.

Gone to float in auntie-bellum parlours
Sing their dirges in long paneled hallways.
Stand at windows gothic in panes
Gauze flutter flying down stairways of marble.

In the wake of the Dart a whirlwind of leaves
Would ride the air then fall to the street.
They rolled in vain but never escaped
And she did not come to save them.

His Old Lady

I see the woman once in awhile. I almost never
see the man.
They never open the door in the front.
The lights blur low through dull gray glass
Passed through by shadows in the dead of
night.

Yellow newspapers cling to the windows
Cardboard boxes on lumpy chair cushions
A shawl draped still in suffocated air
Fluttered and fanned by unseen forces.

The woman squeezes between the screens
A bowing doorjamb under broken Spanish tiles
Throws her arms around a massive garden
That overruns the back of the house.

A thousand pots in a dozen sizes
Red clay blobs that she made herself
Back when her hair fell in auburn waves
Across her sunburnt freckled shoulders.

She pours the streams of water down
It rises to the rims in uplift drips.
They run across the veins of long wooden ta-
bles
Groovy deep with curling paint.

A shuffling movement, first upstairs, then
down
Creaks in the floor and a shape on the wall
His pale eye blinks through a cracked single
pane
But stays behind the half-hinged door.

Will he step out among the reeling pinwheels
And over the mouldy stoned faeries?
Will he dash to the van out back
That they once used to live in?

Only she hears his gauze-thin voice,
Calling in a tongue they invented together.
She answers with a song Paul McCartney wrote
In the year that I was born.

About the Author:

Thea Tomaini is Professor of English (NTT) at the University of Southern California. She is the author of academic books and articles on monster studies, death studies, and the uncanny in Early Mo-dern Literature. She has yet to see a ghost.

ODE TO MADAM CURIE
by Bray McDonald

Ode to Madam Curie

Why
finds no comfort
in reason.

Shouting
doesn't help.
Begging
becomes a fierce round egg
free to ponder.

What whips the cream
of knowledge
is a sacrificial
lamb.

The Madonna of the Lilies
(William-Adolphe Bouguereau, 1899)

The pure white petals of the Madonna Lilies
frame the painting of Mary and Jesus.
Though mimicking the style of the Renaissance
Bouguereau's form of art is Realism which gives the infant
and mother a believable warmth and sense of humanity.
His characteristic technique of layering his paints
give the subjects so much depth you think you can touch them.

Once an emblem of sovereignty to the Kings of Egypt
and presumed to be the Flower of Solomon
the wild lily of Palestine escaped it's dry mountain habitat
and now thrives throughout the world.
One can almost catch the scent of its fragrance
as the hands of the infant Jesus are gestured upward
as though raising the flowers toward the Son.

The Quest for Certainty
After Alfred North Whitehead (1861-1947)

Actuality bridges one nexus to another
and their cohesion ignites a covey of perhaps.

Sense-perception demands sense-reception
so the transmuted feelings can rise like Lazarus.

The principle of process is a subjective obligation.
The categories of the ultimate are always forthcoming.

Beware the logical consistencies.
Prehensions can lead to pitfalls.

Dynamic processes often distort reality.
Eternal objects are pure speculation.

God is conditional and a temporal occasion.
God is differential and His existence bipolar.

Existential Poem with Gertrude Stein in the Shadows
Contemplating the Clarity of Morning Light (3-pgs.)

I.
Gertrude Stein projected refracted light.
The Benedictine Abbey's indefinite depths.
Its colored glass Star Breakers
                              plagiarizing God.
There were movements. However brief.
The Futurist aspiring to become with verbal liberation.
                    Aggressive manifestos.
                    Innovations in Blue.
Chopin inserting bawdy ballads. Mayakovsky spitting diamonds.
Kandinsky scaling the wall between arts. Nietzsche's massive shadow.
An art gallery in Capri on the edge of an urge.
Dada in the heart spreading like Chocolate.
Appollonaire wrote about jock-straps and everyone lamented.
Yeats passion was intense and kept turning and turning.
                                        And Gertrude

placing another painting in morning light
proclaimed the question of identity.

II.
Rilke and his damned elegies. Endlessly knows and craves nothing.
Joyce's Ulysses as a peepofgold. Trilling trilling.
                                        Be tfpritt.
Beckett striking postures with extended overtures.
Ezra expounding to Doc Williams the new measures.
The Objectivist objecting to their personal rages.
The Waste Land and its possibilities and emotional terminates.
Charlie Chaplin with a tulip between his teeth riding an arrow of light.
The indirections of Symbolism seeking romantic clarity.
Russian poetry as music of proof and the curse of Inherent Exile
                              with no lyrical restraints.
Octavio Paz and the radical experiment telescoping Time.
Careless sketches and dismissed missives.
The rhythm of word and image spurred by spiritual obsessions.
Patchen's extended titlings as forms for framing the unframable.
Polish girls of the Ghetto or orphans in Prague.
                              Kodak moments.
                              Hurtful beauty.
Helen and Cleopatra as indigenous wonders.
Horizontal enigmas with questionable faces.
Gertrude stands near an open window dressed in a blue gown
and a breeze moves the curtains which shed dust motes
that dance like stars in the morning light.

III.
Montale expressing the bel canto.
The Italian Metaphysics with mitigated self-irony.
Lorca the graceful gypsy barely covered a tremendous distance.
Breton the real McCoy of process.
                                    Lover turned logician.
Surrealistic aestheticism with dislocated fragments.
Camus' Tongues of Fire in forbidden chambers.
                                    Quick to the core
Language weaves heat. Matches flare and filaments ignite.
Dali the Great Masturbator clinging to ecstasy.
                                    Too luminous.
                                    Unforgiving.
A somber but elegant smile. An intoxicating gaze.
Gertrude cultivating a harvest of canvas.
Gifts held in the hands of time.

IV.
There is no comprehensible stopping place
and the nuances are extremely sensitive.
Artaud exposed the enormity of bosoms
and the scales in a brothel.
                                    The new physicality.
Perpetually on the edge the starless window is deep.
Cezanne and the primitive. Simulations of the present. Emotional fiction.
Gertrude at lunch in the garden. Water in a glass. Spiral woman.

V.
Harlem negritude collectively conceived and assimilated.
Atmospheric struggles and identity rejection.
                                    Raven voices.
                                    Regurgitated heritage.
But Senghor says: "The Spider is Prudence and the Moon is Fecundity.
                                    Buffalo mocks the Lion".
Cesaire in the wee hours licking the deformed islands with a seaweed tongue.
Evidence of wounds and scars on the water.
                                    Veins shocked to the bone.
Bessie Smith deadly calm.
Standing in the wind of change like a Congolese lullaby.
                                    Lungs like cyclones.
Anna Akhmatova under a strange sky.
Seventeen months standing in a shadow.
Life torn from the heart of an emptied house.
                                    A scream amid singers.
Water lilies and red wheelbarrows. Minute basics.
An Alabama song by Brecht circumventing the formal.
Gertrude looking west towards the Atlantic.
                                    Preparing asparagus.
Bamboo fingers testing the texture.

VI.

Neruda just walking about
expelling a turbid rainbow of words. Equivocally human.
Brought to a focus and eclipsed by the visible.
Forming a constellation of difference.
Avant-garde enterprises and Cubist landscapes.

A recombination of elements.

Worms spilling out of beaks.
The translation and renewal of accepted idioms.
The deliberate propositions of the unconscious Symbolists.

To say what one can barely breathe.
The graffiti of Pompeii and Scrimshaw carvings.
Rene Char conserving infinite faces in words
that sneak into one's intimacy.

Assuming.
An underground resistance with poetic cries for the occasion.
Uncomfortable emotions racing toward an orifice.
Raw expressions proclaiming an absurd evidence.
The unpronounceable on the tongue like torture
as Gertrude waters her violets. Face sun drenched.

Her day-dreams rustling.

VII.
Rukeyser opening a way to flow to where still pools are fed.

Directed exploration.
Image by analogy. A metaphor for the mental
dimensioned out of the frame into primal contours.
Responding to the world's strategies.
As Gertrude greets her guests the light moves across the window

unchecked.
Found among those seeking

Wallace Stevens saying:
"It was her song.
She was the maker".
And no matter the occasion
mark the contraries.
Perhaps a book of questions in disguise.

About the Author:

Bray McDonald is an Information Specialist in Chattanooga, Tennessee. Mr. McDonald has been published in many journals recently, including 'Blue Collar Review', 'The Cape Rock', 'Rockhurst Review', 'Third Wednesday', 'Storyteller Magazine', 'Chiron Review', and "Between These Shores Anthology" in the UK. He also has poetry forthcoming in 'Cholla Needles', 'I-70 Review', 'Plainsongs' and 'Avalon Literary Review'.

ONION

by Amanda Leigh

Onion

If I peel off your layers like an onion,

Will I find the ripe in you?

Are you somewhere down under,

Holding an abeyance of the truth?

Your mind is a chasm;

A puzzle I can't seem to fit together.

If I dismantle you,

Will you find a way to reassemble gracefully?

Maybe you are an orange waiting to be peeled;

A gift striving to be unwrapped;

Clothing begging to be unveiled.

Or sadly, none of these may be true.

Perhaps your innermost circle is already exposed.

I hope for your sake that you are the onion,

Eager to be stripped down to the real you.

Lighthouse

Where is your beacon in the night to guide me;

    A sailor lost at sea?

You used to shine so bright for me in those first few years.

    Your arms were my light.

With time comes neglect and you faded.

    I can't find my way through these ripples in the ocean.

When I climb your mossy steps,

    The stairs to your heart are endless.

I can't reach the top to turn on your light once again,

    And so I steer away from you.

I am adrift without your guiding presence;

    A pendulum swinging endlessly.

Sleepy Eyes

when I lay my head down

    tell me beautiful things

        with your sleepy eyes

            plummeting me into my dreams

About the Author:

Amanda Leigh is a recent UNCC grad with a BA in English. She is currently a preschool teacher with 18 amazing students! She has been published in journals such as Askew, Cultured Vultures, Better Than Starbucks, and Tipton. She is working on publishing her first novel.

REFLECTION

by Louise Lever

Reflection

The blended-up shocking-pink skins
Of a handful of frozen cranberries from the USA mixed
With a frozen skinless banana dries
On the sides of my empty smoothie glass. The

Milk looks like sea foam, only it is strawberry blonde,
Pastel, with small geometric berry dots. From where
I sit, I can no longer see through the glass completely.
The reason I am sitting here in the mid-morning sun is

Because today is Saturday and I don't have to go to
Work today. But this is the only day I wished it was
Still Thursday, because on Thursday I still had my job.
Because on Thursday, I didn't know what being 'let go' felt like.

The lolly pink foam on the glass is time and I am the glass:
No longer functional enough to drink time out of, left,
Soaking in discards, clouded Kind Regards, skinless with pink insides,
No truthful explanation, only a summary of earnings.

I remember to take the unused tissues she gave me
Out of my back pockets before I wash my old work pants to stop the
Tissue letting go everywhere in the wash. There is the saying about the
Glass being half-full or half-empty based on your reflection.

A minor repair

The shampoo container feels lighter today as I
Take into account how much is left over to estimate how long it's been

Since you left me while I was on holiday. I am amazed at how long the
Shampoo has lasted me. Although the conditioner

Ran out months ago. I don't feel like my hair is any
Less shiny but I am embarrassed to look too much

Into the mirror. Every time I take a shower, water forms in big
Globules on the beige painted ceiling. The warm water falls from the

Shower head, but every few minutes an enlarged cool wet water drop
Falls down my back and I feel strangely in charge

To take my wrench, watch how-to YouTube videos in order to
Fix this minor repair that you would normally fix.

About the Author:

Louise Lever is a New Zealand artist and writer with an MFA from the University of Auckland. She is a current finalist in the National Contemporary Art Award 2018 and was selected for the first round of judging in the 2018 Arte Laguna Prize in Italy. Recent exhibitions include shows at Enjoy Public Art Gallery, Wellington; Artspace, Auckland and Wharepuke Sculpture Park, Kerikeri. She has previously been published in Poetry New Zealand. Her research interests include examining the intersection of gender, sexuality, film and art history. Most of her work is orientated towards social change and seeks to challenge power disparities. Louise is currently developing a feature-length documentary film (about feminism) in Melbourne.

AMERICA

by Ken W. Simpson

File number thirty-eight

America

The land of the free
a paradox
where hypocrites
without ethics
or moral principles
embraced by hate
are programmed
to cheat the people
destabilise
democratically elected
nations
install dictators
persecute and terrorise.

THE NAMELESS
by Lisa Zaran

The Nameless

Who are we but immigrants too.
Who are we but a lost Country.
Who are we but tin blind, partially broken,
desperado's too are we not.

Who are we but homeless
with our pawnshop belongings,
our tenuous hope. There are padlocks
clinking, yes the beat of our hearts.

Who are we but impoverished
with our rag-bound tenderness
as the child's tear runs down
a dusty cheek, brown river.

Are we not a hobo too, bound
for a home that doesn't exist, lost
in exploration, wayfaring in the making.
We too have no circumference

for the sojourn, no roadmap or compass,
no dominion no bounds, this land is my land
unfurling in our souls, this land is your land
our national anthem, Pilgrims too are we not.

*

Pathos

girl with a broken heart
tends the garden-
drooping rose

*

pawn shop wedding rings
trapped under glass
diamonds of other loves

*

where does the heart end
and i begin-
obtuse separation

*

rain filled Sunday
his leaving footprints
still damp in the doorway

*

water ring
on the oak table-
lonely moon

*

blank journal
by the bedside-
a story unwritten

*

strength in letting go
I dip my toe in the river-
overturn a stone

*

girls night out-
bogo on the appetizers-
I drink for two

*

driving solitary
in rush hour traffic-
one way conversation

*

local florist
daffodils in bloom-
get-well gift to self

*

park birds string lace
limb to limb
just me and my shadow

*

morning cigarette
smoke rings
dissipate

*

unread text message
just to say hi-
soup on the backburner

*

summer storm
even the cacti
yearn

*

a house moth
flutters in the lamplight-
my first smile in months

*

sky alight
with firecrackers-
independence day

****

About the Author:

Lisa Zaran is the author of eight collections including Dear Bob Dylan, The Blondes Lay Content and the sometimes girl. She is founder and editor of Contemporary American Voices, on online poetry journal in its twelfth year of publication. When not writing Zaran works full time for a Community Service Agency in Arizona that serves individuals with mental health and/or substance use disorders.

REEDUCATION CAMP

by Michael Anthony Istvan Jr.

Reeducation Camp

a necktie around your neck brace

becoming the object of a dare

the executioner's daily practice
of axe swings, aware that he can be
called upon anytime

the executioner's daily practice with the axe
of axe swings, aware that he can be
called upon anytime

the headsman's daily practice with the axe,
aware that he can be called upon anytime
to deliver a humane blow saving him from
shame

the artist never knows when he is not creating

rummaging the trash for a used fentanyl patch

repeated checking for symptoms
itself taken as a sign
that you have the disease

once great cities vulgarized by tourist amenities

making him do the crime and then catching him
for it

indifferent to one another, less

as if we were never children
than as if angry for failing to be

as if shouting will make up for the difference
in tongue

the breeze, although it carries
particles of burned persons,
sweeps back the beloved's hair

the stallion unloads his cream
generative in the man who will die
from the depth of the final thrust

pain drugs deemed too habit-forming to give
to the dying man

flannelled men coughing
at dirty jokes on the dock
sipping Styrofoam coffee

a dog waiting outside a corner store

warped ridges of dissolving scum left on the
beach with each wave

families harmonizing in song

first smoky breath of the season

Refugee Droppings

masturbating to historical figures

would you feel accomplishment if one of your
lines became a cliché?

the bright side—
word jumble disorder
a gift for poetry

Rocky Mountain big horn sheep
seek out lichen rocks
tripping

taking up the painted gesture (hand
over face, say) to sort out
what attitude, what inner life, it betrays

arranging the dead one's journal entries by the
locations of writing

hair-mussing from grandpa, and sometimes
more

fashionably emaciated

the urge to pinch cow lips, dog lips

living well as indicated by the practice
of closing and opening refrigerators, drawers,
with the feet while the hands are at work

all day cartoon marathon
filled with commercials
"go outside today"

defense attorneys
put glasses on their clients—
nerds are safe, honest

yellow strips slashing by as you drive yourself
to jail

conditions where phlegm
is intentionally swallowed
for its nutrient value

hat admonitory gesture
of a silent *shh*—forefinger to lips—
implicates its target in the eavesdropping

fixing the drowned victim's face
for the casket, mouth still locked
in a final panicked pull for air

jailed men start to make love

ant mounds mow-riled, dragonflies hover the
lawn

the accidental electrocution of the electro-
fisherman

spreading her ass to a brown butterfly inkblot

blind but resolute
removal of any shafts
just before she squirts

fiends in dawn beds
armed with toys—parents
guarding vitals: eyes, privates

when lowering your face
from the gaze of the maniac
sets him off all the more

fingers crossed for an accident
serious enough to yield
the needed organ

living in a place reputed
to be paradise, the pressure
is to preserve that reputation

geniuses of path-blazing, much more
than those of analysis, leave silly mistakes
for scholars to build careers disclosing

trees give us warmth in their burning

curling iron—cheap weave—fire detector

already one suicide attempt behind her

eating hardboiled eggs
over the sink, salt
straight from Morton

mycelia in this mulch
fruit with rain—
argent withering by noon

silver coins in water
boiling the mushrooms
black coin: poisonous

condemned as nothing but a sketch: strokes
too hurried, too choppy, too enamored
of what is fleeting for micro precisions

opening to the subtleties of drudgeries

freedom to be bored

beetles born eating
their way out of mother—
quick nutrition

those across species
chewing food for their young,
stealing a bit as they do

their caring for baby dolls
an unconscious request
for cock

parental concern about too much
reading became about too much
TV, and now there is the internet

reclined in the grass of a clearing
in the woods, reaching up alone there
to tempt the butterfly to perch

we would be alone were we not separate

the bond formed through talking in whisper

Rejectamenta

the death of those who remembered you

the hot potato of ancestral pain

should we care whether it is cheating to use
numbing spray for deep throating?

leisure construed as but a chance to restore
workweek energy

sandboxes of weeds

if the joy of giving dies
in the giving, then perhaps just *plan*
on giving—keep planning.

the power that your spouse
has over you when she wants
less sex than you

an affair is often the end of a marriage
that everyone knew, but a new marriage
can be formed with the same person

even if life is one season among many,
you are not going to fair better in another season,
because fairing requires living

Jesus not only saves, he sure does pay!

citing that has the same shoes
as the man as evidence
that he is the man's son

attributing feeling better from your chronic
illness
to your invented and promoted protocol
instead of to that you invented and promote it

a father, red-blooded when he looks
at his daughter's filled-out friends, looks
"weird" to them because he never looks

jealous over someone who pains and loves and
struggles too

lifelong servicemen learning to receive help
from others

forging an inner equilibrium
as opposed to sensitizing walls
to weather sonic invasions

in such an age of technology when we all
should not be
slaving away under an employer, we mock
tribespeople
for being too lazy to slave away under an employer

noting how easy it is to waste our time
is no waste of time, for it keeps buried
the thought that everything is a waste of time

feeling death in the room before even checking
the body
is your sensing the absence of the usual
breaths and motions—
and that, despite complaints by the superstitious, is magic enough

the loathing that festers
for your twin, dragged along dead
but still attached at the spine

so often when contaminated
with some contagion
we contract contagiousness itself

fireworks riling up veteran ptsd

however empty the HIV-AIDS distinction
has become, technically you did not lie
in assuring her that you do not have AIDS

letting the city racket below
portal you not into rage
but into reveries of other worlds

prisoners confused, violent almost,
by news that you used your free time
not to do what you so enjoy doing

parents fight at the table each night
over the identity (sexual, racial, cultural)
of the child sitting before them

nurse glares after seeing
bruises on the infant
yet to be diagnosed with hemophilia

About the Author:

M. A. Istvan Jr., PhD, proud member of the
Oregon Trail Generation and long sufferer of
sarchosis, engages in deep play even in base-
line reality where everyone expects truth and
seriousness. He wants to please everyone even
though he is rebellious to the core. Istvan has
butterflied into a philosopher who no longer
attempts to anticipate and respond to all ob-
jections that may arise, even those that may
arise from the most uncharitable readings.

POKHARA, THE CITY OF ANGELS

by Bikal Paudel

Hour Hand's Message to a friend

Dear minute hand,

I wait for you for an hour
And you leave in a minute
Making me wait another 59
Till we are again aligned
We both get life with the same power
Batteries in the core of this Earth that gave us birth
You go through love for numbers

You don't wait for anyone, so I shouldn't have expected you to wait for me
But I can't help it. Every time you come close, I can't feel my heartbeat
I get this feeling that makes me sit and think. And stop. I wait and wait. Tick tock *2
And this is gone before I can say a word like a writer's block
I'd like to think I have a lot of patience but I'm just like you in the end. And together we make a fixed clock.
Maybe if I wasn't a bit odd, and maybe if I was a just a bit tall, I could move fast just like you and with you forever without any mixed thoughts. From society. We could do anything, travel the world and climb mountains to the tip top

My minute hand,
But sometimes I feel bad for you
Maybe it's not you that wants to play with numbers
Maybe you also just want to get settled
Find the perfect place, but more importantly the perfect time to last
But we can't live in the past. Those damn seconds and the second hand. They move way too fast
Those people on top that determine time make me go in circles twice a day

To make us do things, they sometimes hand you fake compliments like you look nice today.
Like I don't look nice everyday.
I used to complain about why I was so slow
Then I realized you've got to go in circles to do 24.
And they don't care about us b/c we don't have a famous brand name and we don't keep score
They just want a rollie, rollie, rollie, Marc Jacobs and Michael Kors
Not really knowing what it's for.

My minute hand,
Every minute you're moving for the next
Just because you've got that extra length
And you've got some extra strength
Just because we don't have the same skill set
Of the new digital watches and the digital age
We've got to work twice as hard
Play games with entities that are twice as large
Is it getting political again, don't let me start

But my minute hand,
I just want to be with you
The same Earth that gave us birth and makes us move is the same reason our love is never approved.
Same reason we can't stop, Same reason you can't be on top. Of me
Even when the sun disappears over the horizon
Even when there is no more moons
Time will go on, Even though we can't live together, breathe together, and tick tock together
I will appreciate that we are both attached to the same thing, and the same energy that we bring
Maybe you'll never be mine
But I'll watch you move flawlessly
Even though we'll grow old and have our own kids
And they'll listen to you when you tell them It's time to sleep
And more. It's time to wake up to a loud ass beep

But minute, you will always be so fine baby
You make them check you out when it's time to leave
When it's time to eat, when it's time to move their feet with a beat
When it's time to drink
Ugh I get jealous when they stare at you so intrigued
I'm not insecure and I understand but I can't help it I'm sorry
The way you move with that beat
Tick tock *2, my heart skips a beat
I mean without you, time will be incomplete
And it will just be me
Trying to tell people I'm not lonely
But with just one hand, they will see

Because you are that missing piece
I'll be useless with no feet
You're sugar to my bland tea, so damn sweet
Even though they won't let us be

Even though they won't stop time
For a little reflection, whether it's happiness or affliction
I'll wait till you're just mine
I'll wait till the batteries die
I'll wait till we're not so accustomed to life
Till we don't all follow the same direction: clockwise
For now, I'll let you live your own life
But please don't run too far away from me like people run away from time

Pokhara, the city of angels

Red boats on the edge of Phewa Lake used to call me
So one day, I rowed one to the other side with Aama
30 feet deep water didn't scare me a bit
Even though I didn't have a life vest
No swimming lessons. If I fell, I would be lifeless
But the blue water savored of life's best
Almost as good as how the Daalbhat waiting for me at home tastes
Perks of being a fearless ten year old looking at a mother's smile
Thinking about home cooked food, when you're in the wild
Though hungry, I was ecstatic
Blood flowed inside my head like the ripples underneath us
A never-ending feeling of home and connection between us
Me, my mother and my Pokhara
The sun glanced at us from behind the Annapurna range
However, before we got to Tal Barahi Temple to worship Ganesh, my favorite God,
My mood changed
Not a single cloud had interfered our morning with rain
But now sky turned grayer than I had ever seen before
Water droplets, the size of my hand-made snowballs in the winter, fell galore
We rowed and rowed for the shore
My many teardrops assimilated with the downpour
Leaving my eyes red, and my heart sore
Aama comforted me with "don't cry, we'll get back home" while the water rose
I had faith in her, of course and we made it back.
Safal and Kushal were waiting for us soaking wet
Their hands felt to mine like the first time they had ever met
I stayed on the porch for a little longer to soak in everything
I was relieved to be back, but a little sad too
About how sometimes life has to take a turn like our red boat had to
And how many things haven't even happened yet
And to how many places I have not gone
But that was the first time I realized this is the best place I will call home

About the Author:

My name is **Bikal Paudel.** I am from Kathman-
du, Nepal. I currently reside in Washington DC
with my family. I love music and poetry.

www.ingramcontent.com/pod-product-compliance
Lightning Source LLC
Chambersburg PA
CBHW080720020726
47502CB00009B/2479